Praise for *Eat Your Garden*

'Harry Holding is one of our most exciting young designers.'

MONTY DON

'*Eat Your Garden* is a joy that will become a well-thumbed entry in the classics. I can't wait to draw on so much of Harry's thinking to transform my own gardens. This palette for the palate is a gift of a Gift. I love it and know that all who receive it will be sincerely grateful for it. Harry Holding has produced a feast of a book.'

SIR TIM SMIT, co-founder, the Lost Gardens of Heligan and the Eden Project

'A feast of invaluable information and a truly inspirational book, coming from a lifetime of curiosity and practical experience.'

DARINA ALLEN, Ballymaloe Cookery School

'Why not eat your garden? Why restrict ornamental gardens to non-edible plants? Harry uses the term *edimental* to describe plants which are both beautiful and delicious. They are the ones we want to grow, and Harry has plenty of ideas for this. *Eat Your Garden* describes how to grow food in an ornamental garden without losing ornamental as a quality. There are so many wonderful opportunities: let Harry guide you to see the amazing possibilities.'

CHARLES DOWDING, author of *No Dig* and *Grow Together*

'When I first saw Harry's Chelsea Flower Show garden, I was blown away by the planting. Once the penny dropped that it was an astonishing tapestry of edible flavours and forms, my brain fizzed with all the new edible delights that unfolded in front of me. I'm all about growing edibles, but Harry takes it to another level and proves just how imaginative and elegant an edible landscape can be.

'Harry makes ecological gardening joyful, accessible and irresistibly inspiring. With clarity and warmth, he reveals how plants can be both delicious and ornamental, transforming borders and everyday spaces into productive, biodiverse ecosystems.

'*Eat Your Garden* is a book we edible gardeners have been yearning for, a gentle shift in perspective, a reminder that our gardens can feed us in more ways than one. May it encourage you to plant boldly, harvest often and see your space through Harry's generous, visionary lens.'

AUGUST BERNSTEIN, head of the Raymond Blanc Gardening School, Le Manoir aux Quat'Saisons

'*Eat Your Garden* will change how we grow our ornamental and edible plants in the same place; it's a book that brings together food and beauty. The case studies give insight into the endless possibilities open to us all, and you will never look at an herbaceous border in the same way again. The plant profiles are full of genuine surprises on the edibility of ornamental plants. I mean, who knew that the young leaves of that beautiful, woolly *Stachys byzantina* (lamb's ear) can be fried in batter for a delicious *amuse-bouche*? Familiar old plants provide new flavours, textures and scents to delight even the most jaded palate. Yes, we can all have edimental spaces, and they can be as small or as large as you can manage. As Mr Holding says, "just give it a go".'

ADVOLLY RICHMOND, author of *A Short History of Flowers*; plant and garden historian and presenter

'Harry's book offers a clear, practical roadmap for creating edible, beautiful and ecologically informed plantings. He absolutely nails the planting design process, offering enormous value in showing how to turn these ideas into reality.

'People often ask me where to learn about edible meadows and edimental plantings. This is the book I recommend – a must-read for anyone interested in ecologically rich edible gardens.'

SID HILL, multi-award-winning ecological gardener and designer

'This book is a gateway to understanding edimental gardening without compromising garden design. When applied to any garden, this concept reveals how edibles can become true architectural showstoppers. Harry elevates the meaning of the potager garden to a refined and contemporary level. Throughout the book, he shares not only the purpose and practicality of edible plants, but also subtly introduces forward-thinking design elements that inspire future garden features. Absolutely love it!'

REKHA MISTRY, author of *Rekha's Kitchen Garden*

'Here is a book that is actually needed – spanning the gap between "landscaping" and food production in an accessible, beautiful layout that you can actually put to use directly. A necessary addition to the world of foodscaping and regeneration.'

BEN FALK, author of *The Resilient Farm and Homestead*

'*Eat Your Garden* by Harry Holding is a joyful and down-to-earth exhibit of the author's memoirs as a landscape designer, world traveller and collaborator with Nature. Through Harry's lens, readers are transported on an international journey to meet gardeners nourishing themselves, their communities and surrounding environments by harnessing synergies with Nature. Harry's guidance, stories and insights will inspire and motivate professional and novice readers alike to befriend Nature and edimentals as their perennial companions and breadwinners.'

VANESSA HARMONY, owner and edimental grower, Colorado Edible Forest

'Using varied real-life examples from high-rise balconies to multi-acre properties, Harry Holding shows how feasible it is to create landscapes that feed us. He makes a passionate and compelling case for gardens that are simultaneously beautiful, ecologically sound and tasty – then goes on to provide the tools for creating them.'

JEROME OSENTOWSKI, author of *The Forest Garden Greenhouse*

'If you are keen to grow what you eat and, at the same time, enjoy creating a garden that is both a joy to be in as well as a place from which to harvest a great diversity of crops, Harry Holding's knowledge and enthusiasm makes this a worthy addition to your garden reading.'

ADAM ALEXANDER, author of *The Accidental Seed Heroes*

'Edimentals have come of age, eighteen years after I first coined the term. I have travelled the world since, talking to permaculturists, urban growers, teachers, foragers, ornamental gardeners and even the walled gardeners of the rich and famous, and they all "get" the low-input, low-carbon edimental garden, of great value also to the biodiversity of the place. One can go on summer vacation without worrying about the veg, fit them perfectly into the school year, and produce food even in very shady gardens and urban areas, along with many other advantages. I welcome Harry's book, as I'm sure it will inspire an equally wide range of gardeners, making edimentalling the next level of ecofriendly gardening, feeding both us and the planet.'

STEPHEN BARSTOW, ESM (Extreme Salad Man); author of *Around the World in 80 Plants*

Eat Your Garden

Eat Your Garden

Edimentals as a Beautiful, Low-Effort Way to Grow Food

HARRY HOLDING

CHELSEA GREEN PUBLISHING
White River Junction, Vermont
London, UK

Contents

Introduction		1
1:	The Power of Edimentals	11
2:	Reimagining the Edible Garden	29
3:	Edimentals for All Gardens	57
4:	Big Ideas from Regenerative Growers	75
5:	Understanding Your Garden	103
6:	Designing with Edimentals	123
7:	Plant Profiles	167
8:	Eating Edimentals	199
Conclusion: Beyond the Garden		223
Acknowledgements		*239*
Notes		*241*
Image Credits		*245*
Index		*247*

Introduction

Gardening has been a part my life ever since I could walk and hold a trowel. Long before I knew what horticulture was, I knew what it felt like to be connected to nature. That spark, so often lit in childhood, can come from many places. For me, it was the Barton Hills National Nature Reserve, just a mile from our house in Bedfordshire.

Looking back, I realise how lucky I was to grow up near the awe-inspiring Chilterns landscape, where the countryside brushes up against the urban edge of Luton, a town just thirty miles north of London. The Barton Hills became my childhood wilderness. My sister and I ran wild through beech woods, splashed in chalk streams and roamed sunlit downlands grazed by semi-wild ponies. It was one big adventure, a magical place for our imaginations to roam. These days, I walk those same hills with a deeper appreciation for it as a biodiversity hotspot and highly protected environment – although stick-sword fighting with my sister has been replaced by boring my wife with my nerdy obsession for the rare wildflowers found there.

My parents ran two nursery schools, and my sister and I spent many weekends and holidays 'helping out'. For me, this invariably meant time in the school gardens sweeping leaves and

The chalk downlands and beech woodlands of Barton Hills.

'Helping' my grandfather, Ian, build a pergola in my parents' garden.

pulling weeds and probably spending more time playing and being a nuisance. For the long summer holiday, they would ship us off to our grandparents.

On my father's side, my grandparents lived in a modest suburban house with a large garden on the outskirts of north London. The garden was, and still is, my grandmother's pride and joy. Over sixty years, they created the garden from scratch – my grandmother taking cuttings from any public planting she passed, propagating them and establishing them throughout the garden, while my grandfather built all the hard landscaping features, including their beloved summer house. I've always admired her no-nonsense approach to gardening. For her, it's all about aesthetics and colour. Vegetable growing? A complete waste of space. In fact, she's endured a lifelong battle to remove the asparagus beds (which resprout from any bits of the deep crowns and roots left behind), a hangover from the site's history as a farm.

My passion for food growing comes from my mother's side. We'd spend holidays on the Norfolk coast in my grandparents' caravan or stay at their home in Luton, a terraced house with a moderate-sized garden. For my maternal grandmother, gardens could be beautiful, but, more importantly, they had to be practical. Raised in a family that grew and sold vegetables at the market, productivity wasn't optional, it was essential. Her tales of how the entire garden was dedicated to food

Hanging out under the hawthorn trees that still stand.

EAT YOUR GARDEN

growing when my mother and her brothers were young captured my imagination. The idea that you could sow seeds, nurture plants and eat them felt revolutionary to me.

My evolving love for gardening spelled trouble for my parents. At the age of seven, I 'knew' I wanted to be a gardener and insisted on taking over one of the borders in their much-loved garden. Having absorbed these different influences from both grandmothers, I set out to create a border that not only looked beautiful but also produced food! A glorious collision of everything I loved about gardening and expressed with the reckless abandon of a child who was not held back by industry norms. Whether it was a success or a visual mess, only golden memories and family anecdotes could say… Whatever the case, it clearly left a lasting impression on me.

Gardening with my grandmother, Rita, working to keep the lawn edges in check. Note the Marigold gloves.

As a teenager, discovering that I could earn money gardening turned my passion into a vocation. Weekend jobs at garden centres evolved into private gardening clients, eventually leading to a small gardening business in Australia in my early twenties. I had travelled there to seek adventure, living in a campervan with my now wife and learning to garden in a very different climate. After a brief career detour into event management following a business degree, I focused wholeheartedly on horticulture. Seizing the incredible opportunity of a scholarship to study at the prestigious London College of Garden Design, based in the Royal Botanic Gardens, Kew, I honed my passion. Today, Harry Holding Studio is a multi-award-winning practice dedicated to creating ecologically sensitive spaces that nurture a deeper human connection with nature.

Food growing remained a constant theme throughout these formative years. While at school, a group of friends and I established a company, Grow Cook Eat, that set out to engage children in the act of growing their own food. This interactive grow guide, cookbook and seed collection recognised the importance of capturing the imagination of children at a young age. What better way to excite and inspire the next generation about the wonders of plants than through food? If more people could have the opportunity to grow at any scale – be it a

Colourful prairie meadow-style planting in the garden of a neo-Gothic lodge in a graveyard in central London. Rich and diverse planting goes a long way towards creating a more ecologically sensitive garden.

window box or vegetable plot – an innate care for the natural world was bound to develop.

For me, this business venture turned into an obsession with growing, and, several years later, I managed to secure a full-sized allotment (known in the US as a community garden plot), where I toiled away at growing neat rows of annual vegetables. Trying to balance time at the allotment – weeding, watering and harvesting – with growing my business and design studio proved too much. I had to give up the allotment. Surely there was a way to balance 'larger-scale' growing with the demands of a busy twenty-first-century lifestyle?

Around this time, I discovered the concept of 'edimentals' – edible plants that are also ornamental. Excitedly, I began working this inspiring group of plants into my designs, whether my clients were aware of it or not, and started to see for myself how beauty and productivity could work hand in hand. Although new to me, this idea is rooted in ancient wisdom and championed by contemporary practitioners, as we'll explore later.

At my design studio, we lean towards the naturalistic end of the spectrum, creating gardens that are as nourishing as they are practical. For me, this approach speaks to the soul: it fosters connection with nature and delivers real biodiversity benefits. It's what I seek in a garden and what many of our clients are drawn to. In urban environments, naturalistic gardens counterbalance the harshness of the built world, offering a remedy for our disconnection from nature. In rural settings, they help anchor a garden in its wider landscape, reinforcing a sense of place and belonging. The edimental garden brings all of this together while adding one crucial extra layer: edibility. These gardens don't just enrich the soul, they provide nourishment.

I was fortunate enough to bring this fascinating world of plants to the Royal Horticulture Society Chelsea Flower Show in 2023. Our 'School Food Matters Garden' – over 80 per cent edible – which we created in partnership with the charity School Food Matters, funded by Project Giving Back, celebrated the power of edimentals. It went on to win the RHS People's Choice Award (Sanctuary / All About Plants Gardens category) and a Silver-gilt medal.

The delight and curiosity the garden sparked in the public's imagination was a clear sign to me: edimentals hold vast, untapped potential. This is about more than just adding a few edibles to your garden – it's about reimagining what a productive, beautiful,

Lush textures and shades of green surround a bench in a woodland-inspired garden surrounding that same neo-Gothic lodge. A demonstration of how colour does not always need to take centre stage.

sustainable landscape can be. Since then, I've been on a journey to tap into that potential and unleash the power of edimentals. This book is part of that journey.

What *Eat Your Garden* Provides

Whether you are a newcomer to edimental gardening or a seasoned professional eager to broaden your relationship with these extraordinary plants, consider this book a trusted guide. It will help sharpen your focus on which attributes you truly want from the plants in your garden, while offering an analytical framework for choosing those plants, rather than simply selecting whatever looks attractive at the nursery. You'll come away with the practical knowledge of how to design, plan and integrate edimentals into your garden. While the theory behind why we want to work with these plants will be explored, the key takeaways will be actionable advice. Edimental plant lists, a glimpse into my planting design process and a unique garden design example will all provide a wealth of practical tips.

Understanding your site is essential, so we'll dive into how to analyse your garden and its environmental conditions. Along the way, we'll explore ideas drawn from perennial vegetable planting, permaculture systems, food forests, agroforestry, edible meadows, and growing on allotments and in kitchen gardens – all practices that support edimentals. These approaches are already widely valued for their regenerative potential, and we'll distil those ideas into a form that works at the garden scale. All of this is brought to life through twelve case studies, featuring world-leading environmentalists, farmers, horticulturists, designers and plant experts. We'll also explore a carefully selected list of edible plants, highlighting some of my personal favourites, before returning to the

Naturalistic design with edimentals in the 'School Food Matters Garden'.

kitchen to see how edimentals can shape everyday living. Finally, we'll step beyond the garden gate to consider the wider opportunities for bringing edible beauty into our shared landscapes and communities.

While many of the ideas in this book can be applied globally, the practical advice focuses on temperate zones – from North America to the UK, Europe to Japan. The journey will take us to environments where edimentals intersect with more traditional ways of growing food

The 'School Food Matters Garden': a foragable landscape with over 80 per cent of the planting being edible. A show garden demonstrating the power of edimentals.

using annual vegetables. Although annual vegetables are an area of great interest to me, they fall outside the scope of this book. Many excellent texts already exist on the topic, including books by experts featured in our case studies. For the same reason, *Eat Your Garden* does not provide detailed practical gardening or growing advice. Instead, it focuses on design thinking, plant selection and sparking a fresh approach to edible gardening.

For too long, growing your own food has often been characterised as only available to those privileged enough to have large gardens, access to an allotment or an abundance of time. This couldn't be further from the truth. As a landscape designer, I've had the opportunity to test these ideas across a wide range of scales and settings, and I've seen firsthand how edimentals can thrive in almost any setting. More importantly, I've witnessed how they spark curiosity and joy in people of all backgrounds and ages. This book brings together my learnings alongside the voices of many inspiring practitioners with whom I've had the privilege of working. My hope is that it will inspire you – not just to grow edimentals but to reimagine what a garden can be.

Chapter 1

The Power of Edimentals

Edimentals are a remarkable group of plants that represent a hugely diverse array of species – from trees and shrubs down to herbaceous perennials, bulbs and ground-covers. Thousands of species across the globe fit under this umbrella, and what unites them all is their dual role – they are as beautiful as they are useful. It is the combination of these two essential qualities that elevates edimentals and makes them incredible, garden-worthy plants. They offer a way to have your (plant-based) cake and eat it too – literally – and I believe they can unlock the joy of growing your own food for many more people. More than simply incorporating edibles into naturalistic plantings, the edimental garden represents a distinct garden philosophy, one that merges aesthetics, biodiversity and productivity.

A staggering number of plant species can be grown in the temperate zones of the world, and, of those, thousands are known to be edible.[1] Globally, there are 40,000–100,000 species of edible plants, and yet fewer than 15 species provide 90 per cent of our food energy intake.[2] Embracing an edimental approach to food

Beauty and food go hand in hand, as shown by this meadow-style edimental planting.

The Korean aster is a delicacy.

growing is not about ripping up the rule book and changing everything we know and love about the plants we choose for our gardens. Rather, it's about taking a fresh perspective on that broad palette while being open-minded to introducing new and sometimes seldom-used species, too. The vast number of plants to choose from and work with is daunting to both professionals and amateurs alike. But do not let those statistics overwhelm you; this book is a guide and roadmap through the world of edible plants.

The fact is, you almost certainly have some edimentals growing in your garden or local park already – like the Mediterranean herbs that many of us frequently use in the kitchen, including rosemary (*Salvia rosmarinus*) and thyme (*Thymus* spp.). They also cover garden classics such as certain species of sedums (*Hylotelephium* spp.), goldenrods (*Solidago* spp.) and Korean aster (*Doellingeria scabra*). We already use some of them widely, and several are among my favourite vegetables.

Key Features & Benefits of Edimentals

In addition to their unique harmony of aesthetics and function, their positive traits are wide-ranging. Their multifunctional nature, immense diversity and dynamic qualities make them suitable for almost any situation. There are many features and reasons to include them in your garden. Below I've gathered some of the key ones.

Edible & Ornamental

There are thousands of edible plants growing in temperate regions. Many are high-quality edimentals offering substantial, reliable harvests and flavours that can hold their own in any kitchen. Others are more unusual and are perhaps grown as much for their story, their history or their novelty as for their culinary value. And then there are the more spurious ones – plants so striking or joyful to grow that they earn their place in the garden, even if they won't revolutionise your cooking. This book embraces all of the above.

Edimentals combine beauty with productivity – the idea that food growing enhances aesthetics rather than compromises them. Edimentals have allowed me to enter a dialogue with my clients with a new focus: one in which beauty, functionality and food coexist in the same space. Beauty is subjective, of course – what appeals to me may not to you – but, with such a variety of forms, colours and textures, edimentals offer something for every taste. They are visually versatile, able to be woven seamlessly into formal borders, naturalistic meadows, cottage gardens, minimalist designs and more. They also provide year-round interest, with value that extends beyond flowers to seedheads, textured foliage and form. Edimentals challenge outdated notions of what food-growing spaces should look like, showing that edible gardens can be just as stunning as ornamental ones.

Beginner Friendly

There are plenty of barriers that stop people from growing their own food: lack of time and knowledge are two of the most common. That first step can often feel like a giant leap. Edimentals offer a gentler entry point. They can be planted once and enjoyed for years, with many being remarkably hardy and forgiving. In fact, they can often thrive even in neglected corners.

A few years ago, after moving to Bristol, I took on an allotment again – this time as a space to experiment

Goldenrods flowers make a wonderful tea and bring vibrant tones into late summer.

THE POWER OF EDIMENTALS

with low-input food growing and to see how edimentals would perform with minimal intervention. One spring, I got my answer. I was away for two months during an uncharacteristically dry, warm spell and the plot went completely unwatered. Yet when I returned, the edimentals were still going strong. They'd held their own, quietly getting on with it, while the annuals we had been establishing were, understandably, a sorry sight. This sort of resilience makes edimentals ideal for those just starting out. They invite experimentation and ease – and with so many underused edible plants out there, they encourage creativity, too, offering beginners a more relaxed, exploratory way into gardening and food growing.

Maximises Space

With over half the world's population (more than four billion people) living in urban areas, space is at a premium.[3] Edimentals allow food production without requiring separate vegetable plots. They're ideal for small spaces, thriving in pots, balconies and a broad range of urban settings. They climb vertical surfaces (like grapevines) and can be integrated into city infrastructure through green walls and living roofs.

Perennial

Being perennial, edimentals return year after year. One of the greatest benefits of this is the time and resources saved by not having to sow seeds and replant annual vegetables. They improve soil health by reducing disturbance, tying into the 'no-dig' approach – a method of leaving soil undisturbed to protect its structure, retain carbon and support a thriving soil ecosystem – and promoting beneficial microbes and mycorrhizal fungi.[4] Dense root systems suppress weeds, reduce erosion and retain moisture. These same roots access deeper stores of nutrients and water, increasing resilience to pests, diseases and drought.[5] The result: lower input, longer returns.

Globe artichoke is bold and architectural, adding striking structure to a garden. In the kitchen, it shines as a dish in its own right, especially when fried whole in the classic Roman dish *carciofi alla giudia*.

Nothing beats the first Wye Valley asparagus of the season – fresh, green and fleeting. It's as valued for its flavour as for its beauty. After harvest, I let it 'fern', enjoying its soft, light-catching foliage all summer long.

Low Input & Maximum Rewards

Once established, edimentals require minimal care: less water, fewer inputs and pest interventions than most annual crops. They are classic low-input, high-output plants and represent the perfect remedy for our over-scheduled twenty-first-century lifestyles that leave little time for intensive vegetable gardening, something I have found to be the biggest barrier for those interested in giving food growing a try. For all those benefits that come from being perennial, they are much easier to grow organically, which is good for the health of our ecosystems as well as our bodies.

Resilient & Climate Adaptable

No matter where you are in the world, the impacts of climate change are becoming increasingly visible, with phenomena such as hotter summers, wetter winters and stronger storms becoming more prevalent every year. Edimentals are well suited to cope. Their deep roots allow them to tap into water reserves inaccessible to annuals, improving drought resilience. Many are cold-hardy or heat-tolerant, helping to extend the growing season and adapt to unpredictable weather.

Some even contribute to carbon sequestration, making them part of the climate solution.

Biodiversity

Alongside the climate crisis sits the biodiversity crisis. Edimentals help restore balance by providing berries, nuts, seeds, shelter and nectar for insects, birds and mammals. They favour polycultures over monocultures, creating resilient, self-sustaining systems. With long flowering periods, they offer vital nectar across the season – a lifeline as pollinator numbers continue to fall.

Low Cost

While the initial investment may be higher, edimentals are cost-effective over time due to their low-input nature. Being perennial, they don't need to be replaced regularly. Many can be propagated by division or cuttings – or may self-seed and spread naturally, creating new plants for free. Because they fulfil multiple roles (beauty, human and pollinator food, wildlife habitat), they eliminate the need for separate ornamentals or pollinator plants as you might choose for a traditional vegetable plot.

Culturally Diverse & Customisable

Edimentals exist in every food tradition. They give people the opportunity to grow plants that reflect their cultural heritage as opposed to being restricted to the local palette of vegetables. They support food sovereignty and reconnect gardeners to traditional dishes and ingredients that can be hard to source. Whether it's Asian perennial greens, Mediterranean herbs or Andean tubers, edimentals open the door to diverse growing and cooking traditions.

Food Security

There's nothing quite like eating a plate of food you've grown, harvested and prepared that same day. Even on a small scale, edimentals can provide fresh, homegrown food year-round, reducing our reliance on distant supply chains and imported produce from industrial farms. They offer a practical way to relocalise food production and encourage a deeper sense of self-sufficiency, allowing individuals and communities to reclaim some control over what ends up on their plates.

Babington's leek standing tall under a quince tree. This perennial leek is poised to flower in a globe-shaped head that will later set tight clusters of edible bulbils.

Crucially, edimentals help fill the tricky gap in early spring and late autumn when annual crops are scarce. They provide a steady source of food that trickles in throughout the seasons, helping you stay connected to what you grow and eat while supporting other food systems you may already have in place.

Challenges of Edimentals

Like any growing method, edimentals come with their own challenges, and it's important to approach them with realistic expectations. Many perennial edimentals play the long game, taking two to three years to properly establish before they offer a meaningful harvest. At the start of your journey, this slower pace can feel a bit underwhelming. And while the long-term benefits are significant, the yields are typically lower, making full 'self-sufficiency' more difficult to achieve.

There's also the matter of establishment. Perennials take time to develop strong root systems – the first year or two is vital. Early care is essential: regular watering, weeding and patience are all part of the deal. Even drought-tolerant edimentals need that initial support and water to get going. Most edimentals are also less common than traditional crops and can be harder to source. You will likely need to search beyond your local nursery to find them.

Compared to traditional veg growing, the world of edimentals is still relatively niche. There's a wealth of insight out there, but it often lives in more specialised spaces. Books, online resources such as Plants for a Future (www.pfaf.org), an incredible database of edible and useful plants, experimental gardening forums and the lived experience of growers around the world. This book is designed to help bridge that gap, and throughout our case studies – including the following one with Stephen Barstow, a pioneer of edimentals – you'll find plenty of inspiration from brilliant practitioners that will help guide your journey.

Case Study
The Godfather of Edimentals
STEPHEN BARSTOW

In 2008, Stephen Barstow, a British-born, Norway-based plant guru, coined the term 'edimentals', a portmanteau of edible and ornamental, in his book *Around the World in 80 Plants*. I came across Stephen's work through his blog (www.edimentals.com) while researching for our 'School Food Matters Garden' at the 2023 RHS Chelsea Flower Show. It was clear from his extensive research, detailed writing and generous online presence (see his popular Facebook group, Edimentals and Perennial Vegetables) that I'd discovered the 'Godfather of Edimentals'. His message is simple but powerful: edible landscapes can be just as beautiful as purely ornamental ones, so why choose one or the other? His decades of dedication and deep botanical observation have influenced horticulturalists, botanists, designers and conservationists around the world. Stephen's life's work has been the single greatest motivator behind my own exploration into edimentals. I knew that I had to meet him. So, when he invited me to his home in Norway to explore his garden, I jumped at the opportunity.

Stepping into Stephen's Edible Garden feels like entering another world. A steep,

One of Stephen's many 'super salads' bringing beauty and diversity into the kitchen.

Hostas: much loved for their bold foliage, glorious textures and delicious flavour – mild, slightly sweet, and reminiscent of asparagus when cooked.

sloping hillside just outside Trondheim, Norway, it overlooks the fjord like a green amphitheatre, the drama of the landscape echoed in the garden itself. Narrow paths wind through dense, layered planting, brushing your legs and drawing you deeper into a world of lush greenery before opening into glades where trees give way to sunlight and cinematic views. Perennials soar – cow parsnip (*Heracleum maximum*) towers above with plate-sized umbels, while angelicas (*Angelica archangelica*) lend an Alice-in-Wonderland atmosphere with their architectural foliage and oversized blooms. At ground level, mashua (*Tropaeolum tuberosum*) tumbles over the paths and jewel-like flowers flicker through the understorey, guiding your eye across the space. The palette is lush and textural: shades of green pierced by sparks of colour and movement. Birds call from the canopy; bees dance around pollinator magnets. It is immersive, abundant and utterly alive.

And that's the point. 'I've observed about eighty-five different species of birds in the garden,' Stephen told me, 'including a first-ever sighting in the county, the red-breasted flycatcher.' Here wildlife isn't incidental, it's integral. The garden buzzes because it was built to host life. Beyond feeding himself and his family, he has always been driven by a desire to create a sanctuary for birds, insects and humans alike.

Stephen has spent the last forty-five years cultivating one of the most diverse and experimental edible gardens in Europe. It all began in the 1970s, when he became vegetarian and moved to Norway for his work as an ocean wave climatologist. 'When I arrived, there were literally three vegetables in the supermarket,' he recalled. 'To continue with an interesting diet, we really had to grow our own.' He started with annuals, guided by a British book on raised bed gardening and John Seymour's *The Self-Sufficient Gardener*. One entry, the only perennial in the book, leapt out: sea kale (*Crambe maritima*). He planted it. Forty-five years later, that same plant is still thriving. Perennial resilience proved transformative.

Around the same time, Stephen joined a local foraging group and discovered more than sixty wild edible plants growing along the coastline of the fjord by his house. He began cultivating them in his garden, and something clicked. 'Perennials look after themselves,' he said. 'No watering. No fertiliser. Low input, high diversity. Ninety per cent of the world's approximately one hundred thousand edible plants are perennials.' Captivated by their beauty, usefulness and self-reliance, Stephen began to seek them out wherever he could. 'Fuelled by my collectomania – which I inherited from my stamp-collecting dad – I started collecting edible plants from around the world.' Since then, he's logged over eight thousand entries in a detailed Excel spreadsheet, tracking what he grew, where and when. The diversity is extraordinary: at one point he was growing over two thousand varieties of edimentals! Nowadays, he has scaled down the number to a 'mere' one thousand-plus in his quest to develop a succession plan to simplify the garden and convert it into a nature reserve.

But Stephen doesn't just grow plants – he has shaped a movement. 'It became more and more obvious that many of these perennial vegetables were great ornamentals too,' he told me. 'If they beautified your garden as well as being edible, they would be more easily taken up by ornamental gardeners.' True to scientific form, he developed a rating system – an 'edimentality scale' of 1 to 5 – and then, with his characteristic humour, extended the system to include *edi-en-to-mentals* (good for insects) and *edi-avi-mentals* (good for birds). 'It was all a bit mental,' he grinned, 'but fun, too.'

The garden itself evolved organically. 'I didn't know about forest gardening back then,' he said, 'but it turns out that's what I created.' The site is far from forgiving: winters regularly drop to −20°C (−4°F), and in the coldest months the sun barely crests the horizon. In summer, it almost never sets. The soils are thin, and the slopes are dramatic. Yet out of this landscape, Stephen has carved a living, breathing plant archive. One small patch of flat ground, at the top of the slope, is

Sea kale was once known as 'the most British of vegetables' and can be seen growing out of shingle and sand along coastlines.

THE POWER OF EDIMENTALS

reserved for annual vegetables, but the rest is devoted to edimental experimentation.

Remarkably, this is just one of three gardens he's created. In the local Ringve Botanical Garden, near Trondheim's city centre, Stephen curates an allium collection of over four hundred varieties. Nearby, the World Garden in the Væres Venner garden at Ranheim, a community space with more than two hundred edible species from across the globe, is open to the public twenty-four hours a day. He's spent a lifetime sharing this message: beauty and food are not separate.

Stephen's creativity extends to the kitchen. 'We have about ten or twenty generic ways of preparing food, and hundreds of plants could be layered into any of those dishes.' These are not novelty meals, they're the edible expression of biodiversity. Each salad, stir-fry or soup becomes a celebration of the living garden outside. With that much edible diversity on your doorstep, it's no wonder he gained the reputation of being 'The Extreme Salad Man', creating what must surely be the most diverse salad ever made. It took three days to prepare and included 537 different plant varieties.

That extreme salad was an ambitious and complex endeavour, but his advice to others is simple: 'Grow the food you enjoy eating. You don't need two thousand plants, but do try a few and don't be afraid to experiment. Perennials are more forgiving than annuals. Bring in the diversity, and life will follow.'

Over time, Stephen has let go of control. 'I've started to loosen the reins,' he told me. 'I noticed small communities of plants finding each other – hogweeds, nettles and Caucasian spinach creating these dynamic, productive ecosystems.' These unplanned partnerships have become some of the garden's most resilient zones. 'It's like extreme companion planting,' he said. 'I didn't plan it – it just happened. That's what I see as the future of the garden: a nature reserve that designs itself.' These days, Stephen sees himself less as a gardener and more as a participant. 'I'm on first-name terms with the butterflies and birds,' he said, smiling. 'It's like I've become part of the ecosystem.'

Stephen Barstow with his prized udo (*Aralia cordata*).

A glade opening within the Edible Garden.

Edimentals set against the backdrop of a Norwegian fjord at Stephen's Edible Garden.

So which plants does the godfather of edimentals choose as his three favourites? First, hosta (*Hosta* spp.), a farmed and foraged spring delicacy in Japan, where the young shoots and leaves are eaten as a seasonal mountain vegetable. Second, Caucasian spinach (*Hablitzia tamnoides*), the hardy climber he helped elevate to global significance as a top edimental. And finally, the plant that started it all: sea kale (*Crambe maritima*). The silver-leaved survivor that still sends up shoots each spring – a living reminder of where the journey began. Sea kale was a much-loved delicacy in Victorian Britain, so much so that it was nearly eradicated by overharvesting from UK coastlines. (I remember the moment I connected the edimental I was enjoying on my plate with the strange plant I'd seen growing out of the pebbly beach as a child.)

Stephen's work is more than a mad obsession or grand scientific experiment; it's a vision of how food, beauty and ecology can come together in a single, symbiotic system. His garden is a classroom, a sanctuary and an act of resistance, showing us that there is always another way. In a world where food systems grow ever more standardised and precarious, Stephen Barstow offers us a different path.

Global Food Production: The Challenges & Solutions

In contrast to Stephen Barstow's expansive vision, I want to briefly look at the current state of the global food production system. An overview of the challenges we face due to industrial agriculture of the past one hundred or so years – alongside an inspiring view on contemporary regenerative and relocalised systems – helps to contextualise why we need resilient, sustainable and connected food today.

Industrial Agriculture Revolution: How We Got Here

Farming wasn't always the way we experience it today – with vast monocultures (endless fields of a single crop), factory farming and food that has travelled thousands of miles before it reaches our plates. Large-scale industrial agriculture, often confusingly referred to as the 'Green Revolution', took hold after World War Two, at a time when we needed high yields and efficiency.[6] While these methods solved short-term food shortages during wartime, the long-term consequences are clear. The industrial food system is one of the biggest contributors to climate change, soil degradation and the collapse of biodiversity.[7] Today, supply chains prioritise profit over sustainability and equality, and the majority of our food is grown using industrial methods that rely heavily on synthetic fertilisers, chemicals (pesticides, herbicides, fungicides) and large-scale machinery.[8] It's important to recognise that many farmers have found themselves locked into this cycle not by choice, but by economic pressures, government policies and corporate control over markets. The system is broken and it often leaves farmers with few alternatives.

Current issues:
- Climate change mitigation
- Offsetting biodiversity loss
- Climate change adaptation
- Enough food for a growing population

Four of the major challenges shaping global food and farming systems today.

Industrial agriculture prioritises short-term yield and scale.

THE POWER OF EDIMENTALS

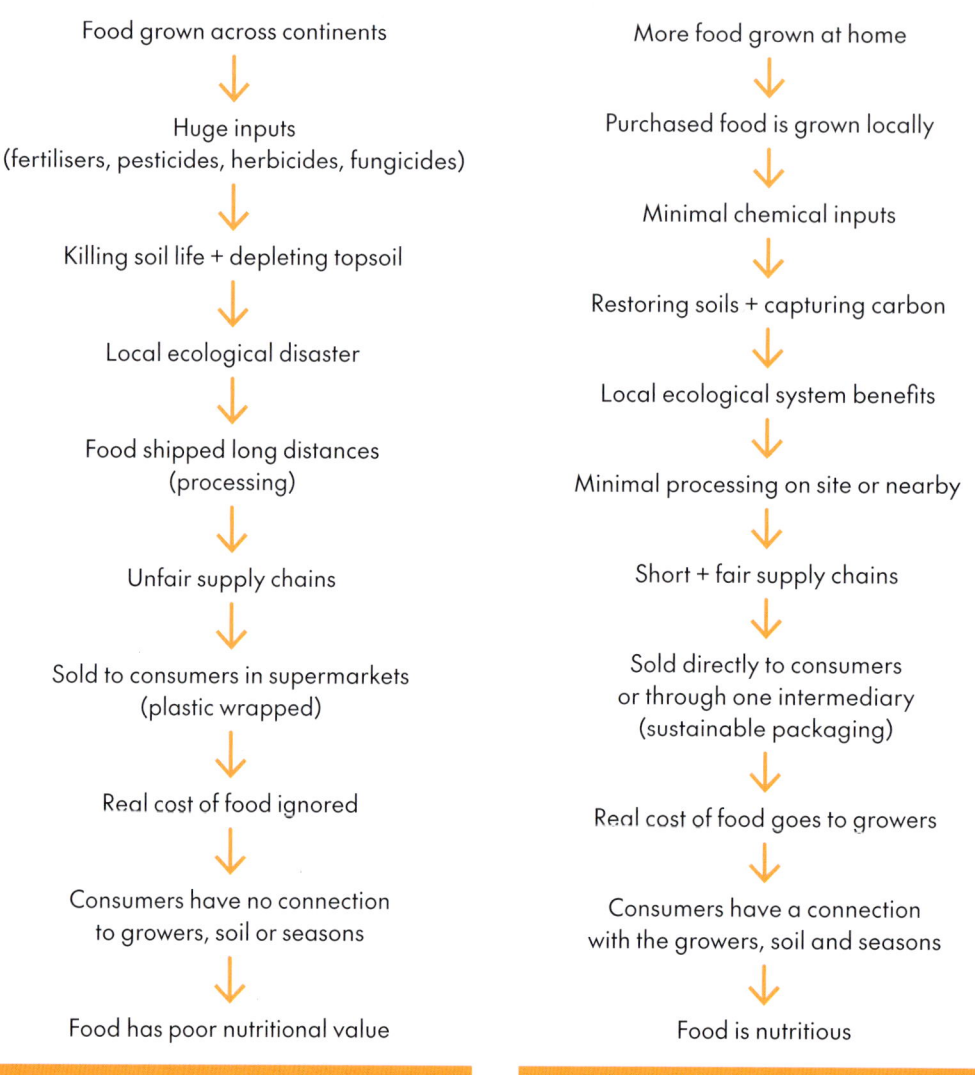

A depiction of the sterile food system – an extractive, globalised model that depletes soils, disconnects consumers from growers and prioritises profit and convenience over ecology, fairness and nutrition.

A vision for a fertile food system – one that restores soils, shortens supply chains, supports growers and reconnects people with the sources of their food, creating a foundation for nutritious and sustainable diets.

Industrial farming has distanced many of us from the origins of our food. Large parts of the world no longer eat seasonally or understand the ecological or nutritional impact of our choices. This disconnection weakens our relationship with nature and dulls our awareness of soil health, biodiversity and localised food systems.

A Different Path: Regenerative & Relocalised Food Systems

Across the world, farmers, growers and communities are embracing regenerative practices that work with nature, not against it. Food systems rooted in ecological balance, diversity and local production aren't just possible, they're already happening. From agroecology and permaculture to organic and biodynamic systems, these approaches prioritise healthy soil, diverse planting, water resilience and relocalised food networks. Many of these farmers and growers are leading the charge, proving that a different approach is not only feasible, but essential.

Rather than relying on monocultures, regenerative systems favour layered, multifunctional approaches that integrate trees, perennials, edimentals and polycultures – creating landscapes that are both productive and ecologically rich. Seasonality and local food are central to this vision, helping to reduce food miles and emissions, while reconnecting us to place and to those who grow our food.

The Road Ahead

This shift offers more than a way forward – it's a chance to rebuild our connection to the land, restore biodiversity and create a more just, resilient food future. At its heart are farmers and growers working to break free from industrial constraints, often in the face of enormous barriers. Supporting them through our purchasing power and conscious choices is one impactful way to help.

To put this into perspective, the collective space occupied by gardens in the UK alone covers an area three times the size of our National Parks.[9] In the US, domestic lawns alone span an area larger than the state of Georgia.[10] This sheer scale presents an extraordinary opportunity – by rethinking how we use these spaces, we gardeners can make a real impact.

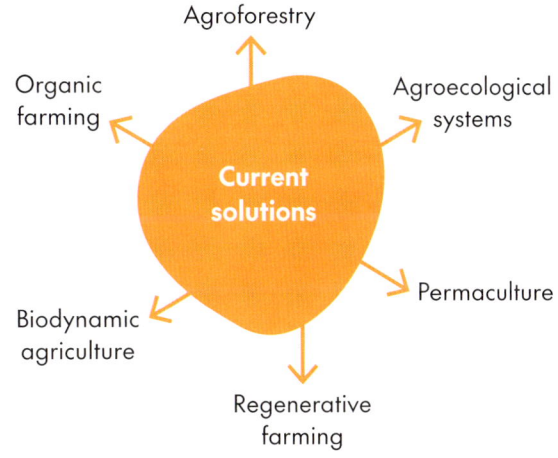

Some of the leading approaches driving positive change in food and farming systems. While each method differs in practice and philosophy, all share common aims – rebuilding soil health, enhancing biodiversity, reducing reliance on synthetic inputs, and creating more resilient, regenerative landscapes.

Chapter 2

Reimagining the Edible Garden

Edimentals are not a magic bullet for fixing our food system, nor should they replace traditional food growing, but they offer something vital. As gardeners, the choices we make may feel small, yet multiplied across millions of households they carry extraordinary weight. Edimentals can supplement our diets, reconnect us with the cycles of nature and remind us that food can be as beautiful as it is nourishing. They sit within the wider movement towards regenerative, relocalised food systems, but their greatest power lies in what they offer at the individual level. Put simply, they help us reconnect with plants, with food and with nature itself.

Nature Connection & Why We Need It

At its heart, nature connection is the deep relationship we share with the natural world – simply being outdoors or engaging with nature in meaningful ways, such as harvesting food, smelling flowers, watching wildlife or swimming in the ocean. These interactions

Late-season colour with Jerusalem artichoke, a perennial species of sunflower.

Edimental systems are already widely used across a range of approaches – from edible meadows to food forests – and they have huge potential to shape spaces like school and community gardens, too.

ground us, foster joy and create a sense of kinship with other living beings. They help us feel rooted in place, grateful for seasonal abundance and emotionally connected to the world around us. Research shows that the deeper the connection to nature, the lower our levels of stress and anxiety and the greater our overall happiness.[1] Spending time outdoors has also been linked to better sleep, reduced blood pressure, improved physical health and enhanced cognitive function.[2]

And yet, despite growing awareness of these benefits, we are steadily moving towards a state of *nature disconnection*. This shift carries profound implications for our individual and collective well-being. One study found that over half of American adults spend less than five hours a week outside, an astounding statistic that highlights the urgency of rebuilding a more nature-connected life.[3] Several forces are driving this disconnection phenomenon. The rise of smartphones, the dominance of screens and increased urbanisation are all pulling us indoors.[4] As we navigate our way through a future with technological advances of unprecedented sophistication, the importance of nature connection will only grow more essential and urgent. The rise of transformative technologies such as artificial intelligence will present great opportunities for us as a species but also profound challenges. Along the way, we must stay grounded in what it means to be human. Whether it's planting, harvesting or simply observing, edimentals encourage mindful interaction and time spent in green spaces, supporting both physical and mental well-being. At our core, we are not separate from nature, we are a part of it.

My exploration of edimentals has led me to believe that they can play a meaningful role in mending our relationship with the natural world. In a time when eco-anxiety often looms large, edimentals offer a way to reconnect, inspire change and generate hope. Their power lies in their ability to spark interest and passion for nature and, ultimately, foster a desire to protect it. Broadening our plant palette

(continued on page 34)

Case Study
The Eden Project, Nature Connection & The Power of a Big Idea
TIM SMIT

Many of you may know the Eden Project – perhaps you've even visited this extraordinary garden in Cornwall. Created in a former clay pit with no soil or plants, it was transformed into a vast global garden, its iconic biomes housing thousands of species from diverse climates. It embodies many of the messages at the heart of this book: reconnecting with nature, using food as a gateway to that connection and the transformative power of bold ideas. I spoke with Tim Smit, Eden's co-founder, to gain a deeper understanding of the vision behind this remarkable place and to explore the lessons we can learn from the big ideas that drive it.

'Eden was conceptually very simple,' Tim tells me. 'Just imagine the crater of a volcano, with a funnel pouring all the world's productive plants into it.' It began as a leap of imagination, a bold belief in what might be possible, rooted deeply in his earlier restoration of the Lost Gardens of Heligan – a once-forgotten Victorian estate in Cornwall, overgrown and abandoned for decades, which he and a small team brought back to life in the 1990s. There, Tim encountered the Victorian concept of the 'hungry months' – a time when food became desperately scarce – and he learned how our survival hinged upon respecting seasonal rhythms. This realisation ignited in him a profound appreciation for those who grow our food: 'Without horticulturists and gardeners, we starve to death. They are applied scientists, every bit as important as medics.'

Inspired by Heligan's seasonal wisdom, Eden emerged as something even more ambitious. 'We wanted Eden to be a living theatre of plants and people,' Tim describes. The fact that they succeeded underscores Eden's fundamental message: what may seem impossible can be just the beginning of something extraordinary.

For Tim, reconnecting with nature isn't complicated. It's a core, innate feeling we

Sir Tim Smit, co-founder of the Eden Project.

REIMAGINING THE EDIBLE GARDEN

'The crater of a volcano': the Eden Project pit, ready for transformation.

experience simply by being outdoors. 'Nature resets me,' he says. 'It touches the wild part of your heart. You don't need science to feel better in nature – just go out in it and tell me you don't feel something.'

Food is central to Tim's vision of this reconnection. 'Why is it that most people vividly remember the picnics they've had in life?' he wonders aloud. Meals shared outside root deeply in our memories. 'It's that old al fresco.' Tim smiles. 'Eating in nature is a return. A reset. A cleansing.'

Growing food at home deepens this bond even further. Tim reminds me, 'You don't need to produce at scale – you can grow small amounts of quality food. That is divine.' He recalls the intense flavour of Royal Sovereign strawberries, rarely available commercially because of their low yield but with an unforgettable taste. Or eating a perfectly ripe peach: 'The juice runs down your front, and you want to laugh.' He laments the loss of nutrition in mass-produced fruit, noting wryly, '"An apple a day keeps the doctor away" – only true now if it's an old variety.' Growing at home allows us to cultivate delicious plants and heirloom fruits and vegetables that aren't available in shops, reconnecting us with foods that are truly nutritious and full of flavour. Even a tiny harvest can leave a lasting impression. 'If you live in a flat in London and grow on your windowsill,' Tim says, 'that one salad a year is going to be the best salad you've ever eaten, and you'll remember it forever.'

Food and beauty, for Tim, cannot be separated – they're inherently linked, nourishing our senses and spirits together. 'The first joy is growing something and creating beauty. Then comes the prize of creating food,' he explains. 'Beautiful food generates a deep sense of abundance, touching our inner contentment.' Eden is, in Tim's words, 'a love child between great horticulture and great theatre,' combining playful exhibitions, large food forests and growing spaces, and engaging sessions that highlight the magic of growing food. Eden makes gardening a joyful, public act – one that reconnects visitors with nature, community and their own potential to create abundance.

While Eden operates at a grand scale, Tim passionately believes its core messages easily translate to our everyday lives. 'Growing food, even modestly, provides agency, resilience and deep satisfaction. Give yourself the absolute rush of learning to grow something and sheltering it until it fruits – that's more valuable than any formal education.'

Eden's true legacy is about more than gardens and biomes – it's about encouraging bold action, empowering people to reclaim spaces and imagine new possibilities. 'The world is filled with derelict land and forgotten spaces. Get your mates together and start a revolution. Reclaim that land and make something beautiful, grow things to eat for you and your community. You know why? Because you can. And if you do it with enough ambition, loads of people who were sleeping will wake up and get involved.'

The Eden Project in Cornwall, with its iconic biomes housing global plant collections, demonstrates the power of a big idea to transform a former clay pit into a living classroom for ecology, art and education. In the foreground, nature play structures invite children to explore and connect with the natural world.

REIMAGINING THE EDIBLE GARDEN

and growing even a small portion of our own food can lead to wider lifestyle shifts, as well as an awareness of how our food is produced and its impact on the planet. This kind of engagement can deepen our understanding of global issues while grounding us in the everyday choices we make. And it's in those individual, local decisions – driven by care, curiosity and conscious consumerism – that regenerative, relocalised food systems can shift from niche to norm.

An Ancient Concept

The Eden Project shows how radical a garden can feel today, yet throughout history people have been combining productivity and beauty in equally visionary ways. The concept of edimentals ties into other contemporary terms you may have come across, like 'foodscaping' – which focuses on incorporating edible plants into traditional landscape settings – or 'edible landscaping', a broader idea that centres edible plants as the foundation of the design. Whatever the name – edimentals, foodscaping, edible landscaping – this seemingly new approach to designing gardens has been rising in popularity. But the concept of edimentals is far from new.

For millennia, civilisations around the world have combined beauty and productivity in remarkably sophisticated ways – from the

Around the world, oak trees were historically renowned for their nutrient-dense acorns.

forest gardens of the Amazon, shaped by Indigenous communities for over ten thousand years through selective planting and soil enrichment, to the managed woodlands of the Pacific Northwest, cultivated by peoples like the Coast Salish and Haida.[5] In Mesopotamia, early irrigation supported ornamental and edible gardens that likely helped spark the rise of complex societies, while Roman villas featured *horti* – enclosed gardens rich with olives, figs, herbs and vegetables – that spread many now-familiar edimentals across Europe.[6] The Aztecs built *chinampas*, floating gardens on lakes around Tenochtitlan, creating one of the most advanced water-based growing systems ever devised.[7] In medieval Europe, monastery gardens integrated food, healing and symbolism, while English cottage gardens brought together fruit, herbs, vegetables and flowers in accessible, small-scale abundance.[8]

These weren't fleeting trends but resilient systems rooted in ecological awareness and cultural tradition. For me, learning about these histories has been transformative – a reminder that edimentals aren't a modern invention but a reconnection with ancient wisdom. Today's gardens can draw on that legacy to create spaces that are nourishing, meaningful and deeply in tune with history, people and place.

A great number of edimentals once held cultural and nutritional importance, yet they have since slipped from common use. We've largely forgotten that they were ever edible at all. Acorns, for example – produced by the majestic oak (*Quercus* spp.) – were once processed into flour and formed a key food source in Indigenous and early European diets. Today, aside from niche revival movements, most people don't associate oak trees with anything edible at all. Indian ricegrass (*Achnatherum hymenoides*) is another example. Once a vital grain for Indigenous North American communities, it provided a protein-rich staple before wheat and maize took over. Now, where ricegrass once thrived, vast monocultures dominate. These ingredients haven't disappeared because they weren't useful, but because industrial agriculture prioritised crops that could be bred, processed and scaled more efficiently.

Although humans have a deep history and connection with these plants and the natural world in which they originate, we have largely decoupled our link to the sources of food we eat, and we are on a path to disconnection from nature. The foraging-like qualities of edimentals blur the line between the wild and the cultivated, offering a way to bring the act of foraging into our own gardens and daily lives and reclaiming meaningful connections between us and the food we eat.

Foraging

At its core, foraging is the act of searching for, identifying and harvesting wild food. For humans, foraging is an ancient practice. It predates agriculture, precedes the garden gate and remains integral to many cultures around the world today. Our connection to foraging runs deep even though, for many of us, the ritual has been dormant for generations.

Although rooted in rural landscapes, foraging is far from limited to these environments. Cities, in fact, are rich with edible opportunities – that's where I've explored much of my own foraging. Once I'd taken a few steps along the foraging path, my view of the urban landscape changed entirely. I began to see living, edible ecosystems. Nettles (*Urtica dioica*), elder (*Sambucus nigra*), wild greens and a patchwork of seasonal fruits have all featured in my city harvests. Much of this urban bounty goes unnoticed or wasted. Of course, foraging in cities comes with caveats – pollution, for example, is a valid concern. The key is common sense: avoid areas near heavy traffic, polluted waterways and low-growing edibles in dog-walking hotspots. As a general rule, if I wouldn't want to sit and eat my lunch there, I won't forage from it.

Dietary Diversity & Health

Edimentals encourage greater diversity in our diets, with meals often easily consisting of ten, twenty or even more varieties of different plants. Along with this diversity comes a whole new world of flavours. The industrial agricultural revolution, particularly from the mid-twentieth-century 'Green Revolution' onward, limited our diets to

Foraging awakens something ancient within us – the instinct to seek, notice and harvest from the land – rekindling our bond with the natural world.

Stinging nettles don't make it onto my edimental list but they are one of my most valued foraged foods.

a measly palette of just thirty or so crops, all bred for yield and transportability over taste or nutrition.[9] Edimentals, meanwhile, open that door wide again – to flavour, colour, culture and nourishment.

Most of us know the fiery kick of horseradish (*Armoracia rusticana*), the gentle savoury lift of chives (*Allium schoenoprasum*) or the tart, mouth-puckering pull of rhubarb (*Rheum × hybridum*). But common plants can feel completely unfamiliar at first – like sorrel (*Rumex acetosa*) with its citrusy tang; skirret (*Sium sisarum*) with its sweet, nutty root; biennial plant alexanders (*Smyrnium olusatrum*) with its bold, peppery flavour; or salsify (*Tragopogon porrifolius*), another biennial, with an oyster-like taste. You may not love them all straight away, and that's okay. Studies show it often takes repeated exposure to develop a liking for new tastes, much like children learning to enjoy broccoli.[10] Our taste buds evolve over time, and adults can retrain theirs just as children can. It's important to keep an open mind when trying new textures, flavours and colours. Let's face it, not many of us loved our first coffee or pint of lager!

The benefits of experimenting with the vast array of edimental flavours extends beyond our palate into our gut microbiome. Our ancestors regularly consumed hundreds of different

Even in the heart of a city, edible plants thrive in overlooked places – reminding us that urban environments hold abundant foraging potential for those who know where to look.

REIMAGINING THE EDIBLE GARDEN

Today our limited diet consists of just a few staple vegetables despite the thousands of edible plant species once part of human diets.

plant species each year, from wild greens to roots, flowers, fruits and tree crops.[11] In contrast, today the average Western diet relies on fewer than twelve plant species, with common wheat (*Triticum aestivum*), maize/corn (*Zea mays*) and rice (*Oryza sativa*) dominating.[12] But modern research confirms what our ancestors knew intuitively: diversity is vital. People with fibre-rich, varied diets – similar to those still seen in traditional or foraging communities – have more beneficial gut bacteria and experience better overall health.[13] Edimentals and perennial foods are often higher in prebiotic fibre and beneficial phytochemicals. They're also typically more nutrient-dense than intensively farmed crops, and they offer more varied, complex flavours than many of the mass-produced vegetables.[14]

The human body is made up of roughly equal numbers of human and microbial cells, with trillions of those microbes living in our digestive system.[15] A thriving gut microbiome feeds on variety – especially diverse, plant-based foods – and the edimental diet is naturally rich in the very ingredients it craves.[16] Just as regenerative landscapes rebuild the microbiology of soil, diverse diets rebuild the microbiology of our own internal ecosystems.

An array of edimentals brings diversity into the kitchen.

The Broad Range of Edimentals

Edimentals encompass an extraordinary diversity of plants, spanning climates, functions and ecological niches. They can be native or non-native, adapted to a wide range of environmental conditions, and grown in layers to mimic natural plant communities. Their multipurpose nature means they offer much more than food or beauty alone, playing vital roles in pollination, soil health, climate resilience and more.

Native vs Non-Native Edimentals

Depending on where you live in the world, the terms native and non-native (or exotic) carry a wide range of connotations. There is a long-standing debate – often between ecologists and horticulturalists – about the merits and limitations of each, and how they interact with surrounding wildlife. Edimental planting typically takes a blended approach. I believe there are significant benefits to both native and non-native species. The key is to embrace a sensible, holistic perspective that considers your location, local ecology and personal needs.

Sorrel is an essential species for the small copper butterfly.

Native plants are important as they have co-evolved with local wildlife and offer crucial ecological benefits, as well as providing food and habitat.[17] Some species have evolved to have a dependency on specific native plants. For example, the small copper butterfly depends almost entirely on the edimental sorrel (*Rumex* spp.) as a larval food plant. Females lay their eggs exclusively on sorrel to ensure that newly hatched caterpillars have immediate access to food.[18] Native species typically require less maintenance, as they are well suited to local soils and climate.[19] However, with a rapidly changing climate, they are often being pushed to the extremes of their tolerances and, in some circumstances, it could be argued that carefully chosen non-native species may be more resilient and appropriate for the long-term future of a place.[20]

Wild garlic is my favourite basil substitute when making pesto.

Beyond ecological benefits, native plants carry a rich cultural significance.[21] They help define a sense of place and mark the changing seasons in meaningful ways. I treasure those key calendar moments tied to local flora – like the wild garlic (*Allium ursinum*) that carpets woodland floors in spring and quickly becomes jars of vibrant pesto stored for weeks to come. Or the sight of hawthorn (*Crataegus monogyna*) branches heavy with haws in autumn, decorated red and perfect for a rich, hedgerow-style ketchup. Preserving and celebrating these seasonal rituals is one of the most beautiful and nurturing aspects of using native edimentals.

Hawthorns are resilient, diverse and widespread across the temperate zones.

On the other hand, non-native (or exotic) plants can help extend the season of interest and productivity. They may flower, fruit or remain evergreen outside the peak windows of native species, providing valuable resources for us and wildlife. For example, most of the UK's native plants flower in spring or early summer, with relatively few continuing into autumn. By incorporating North American native edimentals, such as prairie plants like anise hyssop (*Agastache foeniculum*) or Jerusalem artichoke (*Helianthus tuberosus*), you can stretch the flowering season through the latter part of the year. The reverse is true as well: in North America, integrating hardy UK-native edimentals like sea kale (*Crambe maritima*) can offer early-season interest and valuable forage for pollinators before many North American natives have begun to bloom.

Not all wildlife are specialists – many are generalists who can thrive on a variety of food sources and habitats. While this doesn't mean we should overlook the needs of specialist species (which are often the most endangered), it does suggest that a mixed edimental approach is likely to bring wide-ranging benefits for local biodiversity, and for us. My harvests would not be the same without the integration of non-native species. A moment's rest at the allotment on a summer's day is often accompanied by juicy, aromatic berries from the

Sea buckthorn has one of the highest vitamin C contents of all fruits.

Japanese wineberry (*Rubus phoenicolasius*). Autumn lunches in the garden are followed by foraging for bright orange sea buckthorn (*Hippophae rhamnoides* – native only to the UK coastline) berries, a zingy hit of vitamin C to round off the meal. And when the season's been warm and kind, harvesting sun-ripened figs (*Ficus carica*) straight from the tree instantly transports me back to idyllic holidays in Mediterranean landscapes.

Of course, we can't ignore the very real risks associated with non-native species. There are countless examples of exotic plants becoming invasive and disrupting local ecosystems.[22] It's vital to do your research, and to understand what's appropriate for your specific environment. Just because a plant thrives in one region of the country doesn't mean it won't cause problems somewhere else.

At the heart of an edimental approach is the understanding that native and non-native plants aren't opposing forces. It's about taking a pragmatic, place-based view drawing from both to create edible landscapes that are resilient, generous and ecologically attuned.

Matching Plant to Place

Edimentals can thrive in a wide range of conditions – from damp meadows to dry gravel gardens. Just as many wildlife species are generalists, some edimentals are, too – they don't need overly specific conditions and can adapt to a broad range of settings. This includes several classic garden plants. Some edimentals might be able to tolerate extreme conditions in the wild, and, in many cases, they actually perform best when planted in environments that echo those origins. Take rosemary (*Salvia rosmarinus*) and lavender (*Lavandula* spp.), for example. These Mediterranean sub-shrubs (small, semi-woody plants that sit between perennials and shrubs) are tough – adapted to drought, poor rocky soils and full sun. Plant rosemary and lavender in rich, moist UK soils and they grow rapidly, seemingly thriving, only to burn out early, becoming woody and short-lived. Just because a plant can survive outside its preferred conditions doesn't mean it will flourish there. It's still essential to match plant to place thoughtfully.

Layers & Companion Planting

In a typical edimental scheme, you might find canopy layers rich with fruits and nuts emerging from a matrix of herbaceous perennials – plants of all sizes offering an abundance of vegetables, leaves and flowers. The soil is knit together by delicious creeping groundcovers and bulbs, while climbers twine their way up woody plants, reaching for light and showering down their bounty. From ginkgo trees (*Ginkgo biloba*) producing edible seeds in the canopy, down to wild strawberries (*Fragaria vesca*) offering tiny gems along the ground – the possibilities for layering edimentals are endless.

To enjoy their bold foliage set against a wall, figs are great to grow against south-facing elevations of buildings.

REIMAGINING THE EDIBLE GARDEN

Multipurpose Plants

Many edimentals often serve several functions beyond simply being edible and beautiful. A short walk around my allotment reveals just how diverse those benefits can be. Chives (*Allium schoenoprasum*) – and alliums more broadly – are prolific in the edible meadow edges and polytunnel. They're pollinator magnets, and I use them constantly, not just for their flavour, but as excellent companion plants for more traditional annual vegetables. Yarrow (*Achillea millefolium*) dances through the meadow, offering soft texture and powerful medicinal qualities. In moderation, it's known to support the immune system, aid digestion and act as an anti-inflammatory. I use it to make tea (read more about my favourite herbal edimental teas in chapter 8), and a brewer friend has even swapped it in for hops when making beer, although I can't vouch for the health claims of that recipe!

Hazel shrubs (*Corylus* spp.), carefully placed as natural windbreaks, are essential on my open, exposed plot. Beyond shelter, they produce nuts, and their coppiced wood is a resource for firewood and craftwork. And in and around nutrient-hungry plants, a living green manure of leguminous species – such as clovers (*Trifolium* spp.) – improves soil fertility by fixing nitrogen and boosting long-term productivity.

These are dynamic, responsive plants with far-reaching impacts – often triggering unexpected interactions and positive outcomes. You may plant an edimental for one standout trait, only to discover a whole raft of additional qualities over time. That's part of the magic.

Yarrow is a magnet for pollinators and can be brewed into a fragrant herbal tea when used in moderation. Historically, it was also used in beer brewing before hops became common.

Vibrant pink chive flowers bring colour and flavour to the garden. They belong to the diverse allium family – one of the most accessible and rewarding groups of edible plants.

REIMAGINING THE EDIBLE GARDEN

Case Study
Edimental Nurseries & the Growers Behind the Plants
MANDY BARBER OF INCREDIBLE VEGETABLES

For Mandy Barber, the journey into perennial vegetables began with a chance discovery. 'The plant that started it off was a perennial "Nine Star" broccoli [*Brassica oleracea* (Botrytis Group) "Nine Star Perennial"],' she says. 'It was like, wow, this variety will produce for five years. How come I didn't know about this?' That moment lit a spark. 'It got me down the perennial brassica avenue. Then I realised there were perennial

Mandy Barber, founder and grower at Incredible Vegetables.

kales (*Brassica oleracea* var. *ramosa* Acephala Group) and collards (*Brassica oleracea* Acephala Group), and that opened up all these pathways of research into perennial edible plants.'

Over time, Mandy's garden transformed into 'a wild perennial garden, a bit of a topsy turvy forest garden.' She started from the ground up – literally – with vegetables first, then added trees later. Now, it's a place where 'perennial veg can stand up to the kind of wildness and low maintenance. Every year, they just come back up through everything.'

Mandy's nursery, Incredible Vegetables, in Devon, UK, grew out of scarcity. 'People would approach me saying, I hear you've got such-and-such,' she recalls. 'I'd post on social media, and a whole flurry of people would descend.' Though demand now far outstrips supply, especially since the pandemic surge, Mandy resists scaling up. 'I can't grow things fast enough. But the reason I got into this is because I love the plants. I don't want to be removed from that. They're all nurtured and cared for by me.'

Her deep sense of purpose runs through everything. 'I feel like this is my life's work, my contribution; it can only improve things by making the country more biodiverse.' Whether it's carbon capture, habitat creation or simply 'if the beetles are happy because you haven't dug that area' – to her, that matters.

Mandy embraces the term 'edimentals'. 'You don't have to separate everything out –you can have this naturalistic polyculture, which is incredibly ornamental and still delicious.' When asked what edible plants she found most attractive for gardens, Mandy couldn't tell me a perennial veg that she thought was ugly. For Mandy, they're all delightful plants. 'Even when they're in their seed-head phase – like sea beet – I find that beautiful.'

Mandy's advice for someone wanting to try at home? 'Start with perennial kales or perennial onions and leeks. They're easy to grow, and people know what to do with them in the kitchen. It's a way in.' From there, you can begin to experiment with giants like giant Korean celery (*Dystaenia takeshimana*) and create your own edible oasis. One of Mandy's greatest joys has been learning to let go. 'The biggest lesson has been allowing nature to find its own way. I came back to my garden after a month and found American groundnut twining up fennel, both flowering in this beautiful, mad tangle. Nature knows how to design better than we do.'

Mandy Barber's garden in Devon showcases the beauty and productivity of perennial food.

REIMAGINING THE EDIBLE GARDEN

Edimentals vs Traditional Food Growing

I want to clarify what I mean by traditional food growing and draw some comparisons to the edimental way. When I refer to traditional systems, I'm talking about the cultivation of staple crops and vegetables – typically annuals and biennials. I'm deliberately simplifying here, because it's more helpful to view growing methods as existing along a spectrum. For the purposes of this book, I'm using the term 'traditional' to describe the classic allotment or kitchen garden. These conjure images of neat rows of monoculture veg, an abundance of produce

Neat, weed-free rows of veg are the gold standard of traditional food growing yet challenging to achieve with our busy twenty-first-century lifestyles.

and beautiful, friable soil worked to a fine tilth, ready for the next sowing. In these systems, yield is king, and time demands are high.

There's huge potential for edimentals to integrate beautifully into traditional systems – whether in market gardens, walled gardens, smallholdings, allotments or annual veg plots. My allotment is a blend of approaches. Fruit trees provide height and take advantage of vertical space. Below is a structural layer of soft fruit bushes and architectural edimentals such as globe artichokes (*Cynara cardunculus* Scolymus Group). Interwoven throughout is an edible meadow yielding a diverse tapestry of salad leaves, flowers, seeds and tubers across the seasons. Annual crops still occupy a solid place, woven

An alternative approach: the edible meadow at my allotment, punctuated by fruit trees and flanked by berry bushes and annual crops.

REIMAGINING THE EDIBLE GARDEN

through open gaps and thriving under the shelter of the polytunnel. I treat the space as a dynamic, evolving experiment. It's as much about the learning process as the harvest. That's where the joy lies.

Benefits & Challenges of Traditional Food Growing

One of the biggest advantages of traditional food growing is its high yield. Annual crops have been selectively bred for productivity, offering abundant harvests within a single season. These systems are also easily scalable, which explains why they've become the foundation of modern commercial agriculture.

Another benefit lies in the familiarity of staple crops, which form the backbone of most culinary traditions. These are the flavours many of us have grown up with. They're easy to prepare, straightforward to cook and don't require any adventurous taste-testing. For many of us, they bring comfort and ease in the kitchen.

Finally, there's the visual satisfaction and a level of instant gratification. Few experiences compare to seeing a once-bare patch of soil transformed into orderly rows of lush, edible crops. The rituals of preparing soil, sowing seeds and tending the beds tap into an innate satisfaction, imprinted within us after twelve thousand years of farming.[23] For many of us, this process is deeply therapeutic, offering both structure and a rewarding physicality.

But there are practical challenges to consider, too. Traditional food growing is time-intensive. Since most crops are annuals, there's a constant cycle of sowing, watering, feeding, weeding and replanting. Traditional systems can also require regular interventions like crop rotation and companion planting to maintain balance. It often demands regular attention and consistent effort – something that's not always compatible with our modern, busy lifestyles.

Traditional food growing often comes with a heavier reliance on external inputs. Regular soil disturbance encourages weed growth. Sowing seeds, fertilising, watering thirsty crops and keeping pests at bay all require consistent intervention. Over time, this often leads to a dependence on added materials – compost, feed, mulch, slug traps – and these inputs carry ongoing costs. Plastic seed trays, netting, fleece and other protective materials are commonly used and, while often essential, add to both the financial and environmental footprint of the garden.

Pests and diseases are another issue. Straight rows of vegetables can look like a buffet to caterpillars, slugs and countless other pests.

Familiar problems like carrot fly, cabbage white caterpillars and fungal blights can wipe out crops unless managed carefully. This often leads to reactive gardening, including applying pesticides and other chemicals in response to the oncoming hordes.

Lastly, space can be a barrier. Traditional food growing generally requires dedicated ground – veg beds in your garden, a walled kitchen garden or an allotment away from your home. But as gardens shrink and urban living increases, many people simply don't have access to enough growing space.

Diverse, Resilient Systems

Ultimately, a multifaceted approach is required for us to adapt to the changing climate and to build diverse, resilient ecosystems. It's not about choosing between edimentals and traditional food growing. It's all about a diverse approach and multidisciplinary practice. It's helpful to take a view of your life situation – your time, passions and the space you have available. Design a system that works for you and create an edible environment that speaks to your soul.

Perennial Veg vs Edimental

You might be wondering about the difference between a perennial vegetable and an edimental? The two categories overlap considerably, but they're not completely interchangeable. Edimentals span a wide range of plant types – from trees and shrubs to herbs, bulbs and climbers. And not all the edible parts are

Perennial veg or edimental? Perennial brassicas are often vigorous, woody and a little unruly. While valuable as a long-lived food crop, they lack the ornamental qualities that characterise true edimentals. I'm afraid they wouldn't make their way into my borders.

REIMAGINING THE EDIBLE GARDEN

vegetables in the traditional sense. Some offer seeds, fruits, nuts or legumes. On the other hand, most perennial vegetables could be considered edimentals, but here's where I draw a personal distinction: not all perennial vegetables are what I'd consider classically beautiful – and for me, beauty matters. It's a deciding factor as to whether a plant earns a place in one of my designed borders.

Of course, beauty is subjective. What I see as unruly or awkward, you might see as charming and full of character. There are some true 'ugly delicious' of the perennial veg world – in fact, some of the least ornamental perennials are among the tastiest. Perennial kales like Daubenton's (*Brassica oleracea* var. *ramosa*) or Taunton Deane (*Brassica oleracea* var. *acephala*) are perfect examples. They're incredibly hardy, generously productive and low maintenance, but, left unchecked, they can grow into sprawling woody masses. Good King Henry (*Blitum bonus-henricus*) is another. A fantastic spinach alternative, packed with nutrition, but visually... Let's just say it hasn't won any design awards. I draw the line somewhere, and my design sensibilities take over. These kinds of plants have a home on my plot, but usually tucked away in a corner, doing their thing with quiet diligence.

Perennial veg systems often feature a combination of edimentals and more utilitarian plants. They lean into beauty through their structure and diversity, but the primary driver is food. Productivity, resilience and regeneration take precedence over show-stopping aesthetics. These systems still feel wild and alive, but with a slightly different design focus than, say, an ornamental border filled with edimentals. As we will see, perennial vegetables sit at the heart of permaculture thinking and many of the regenerative movements – such as food forests (as we will see in chapter 4), polycultures and low-input systems – growing happily alongside herbs, fruit trees and other multifunctional plants. Much of what we explore in this book draws on the potential of these long-lived, low-maintenance crops. Semantics aside, one thing is clear: if we want to build resilient, edible landscapes, perennials need to form a big part of the picture.

Case Study

Polycultures & Diversity at Birch Farm

JOSH SPARKES

When thinking about diversity and resilience, there was one place I knew I had to visit: Birch Farm in North Devon, UK. Spread over seventeen acres, the site is a living experiment in natural and regenerative farming, vividly showcasing the potential of combining edimentals, perennial crops and ecological design. Birch Farm is part of a local collective and supplies seasonal produce to the Farmers Arms pub and village shop in Woolsery. The farm's ethos embodies the principles of relocalised and regenerative agriculture: producing nutrient-dense food while restoring the land that sustains it.

The farm feels like a vibrant mosaic of life. Trees stretch upwards, perennial vegetables and edimentals flourish beneath and wildlife thrives. While walking through the fields with visionary head grower Josh Sparkes, we spotted both a grass snake and an adder – an increasingly rare sight in UK agricultural settings. 'When we started, there was no birdsong here,' Josh recalls. 'Now, after just four years, the place is bursting with life.'

'Diversity isn't just the range of plants,' Josh explains. 'It's about integrating different growing systems together, layering them so each enhances the other.' At Birch Farm, annual crops are grown in highly diverse polycultures. Food forests, perennial beds and syntropic rows weave across the landscape. What binds it all together is a guiding philosophy of working with nature, not against it.

Rather than sowing traditional cover crops – plants grown between harvests to protect and enrich the soil – Josh uses wild plants already thriving on site. 'Weeds provide free fertility, pollinator habitat, forage for wildlife and even edible harvests,' he says. 'They're perfectly adapted to this ecosystem. Nature has already done the work.'

The mastermind behind Birch Farm, Josh Sparkes.

REIMAGINING THE EDIBLE GARDEN

Stunning polycultures bring diversity and complexity to traditional crops at Birch Farm.

Perennials form the backbone of the farm. 'They stay in the ground, reducing our need for compost, seed and labour. They're more climate resilient and fill the hunger gap brilliantly when most annual veg is still getting going.' Among his favourite edimentals are sea kale (*Crambe maritima*), Turkish rocket (*Bunias orientalis*), and Korean aster (*Doellingeria scabra*). 'The perennials are key for biodiversity,' he adds. 'They adapt much better to a wetter spring or hotter summer, and reduce irrigation needs because of their deeper roots.'

That said, annuals still play a vital role, especially for the pub's chefs and local customers. But they're never grown in monoculture. Rows of beetroot (*Beta vulgaris* subsp. *vulgaris*, Conditiva Group), coriander (*Coriandrum sativum*), chard (*Beta vulgaris* subsp. *vulgaris*, Cicla Group) and kale (*Brassica oleracea*, Acephala Group) are interplanted with flowers and herbs. 'I don't understand why growers shy away from polycultures,' Josh says. 'People say it's about efficiency, but we're not inefficient, and we've proven the results after years of creating annual polycultures.'

His approach builds fertility through plant diversity rather than fertilisers. 'By having so much root variation – different

depths, nutrient demands, plant families – you're naturally going to build soil health.' The above-ground beauty, it turns out, reflects an underground richness. This commitment to combining productivity with aesthetics stems in part from Josh's background in ornamental horticulture. 'Growing food doesn't have to look boring,' he says, smiling. 'Beauty engages people. It sparks curiosity and opens up conversations about ecology and sustainability.'

That belief extends beyond the field and into the kitchen. Josh works closely with chefs at the Farmers Arms to introduce lesser-known perennial vegetables into the culinary mainstream. 'We need chefs using perennial foods and edimentals first. Once chefs introduce these flavours, it trickles down into home gardens and community diets,' he explains. 'When diners experience their amazing flavour, demand grows organically.'

For home gardeners, Josh's advice is simple: 'Don't be afraid. Horticulture isn't concrete. Have fun, experiment and enjoy it. Efficiency isn't necessary in home gardens – beauty and enjoyment are.'

Birch Farm is a compelling model of what regenerative food systems can look like in practice. 'Birch Farm has proven how quickly ecosystems can be restored,' Josh reflects. 'In four years, birds, snakes and biodiversity returned naturally. It's deeply hopeful – we really can reverse ecological decline.' As he puts it, 'Small-scale farming is what we need. We don't need to upscale. We need to put diversity, beauty and resilience back into our food-growing systems. Our responsibility as landowners is to care for nature, rebuild ecosystems and grow food in ways that enhance biodiversity, not diminish it.'

Chapter 3

Edimentals for All Gardens

Edimentals can be worked into existing herbaceous borders, used as the main feature of a newly planted garden, or rolled out across spaces large or small. You can transition gradually, filling gaps, moving plants and shifting your space into an edimental scheme over time. Edimentals allow every gardener to maximise the potential of their space, no matter the size. Whether you have a windowsill, a rural estate, an urban garden, a smallholding or manage a school garden, the principles of layering and integrating edibility are universal.

There is a huge diversity in garden styles and planting approaches. I love the fact that gardens reflect the people who make them, and, when designing for my clients, I try to capture their spirit and draw it out into the garden. This is especially true in British gardens, where a long history and deep relationship with gardening have resulted in a wonderfully eccentric mix of styles. I've had the great pleasure of visiting many private and public gardens, and no two are ever the same. Even along a single London street, you might come

Sun-loving herbs like those on this windowsill can provide a steady supply of fresh flavour, even in the smallest indoor spaces.

across classical, historic, formal, cottage, romantic, arts and crafts, minimalist or naturalistic gardens. The beauty of edimentals is that they're for every type of garden.

Small Spaces

Not all of us have gardens or large outdoor spaces – but that shouldn't hold you back from growing your own. Even the most compact areas can be transformed with edimentals. Whether it's a sunny windowsill, a shaded courtyard or a city balcony, there are always creative, productive ways to integrate food into your life.

Windowsills

A sunny windowsill is all you need for a mini edible haven – pots of rosemary (*Salvia rosmarinus*), thyme (*Thymus vulgaris*), oregano (*Origanum vulgare*), chives (*Allium schoenoprasum*) and basil (*Ocimum basilicum*) offer both fragrance and fresh pickings within arm's reach. Add colour and interest with nasturtiums (*Tropaeolum majus*) or small chilli plants (*Capsicum annuum*).

Balconies

On balconies and small roof terraces, you often have great opportunities for vertical layering. Even in the tightest spaces, you can grow upwards – passionflowers (*Passiflora caerulea*) trained against walls or balustrades create a lush, edible backdrop. In cooler regions, this climber may not fruit reliably or persist as a perennial, but sheltered balconies can often benefit from the residual heat of the building, creating microclimates where more tender edimentals can thrive. Beneath these climbers, pots of herbs and fresh salad leaves make use of ground level. It's a simple way to turn even the most urban setting into a thriving edible escape.

There's an edimental for all scenarios, even balconies and rooftops.

Patios & Courtyards

A small patio or courtyard needs careful consideration of scale and planting style. I often notice raised beds in compact city spaces, but these can feel bulky and will box everything in. If you're in a rental apartment and stuck with imposing beds, work with what you've got – trailing edimentals like prostrate rosemary (*Salvia rosmarinus* 'Prostratus') can soften the edges. I had this exact setup in a London rental – a 3-by-3 metre (10 × 10 foot) courtyard boxed in by concrete beds. Trailing plants were essential to transforming the space, adding green softness to an otherwise stark layout.

If you have the option, planting directly into the ground creates a more fluid, natural feel. It allows plants to spill and soften the space. It also gives them access to groundwater and the nutrients in the native soil, making the garden more resilient. Layering diverse perennials builds a rich tapestry of textures, heights and seasonal shifts. Don't be afraid to go big either – small fruit trees or shrubs add mass and structure while bringing depth and seasonal dynamism. One of my favourite tricks in a small garden is to fill it with scent. Brushing past herbs by the door, catching a waft of citrus blossom, or enjoying night-scented plants like the biennial evening primrose (*Oenothera biennis*) perfuming the night air – it all creates a deeply sensory experience. Small gardens can be the most intimate and immersive. The key is making every element work hard for its place.

Pots & Planters

One impactful strategy in small spaces is to use fewer, larger pots. We often default to filling a patio with lots of small containers, but I find going bold, with one or two large statement planters, creates more visual impact and greater growing potential. A sculptural tree in a single oversized pot adds presence and structure all year round. Larger pots are also more resilient: they dry out less quickly and give plants room to develop strong root systems.

By mimicking the layers of a natural ecosystem, you can maximise productivity and biodiversity. A single large pot can become a miniature food forest. In warmer climates, this might include a small fruit tree, like a pomegranate (*Punica granatum*), underplanted with herbs such as oregano (*Origanum vulgare*), French tarragon (*Artemisia dracunculus*), and a creeping thyme (*Thymus serpyllum*) groundcover. It's a beautiful, low-maintenance system where the layers support one another. For renters, edimental pots and planters are ideal – they are portable, productive and easy to take with you when you move.

Case Study
Balcony Gardening with the Cloud Gardener UK
JASON WILLIAMS

When furloughed during lockdown, Jason Williams turned to his high-rise Manchester balcony for solace. 'I had nothing else to do, and there was no advice out there for balcony gardeners,' he recalls. 'I just stopped following the traditional gardening rules and went with the flow.' That shift – from frustration to experimentation – became The Cloud Gardener UK, an individual balcony project that grew into a movement.

Sharing both successes and failures online, Jason quickly found an audience of thousands who felt equally unseen in the mainstream gardening world.

His balcony today is a thriving patchwork of edimentals, annuals and purely ornamental plants. Herbs form the backbone: mint (*Mentha* spp.), chives (*Allium schoenoprasum*), basil (*Ocimum basilicum*), and salvias (*Salvia* spp.) – 'low-input plants

Jason Williams, the Cloud Gardener, transformed his high-rise balcony in Manchester into a thriving edible and ornamental garden, proving that even the smallest urban spaces can nurture biodiversity and community.

Jason's balcony garden sits eighteen floors above the city, filled with fruit, herbs, flowers and even edible ponds.

that can take a beating but still bring so much into the kitchen'. He plays with colour in crops like radishes (*Raphanus sativus*) and pak choi (*Brassica rapa* Chinensis Group), while his ponds (he has four of them!) brim with sorrel (*Rumex acetosa*), taro (*Colocasia esculenta*) and watercress (*Nasturtium officinale*). 'Even my mini ponds are edible,' he says, laughing. 'It's about maximising every opportunity – creating habitats and growing food, all at once.' For Jason, every plant must earn its place by offering multiple functions: food, beauty and biodiversity.

Designing for balconies demands invention. 'Levels are everything,' he tells me. Jason layers pots of different sizes for depth and rhythm, then uses trellises pinned against the wall by containers, rose arches and vertical herb towers to grow upwards without drilling into walls. He encourages people not to fear scale: 'Don't be scared of big plants in small spaces. They bring drama – just remember the wind and weight.'

Beyond harvests, Jason values the well-being his balcony offers. 'I can pick a tomato for dinner while watching butterflies feast on the plants around me. That's why I do it – food for me, food for wildlife.' He avoids screens outdoors, treating his balcony as a refuge that supports his mental and physical health.

Jason's vision extends far beyond his own garden. 'The goal is to connect as many people in the city to nature as possible,' he says. Travels to Singapore and China left him inspired: 'You walk through these dense cities and they're fantastically green. Why aren't we doing the same here?' He imagines a future where every balcony and rooftop contributes to urban biodiversity, and where tenants are granted the 'right to garden'. For now, his Manchester balcony proves the point: even the smallest space can be abundant, beautiful and alive.

Medium-Sized Gardens

You might already have a well-established and well-loved space that you've evolved over the years, or perhaps you're staring at a blank patch of earth, wondering where to begin. A medium-sized garden – whether urban, suburban or semi-rural – holds huge potential to transform into an edible landscape.

The first step is to take stock of what's already growing. As we've seen, it's surprising how many classic garden plants are already edible. Sedums (*Hylotelephium* spp.) are a popular garden staple with hidden culinary qualities. Use their fleshy young leaves in salads for a mild, cucumber-like crunch. Another example is the peppery bite of daylily flowers (*Hemerocallis* spp.), which can be tossed into a salad or dipped in batter for tempura. When assessing your existing plants, a great resource is Plants for a Future (www.pfaf.org), an invaluable online database for checking the edibility and medicinal features of plants.

Once you've explored what's already there, the next step is identifying the areas of opportunity. Some of the most overlooked spaces are vertical surfaces, and they're one of the first elements I consider when designing. Naturally, we tend to focus on ground-level planting, but vertical surfaces in a mid-sized garden can offer just as much potential. Take a 15 × 5 metre (or a 49 × 16 feet) garden – at first glance, you've got 75 square metres (or 784 square feet) of planting opportunity. But once you factor in terraces, pathways, storage, water features and lawn, you're often left with only half that measurement. Meanwhile, the boundaries – walls, fences and trellises – can provide around 60 square metres (646 square feet) of growing area, yet they so often remain bare.

Climbing edimentals are an obvious and incredibly rewarding solution. Hops (*Humulus lupulus*) will tangle their way up fences,

Bringing trees into even relatively small spaces is an effective way to add layers, depth and structure to the garden. Here a crab apple holds the border with seasonal interest and edible fruits.

offering visual impact and tender hop shoots in spring. Caucasian spinach (*Hablitzia tamnoides*), a vigorous shade-tolerant vine, scrambles effortlessly up tension wires or mesh. Even more traditional climbers like grapevines (*Vitis vinifera*) can be trained to make the most of these underused vertical spaces. Beyond walls and fences, even hedges can be made productive. An edible hedge might include elder (*Sambucus nigra*), crab apple (*Malus sylvestris*), hazel (*Corylus avellana*) and quince (*Cydonia oblonga*). A rather magical trick I love is grafting apples (*Malus domestica*) or pears (*Pyrus communis*) onto existing hawthorn (*Crataegus monogyna*) hedges – seamlessly blending wild and cultivated, enhancing an existing feature while layering in productivity at zero cost.

Strawberry gems tucked in between stepping stones in a garden that draws on forest garden principles of layering edimentals.

Edimentals aren't just for the obvious spots like borders; they're also perfect for the forgotten corners of a garden. Pathways, paving cracks and the spaces beneath trees all hold potential for low-growing edibles. Wild strawberries (*Fragaria vesca*) are brilliant for sprawling along pathways – brushing past them in summer, catching their scent and spotting tiny ruby fruits nestled among the foliage is one of those quiet joys an edimental garden brings. The dappled shade beneath trees, where little else thrives, is perfect for wild garlic (*Allium ursinum*). In spring, it erupts into a lush green carpet, and, beyond its well-loved use in pesto, its delicate white flowers can be sprinkled over salads and the strappy leaves cooked like spinach. Even ponds and water features can play a part – watercress (*Nasturtium officinale*) and water chestnuts (*Eleocharis dulcis*) are wonderful edimentals for water or boggy edges.

What I love about this approach is that it encourages you to work with what's already there, adding layers of interest and function over time. A mature, well-loved garden can transition into something richer, more dynamic and deeply intertwined with the seasons. But sometimes, you may want to go further by creating entirely new features, dedicating areas to edimentals, or even starting from a blank slate, something we'll explore more in chapter 4, Designing with Edimentals.

Large Gardens, Smallholdings & Estates

When working with large gardens, rural estates or productive smallholdings, the approach shifts from the intensive management of smaller spaces to a broader, more adaptive way of thinking. At this scale, it becomes more about working with the land and natural processes – introducing edible diversity, allowing plants to establish naturally and managing the landscape in a way that balances productivity with biodiversity. Instead of imposing a rigid design, the first and most valuable step is observation.

I've been going through this process on my own land in Wales, where in 2024 we began the slow transformation of eight acres of former pasture, scrub and woodland into a diverse edible landscape. Rather than rushing in with a masterplan, I've started by walking the land, taking stock of what's already there. So much of the groundwork is about noticing: where the light falls, where the soil holds moisture, which areas hum with biodiversity and which feel depleted. There's already an abundance of edibles if you know where to look – fruiting hedgerows, self-seeded herbs, wild greens tucked into the undergrowth – and foraging has been my first way into understanding the rhythms of the land before making more permanent interventions.

Over time, our aim is to build a home and design studio here, allowing many of the ideas in this book to play out across the site in a way that meets the needs of the land, our family and my work. Food forests and orchards will take root in open areas, while traditional veg beds will sit closer to the house. Edible hedges, syntropic agroforestry systems (dense, layered plantings that mimic natural succession to build soil and productivity) and a coppiced woodland of edible species (trees cut back to the ground periodically to promote vigorous regrowth) will weave across the slopes, with an edible wetland nestled into the damp low point. It's a slow, evolving project, but that steady approach allows for creativity, experimentation and a deeply personal expression of an edimental landscape.

The next step is to consider how to intervene, whether through subtle enhancements to existing systems or through the introduction of new elements. Larger spaces offer an incredible opportunity to shape edible landscapes that are immersive, biodiverse and productive. This

My plot in Wales, Long Barn Farm, in its early days. It is now on its way to becoming a richly layered edible landscape.

doesn't mean high-maintenance planting schemes – quite the opposite. At this scale, resilience is key. Any intervention needs to align with natural systems, ensuring the landscape remains low-input and self-sustaining over time.

There are countless ways to introduce productive layers into a landscape, whether by creating edible meadows or shaping new features like food forests, agroforestry systems and walled kitchen gardens. What's exciting about working with larger spaces is the freedom to experiment, to carve out new edible ecosystems, to play with structure and succession and to create something that not only feeds people but also restores and enriches the land.

I find these dualities – observation and intervention, patience and boldness – some of the most rewarding aspects of working at scale. With land, there is space to think big, but the best results come from a balance of careful listening and creative ambition. Some areas will remain semi-wild, enhanced only through thoughtful management, while others will take on newly designed forms, layered with productivity and intended to flourish over time. The most exciting thing is that this is just the beginning.

Green Infrastructure

In recent years, green infrastructure – features like living walls and green roofs – have moved from large-scale urban projects into private gardens and homes. These systems offer a creative way to introduce greenery and food production into overlooked spaces, making use of roofs, walls and vertical surfaces that would otherwise remain bare. Step back and look at any home, neighbourhood or city, and the sheer amount of unused vertical and rooftop space is striking. It's an untapped opportunity, particularly for bringing edimentals into the most unlikely of places.

Living Walls

For several years, my studio has been developing a 'Green Walls in Schools' initiative in collaboration with The Cabin Charity (a London-based organisation supporting children's well-being and education through nature and creativity). The goal is to make real change in urban schools, many of which are surrounded by seas of concrete and completely devoid of green space. By leveraging

'Green Walls in Schools' initiative in action – inspiring the next generation and planting an array of edimentals such as strawberries, rosemary and thyme.

government grants, we've been transforming barren playgrounds into living, breathing classrooms. The project focuses on the schools that need it most – those in areas of high pollution with little or no access to the soil beneath the tarmac. These living walls support biodiversity, improve air quality and give children hands-on opportunities to engage with nature.

Living walls are particularly valuable in dense, built-up areas where traditional gardens either aren't possible or would come at great expense. Trailing edimentals like strawberries (*Fragaria* spp.), salad burnet (*Sanguisorba minor*) and wild rocket (*Diplotaxis tenuifolia*) thrive in vertical planting systems, offering both greenery and a source of fresh, edible produce. That said, while living walls are an exciting solution for bringing life into urban environments, I still believe that planting in the ground is preferable wherever possible. Soil-based plantings are more resilient, require fewer inputs and support more complex ecosystems. But in spaces where access to soil simply isn't an option, living walls present a powerful way to introduce both greenery and food into even the most unlikely places.

Green Roofs

One of my most unusual projects was The Lodge, a neo-Gothic gatekeeper's cottage set within a graveyard in central London. The project gained attention when it was featured on Channel 4's *Grand Designs* and, with its historic and unexpected setting, it was clear that any landscape intervention needed to be handled sensitively.

The green roof at the central London neo-Gothic lodge transitioning to an edible meadow with the introduction of edimentals like chives.

As part of the planning requirements, a large green roof was specified. Often, these end up as sedum roofs (lightweight, low-maintenance living roofs planted with hardy, drought-tolerant sedum species, *Sedum* spp.), which provide some benefits but lack the richness and ecological value of more complex plantings. Instead, working with Pictorial Meadows, a UK-based wildflower meadow and seed supplier, we created a wildflower meadow on just 80 millimetres (3.2 inches) of substrate, turning the roof into a thriving, biodiverse habitat that softened the building and tied it beautifully into its surroundings.

Because we are involved in the ongoing management of the garden, we've had the opportunity to gradually introduce edimentals into the planting. Over time, that wildflower meadow has evolved into something even more dynamic – an edible meadow. What began as an ornamental roof has become something productive, too. Mediterranean herbs like chives (*Allium schoenoprasum*), thyme

(*Thymus* spp.) and oregano (*Origanum vulgare*) now weave through the wildflowers, enhancing biodiversity while also making the space more functional. The result is a roof that not only looks beautiful and supports wildlife but also provides fresh herbs and salad for our client, right in the heart of London.

This project proves that green roofs can be far more than a box-ticking exercise. They can become vibrant, functioning edible ecosystems that blend seamlessly into their surroundings while offering genuine ecological and culinary value. The Lodge remains a flagship example of how even a shallow layer of soil can sustain abundant, biodiverse and delicious planting.

Edimentals for All Ages

Much of this book focuses on what you can do as a keen gardener or professional practitioner, but the process of creating an edible landscape, and its impact, extends far beyond the individual. A garden doesn't exist in isolation; it is experienced by everyone who interacts with it, and, perhaps most powerfully, by children. In my experience, children love edimentals. They seem to instantly understand the foraging concept and are naturally drawn to the idea that food can be picked straight from the landscape. At my design studio, we've worked with schools and children from all different walks of life, and time and time again I've witnessed the same innate love of nature. It's something we are all born with, yet for many that spark fades as we grow older. A naturalistic, edimental garden plays into the sheer joy that children get from scrambling around and exploring the outdoors, layering in an element of edibility that opens their eyes to the living world around them. These early experiences can foster lifelong connections with nature and food, shaping how they engage with both for the rest of their lives.

When designing a garden that enriches a child's experience of nature, it's important to put yourself in their shoes. Children see the world through a lens of curiosity and wonder, where the smallest details can become an adventure. A garden should embrace this, offering opportunities for exploration and play rather than simply being a passive, ornamental space. A dream children's garden isn't about static, purpose-built play equipment – it's about a landscape that sparks the imagination. Children are natural explorers, and edimentals provide a sensory-rich experience that engages them on multiple levels. Their palates are still developing, and they delight in trying weird and wonderful flavours. By incorporating unusual edimentals and surprising tastes, you can create moments of joy and discovery that stick with them long into adulthood.

Beyond their edible qualities, the magic of an edimental scheme for children lies in how it excites curiosity through scale, colour, scent and texture. A garden that feels immersive – where they can weave their way through layers of plants, stumble upon hidden corners and experience a sense of mystery – is one that invites them to engage deeply with their surroundings. Think of the vivid orange of nasturtiums (*Tropaeolum majus*) tumbling over a path, the towering height of annual sunflowers (*Helianthus annuus*) or the unexpected sweetness of daylily petals (*Hemerocallis* spp.). Many edimentals are plants that, by their very nature, captivate the senses and spark intrigue.

More than just an experience of beauty, an edimental garden also offers a powerful lesson: food doesn't come wrapped in plastic on supermarket shelves. Giving children the opportunity to participate in a more raw and wild experience of food growing makes this abundantly clear. It's a stark contrast to what they see in everyday life. Of course, when engaging children in foraging or edible gardening, there is an essential responsibility to teach them what is and isn't safe to eat. Rather than overwhelming them with plant identification, start with guiding principles or a handful of memorable species. The key is to join them in the process, nurture their curiosity and inspire a lifelong love of learning.

Case Study
Royal Horticulture Society Chelsea Flower Show
THE 'SCHOOL FOOD MATTERS GARDEN'

The RHS Chelsea Flower Show is a world of its own. It's the pinnacle of horticulture and garden design, a melting pot of creativity, craftsmanship and plant obsession that has been running for over a century. For one week in May, the grounds of the Royal Hospital Chelsea, London, transform into a showcase of the most cutting-edge ideas in the gardening world. The pressure is high, the media buzz is intense and the scale of ambition is mind-boggling. To secure funding and a space at Chelsea is a rigorous, months-long, if not years-long, process where many apply and not everyone makes it through. Once selected, it's a whirlwind of planning and off-site development leading up to a three-week, high-stakes build onsite.

Being involved in my first Chelsea garden was a surreal experience – equal parts exhilarating, exhausting and utterly addictive. The energy is incredible, with an atmosphere unlike anything else I've been a part of. It's not just about the final garden; it's about the collaboration, the problem-solving, the camaraderie of the build teams and the sheer madness of bringing an ambitious vision to life in such a high-pressure environment. Chelsea is a test of patience, resilience and the ability to adapt when things don't go to plan – because they never fully do.

The 'School Food Matters Garden' was created in collaboration with the brilliant

Dame's rocket, asphodeline and Californian poppies bring a splash of colour while the pomegranate tree and globe artichoke leaves provide architectural presence in the 'School Food Matters Garden'.

charity School Food Matters, which works to teach children about sustainable food, healthy eating and climate change. The brief was clear: food and children must be at the heart of the design. More than just a beautiful space, it had to be immersive, engaging and, most importantly, edible. Funded by Project Giving Back, the garden wasn't just for show. After Chelsea, it was relocated and reimagined as two permanent school gardens in London and Liverpool, where it now has a lasting, educational impact.

From the outset, I knew I wanted to move away from the traditional kitchen garden aesthetic and showcase a more naturalistic, foragable approach to food growing – an edimental garden in its truest form. The planting was over 80 per cent edible, designed to be as beautiful as it was productive. I wanted visitors to experience the magic of discovering food within a naturalistic landscape rather than in neat rows of crops – wandering through, brushing past plants you could pick and eat and engaging all senses in a way that felt instinctive and joyful.

The garden was a perfect embodiment of many of the principles explored throughout

Ribbons of hot colour work their way through the planting and contrast against softer tones and calming greens.

this book – integrating layers, succession, edible diversity and resilience into a cohesive, immersive landscape. It showed that a space could offer nourishment, biodiversity and beauty all at once and that food growing needn't be separate from ornamental gardening. At the heart of the garden was a characterful pomegranate tree (*Punica granatum*), a symbol of nature's bounty. Along the rear, an edible hedge of hazel (*Corylus avellana*), hawthorn (*Crataegus monogyna*) and crab apple (*Malus sylvestris*) framed the space, while structural edimentals like rosemary (*Salvia rosmarinus* 'Miss Jessopp's Upright'), globe artichoke (*Cynara cardunculus* Scolymus Group), fennel (*Foeniculum vulgare*) and sea kale (*Crambe maritima*) formed the garden's backbone.

Mid-layers were filled with flowering plants such as dame's rocket (*Hesperis matronalis*), king's spear (*Asphodeline lutea*) and yarrow (*Achillea millefolium* 'Moonshine'), adding texture and colour. Ground-level edimentals like bladder campion (*Silene vulgaris*), chives (*Allium schoenoprasum*) and wild strawberry (*Fragaria vesca*) stitched everything together. Hidden throughout were more familiar crops, like asparagus (*Asparagus officinalis*), beetroot (*Beta vulgaris*) and salad greens, all subtly integrated into the wilder aesthetic. The planting was designed for succession, so as one layer was harvested or faded another would step in, keeping the garden productive and beautiful through the seasons.

Climate resilience was also a key focus. Many of the plants were chosen for their ability to thrive in hotter, drier conditions, acknowledging the reality of the changing climate and the future that today's children will inherit. This wasn't just about growing food, it was about designing for resilience, adaptability and biodiversity, mirroring the principles we see in thriving natural ecosystems.

During show week, standing back and listening to visitors' reactions was a powerful experience. There was a real sense of wonder – people were amazed that an edible garden could be so beautiful. I overheard conversations of surprise as visitors recognised familiar garden plants and clocked that they were edible. These moments reinforced something I had long suspected: there is an untapped excitement around reimagining food growing. People are instinctively drawn to it, but so often, they simply haven't been exposed to the possibilities. Seeing this firsthand was a pivotal moment for me. It inspired me to push deeper into this way of thinking, explore the potential of edimentals further and, ultimately, to write this book.

The garden's success was overwhelming. It won the coveted People's Choice Award (Sanctuary / All About Plants Gardens category) – an incredible endorsement of the ideas behind it. More importantly, it sparked conversations about food growing in a changing climate, the importance of access to nature and how we can rethink the way we integrate edibles into our gardens. After the show, the garden was relocated and transformed into two permanent school gardens where hundreds of children now get to experience it every day. What started as an 8 × 8 metre (26 × 26 feet) Chelsea show garden has evolved into something much bigger, something that will continue to inspire and educate for years to come. In the conclusion of this book, we'll visit one of these schools, Alec Reed Academy, where the garden is now used as an outdoor edible classroom, engaging children in food growing in a hands-on and meaningful way.

Chapter 4

Big Ideas from Regenerative Growers

Edimentals already sit at the heart of many regenerative approaches – permaculture, agroforestry, food forests, edible meadows and no-dig market gardens – most of which share a bias towards perennial food crops and a common ethos: read the land, value soil and water, work with nature's patterns. Let's pull out the lens and take a tour through those landscapes, not to turn us into farmers, but to spot the transferable patterns. As we journey through, we'll distil the big ideas into practical actions at garden scale.

My Journey to Permaculture

For many, the word 'permaculture' conjures images of food-growing communes, lots of straw and kombucha-brewing hippies. There may be a sliver of truth to that, but it's far from

Wild garlic (*Allium ursinum*) and false strawberry (*Potentilla indica*) knit together the ground layer of Martin Crawford's food forest in Dartington, Totnes, suppressing weeds and offering seasonal delights.

the whole story. First and foremost, permaculture is a design system – one rooted in three core ethics: earth care, people care and fair share. It's about creating human environments that align with the rhythms and intelligence of nature.[1] Drawing on the principles of natural ecosystems, it offers a way to design self-sustaining, regenerative systems that serve both people and the planet. Food is a central thread in this fabric, and enhancing productivity in our landscapes is key.

It's easy to think of permaculture as a system for large rural landscapes or off-grid homesteads, but its real power lies in its adaptability. The core ideas scale down beautifully. Whether you have a sprawling garden, a small urban plot or a balcony, these principles can help you create a space that's productive, resilient and deeply connected to nature. Permaculture invites us to see our gardens not as isolated collections of plants, but as whole systems – alive, responsive and full of potential. This is where edimentals shine: perennial, low-input, multifunctional and beautiful, they embody permaculture values perfectly.

Permaculture is rooted in many of the holistic land practices used by ancient civilisations. These age-old ideas have been reinterpreted for the modern world with all the challenges we face and the opportunities that lie ahead. It fosters dynamism and adaptability and encourages systems thinking. In the face of climate breakdown, multilayered collapse and accelerating technological change, I believe permaculture design could be one of the most vital tools we have – not just for survival, but for thriving in a future that we can help shape.

I first encountered permaculture at the age of twenty-one while staying at an ashram in northern India. A key part of ashram life is karma yoga, the practice of selfless action for the benefit of others. My karma yoga took the form of food growing, and much of my free time was spent in the gardens. The meals we harvested and cooked communally remain some of the most nourishing I've had.

I'd already been growing annual vegetables on my first allotment back home. I was fully immersed in traditional food growing and, in some ways, had created that ideal-

Some of the core concepts that underpin permaculture design – from working with living soils and perennial systems to creating diverse, multi-layered and circular growing models.

ised image of the productive veg patch – back-breaking double-digging, meticulous weeding, endless watering. The contrast to what I experienced in the ashram garden couldn't have been starker. The array of regenerative practices used there profoundly shaped how I came to understand gardening and food growing.

Little did I know then, but I was living inside a holistically designed permaculture system. Every available space had a purpose; nothing was wasted. A mosaic of microclimates had been carefully shaped to create optimum conditions for both plants and people. Although the climate was different from what I was used to, the principles had a universal quality.

Soil health was the first priority. With healthy soil, everything else could flourish. We used mulch to protect and feed the earth, laying cardboard topped with compost and organic matter (including generous contributions from the resident cows) to build fertility and suppress weeds. Planting was multilayered and diverse, mirroring the wild environments beyond the ashram walls. Trees and climbers reached for the sun, casting shade below, while edible groundcovers and herbaceous plants filled in the lower storeys. It felt abundant, but also deeply intentional. Water was treated with reverence. Every drop that entered the garden was valued, captured through inventive systems and channelled straight to thirsty plants or into retention ponds for future use. And just as the garden sustained the body, it also nourished a sense of community. We worked together with shared purpose and care. Food growing was more than just practical – it was a social glue, and the garden was designed to encourage human connection.

Years later, I studied the theory and language of permaculture, learning the frameworks that underpin the practice and becoming a certified practitioner. Permaculture isn't about fixed techniques. It's a way of thinking. It offers a set of guiding principles that allow growers to develop context-specific approaches based on their environment, needs and values. That flexibility is what makes permaculture so powerful. It has become a lens through which I view the world, and it continues to inform how I design both gardens and the wider landscapes we inhabit.

This book isn't a guide to permaculture – there are many excellent texts that cover the subject – but it's important to explore it here because its concepts form the backbone of so many regenerative practices. Permaculture isn't just compatible with edimentals: it actively encourages their growth. Perennial, productive, low-maintenance plants that support soil, wildlife and people? That's permaculture thinking in action! Nowhere have I seen that thinking brought to life more vividly than in the work of Ben Falk.

Case Study
Permaculture in Practice
BEN FALK

If you spend time exploring permaculture, you'll come across Ben Falk. Designer, educator and land steward, he's the founder of Whole Systems Design in Vermont, and the author of *The Resilient Farm and Homestead*. For almost three decades, he has tested how to make abundant, resilient, beautiful and edible landscapes in a cold-temperate climate – and shared what works. I've followed his work for years and wanted to experience it firsthand – to understand what we could borrow at garden scale. The best way was to immerse myself, so I joined his summer Permaculture Design Course. Forty of us gathered from across North America and beyond and, for ten days, learned inside the landscape he has shaped. It was the best kind of classroom.

Ben's hillside is abundant and considered. Timber-framed barns and teaching spaces sit within a web of paths and nature trails. Ponds hold light and life, their margins thick with edimental aquatics like arrowhead (*Sagittaria latifolia*). Fruit trees run in gentle alleys on contour, with berry bushes and herbaceous perennials layered below. Annual beds sit close to the house; perennial vegetables and edimentals weave along path edges and around buildings. Farther out, the pattern loosens into larger scale agroforestry practices – rows of fruit and nut trees with soil-building groundcovers and shrubs beneath – before blending into woodland and more open, savanna-like pasture. Animals move through the landscape; Jersey-cross cattle graze and leave fertility behind. It is a productive haven, but it is also a home: a place to swim, gather, teach and be still. One evening, I watched swallows skim the pond at dusk while a beaver paddled below – the whole place is captivating and inviting.

Permaculture here isn't a label, it's a way of working. Ben defines it simply as 'applied ecology'. In practice, that means learning from how nature functions and arranging human life to collaborate with those patterns. As he put it during the course, 'Ecosystems are multidimensional and have many layers to them, so good design stacks

Ben Falk tending his beehives. Another yield that can come from an abundant, diverse permaculture system

EAT YOUR GARDEN

Water capture, management and use are an essential part of permaculture design thinking.

space and time rather than flattening them.' He's pragmatic about where to begin: 'Start with what's easy and what you like, then build from there.' That blend of principle and practicality runs through everything on his land and is a useful approach for creating a garden at any scale.

The guiding principle of multidimensional design shapes this expansive Vermont landscape. A chestnut (*Castanea* spp.) or apple (*Malus domestica*) gives height and canopy. Understorey fruit and nut trees fill the mid-layer – plum (*Prunus domestica*), sea buckthorn (*Hippophae rhamnoides*), hazelnut (*Corylus* spp.), blueberry (*Vaccinium* spp.). Herbaceous edimentals are woven throughout – rhubarb (*Rheum* × *hybridum*) and daylily (*Hemerocallis* spp.), sorrel (*Rumex acetosa*) and wild bergamot (*Monarda fistulosa*), yarrow (*Achillea millefolium*) and Jerusalem artichokes (*Helianthus tuberosus*). Groundcovers stitch everything together and climbers twine their way up whatever will take them. Each layer helps the next – wind softened, soil shaded, pollinators fed, water held. Perennials form the bones. As Ben puts it, they 'do a lot of ecosystem services from pollinator habitat to soil building, beauty and yields'. Annuals are still part of the picture but kept close to the kitchen door and modest in scale. 'I'm not against annuals, I grow them in my veggie garden.' Ben grins. 'Start simple, grow what you love, then let perennials carry the long-term load. Layering and species diversity are how resilience is built here.'

Edges offer productive havens. Where woodland softens into meadow, where a path becomes a bed, where water meets land – those transitions are treated as hubs of diversity. Around a pond, cattail (*Typha* spp.), watercress (*Nasturtium officinale*) and water lilies (*Nymphaea* spp.) share space with amphibians and insects. Along a woodland fringe, blackcurrants (*Ribes nigrum*) and raspberries (*Rubus idaeus*) thrive in dappled light. The result is more niches, more flowering across the season, more habitat for predators and pollinators and more microclimates to grow into.

Succession (the natural progression from open ground towards long-lived, woodland plant communities) runs through Ben's permaculture thinking. Rather than fight that direction, he works with it. Pioneers go in early to lift nutrients, break compacted soil and cast shade; as conditions improve, the planting shifts towards fruiting and flowering species. One of his clearest markers of ecosystem recovery was unexpected: 'Ten years in we started having crazy flushes of mushrooms – the winecaps (*Stropharia rugosoannulata*) were so abundant in a field that had been lifeless before we arrived.' That story captures a core permaculture idea: get the processes right (soil building, microclimate creation, plant layers) and the outputs take care of themselves.

'Wild soil' is the foundation of the landscape. 'If you're on a slope, water will take

BIG IDEAS FROM REGENERATIVE GROWERS

Ben's magical edible landscape in Mad River Valley, Vermont.

your soil away, and even on flat ground, if you're not managing your water, you're not managing your soil.' On the homestead, interventions like minor earthworks and tree planting are designed to slow, spread and sink rainfall so living topsoil can build and stay. Day to day, the soil is protected and fed with practices like applying compost and woody mulches, ensuring roots in the ground year-round and minimal disturbance where possible. The effect is visible. The planting beds hold moisture through a hot week and drain cleanly after a storm. 'Ensuring you build a healthy soil makes growing abundance that much easier.'

Ben's land reflects other key permaculture principles such as 'obtain a yield', where every feature is designed to provide some output – be it food, useful materials or less tangible benefits like recreation. Another is to 'stack functions' so each element earns its keep in more than one way. Rows of trees filter wind, build soil and produce fruit. Ponds store irrigation water, moderate frost, grow food and allow for swimming. Edimentals and other perennial vegetables cover soil, draw up minerals with deep roots and offer edible parts throughout the year. Beyond the homestead's integral functions, place-making and creating a landscape that speaks to the soul are of great importance to Ben. 'Beauty emerges when a place is taken care of. When it is living and healthy, it will be beautiful.'

I set out to immerse myself in Ben's world to see how we could all translate decades of whole-site thinking into everyday gardens. The pattern is clear – think in layers, welcome edges and microclimates, design with time, build living soil and look for harvests in every element. At home that might look like catching rain and letting it soak in – a water butt or barrel on the downpipe, a shallow swale (a shallow ditch dug on contour that is designed to slow the movement of water and sink it deep into the soil) along the high side of a bed, even a tiny pond. Pair that with continuous cover – borders knitted with edimentals and mulched with homemade compost – and your soil begins to do the work for you. Plant an edible hedge to soften prevailing winds, add fruiting trees or shrubs where none exist, and invite water, insects and birds in. Then give it your attention and become a part of the ecosystem. Care for your garden and observe how it responds.

My time at Ben's homestead was clarifying. Permaculture isn't a style to copy – it's a way of seeing and arranging. On that Vermont hillside, applied ecology feels generous, not just to people but to wildlife. You don't need a hillside or decades of experience to begin. Start small. Plant something perennial, edible and beautiful. Observe, tend and let the garden teach you. You will build resilience – a garden that feeds you and gets better every year because you are part of it.

One of the many ponds scattered across Ben Falk's landscape, serving multiple functions – from water management and irrigation to swimming, storm resilience, microclimate creation and food production. Arrowheads grow along the margins, adding beauty and edible abundance.

BIG IDEAS FROM REGENERATIVE GROWERS

Food Forests (or Forest Gardens)

Forest gardens – interchangeably known as food forests – mimic the layered structure of young, open woodlands, with every plant chosen to serve a function. These systems bring together beauty, productivity and ecological resilience, offering a model for food growing that feels both deeply rooted in the past and strikingly relevant today. While their origins lie in tropical regions – from the edible 'home gardens' of Kerala, India, to the layered agroforestry systems of the Amazon – they've been passionately adapted for a range of climates by pioneering practitioners such as Robert Hart, Martin Crawford and Jerome Osentowski (all of whom published wonderful books that explore the subject in more depth than we can here).

Permaculture thinkers quickly recognised their potential. Inspired by the abundance and efficiency of tropical food forests, they made forest gardening a core strand of permaculture, applying its logic to gardens, smallholdings and farms worldwide. Their work translated a system rooted in lush ecosystems into one that thrives in cooler, seasonal landscapes.

These ecosystems are among the most productive in the temperate world, with layered, interconnected structures that maximise space and resources. Like permaculture systems, forest gardens rely on no-dig practices, perennial planting, closed-loop thinking and multilayered design. The aim is to fill as many ecological niches as possible, creating spaces that feed us, support wildlife, build soil and sequester carbon – while offering a deeply nourishing place to be. (We'll explore ecological niches in more detail in chapter 6.)

Most forest gardens follow a seven-layer model (eight if fungi are included): canopy trees, understorey, shrubs, herbaceous perennials, groundcovers, climbers, root

Layers in action at Central Rocky Mountain Permaculture Institute with plant communities that include fruit, berries, perennial crops and nutrient accumulators like comfrey.

crops and fungi. At the top, trees like pear (*Pyrus* spp.) or sweet chestnut (*Castanea sativa*) offer structure and harvests, while nitrogen-fixing species such as Italian alder (*Alnus cordata*) enrich the soil. Beneath, shrubs like goumi (*Elaeagnus multiflora*), saskatoon (*Amelanchier alnifolia*), blackcurrant (*Ribes nigrum*) and black chokeberry (*Aronia melanocarpa*) provide fruit and fertility. The herb layer might include lemon balm (*Melissa officinalis*), Turkish rocket (*Bunias orientalis*) or Babington's leek (*Allium ampeloprasum* var. *babingtonii*), with groundcovers such as Siberian purslane (*Claytonia sibirica*) or false strawberry (*Duchesnea indica*, invasive in parts of North America) suppressing weeds. Climbers like hardy kiwi (*Actinidia arguta*) or groundnut (*Apios americana*) add vertical yield, while roots like greater pignut (*Bunium bulbocastanum*) extend productivity underground. Fungi – whether wild or introduced – knit the system together, recycling nutrients and closing the loop of renewal.

Crucially, many of these plants are edimentals, uniting food, beauty and biodiversity. A forest garden is more than functional: it is immersive, alive with texture and colour across the seasons. Its resilience comes not from a single element but from many overlapping ones – each plant contributing to the whole.

The 'Home Gardens' of Kerala, India

I'm riding in a rickshaw in Kerala weaving through a landscape that is lush, humid and intensely alive. Our driver, Arun, is the kind of person you often meet in Kerala – warm, welcoming and deeply connected to his land. He's thrilled to be showing us around, pointing out landmarks, chatting about life and, as we quickly discover, brimming with knowledge about the plants that surround us. When he learns that I'm a garden designer, his face lights up. 'Then you must see my home,' he insists.

As we pull up to his home, it feels like we've walked into another world. Set within the jungle, his single-storey house is nestled among the trees, barely distinguishable from the vegetation around it. The air is cooler here, the canopy filtering the harsh Keralan sun, creating a dappled, shifting light. There's a stillness, broken only by the hum of insects and the occasional rustle of movement in the undergrowth.

At the time, in my mid-twenties, I didn't know about Kerala's long history of forest gardens, or *kaanam* (home gardens) as they are known locally. My delight in discovering Arun's fully edible garden was pure and immediate. Even before we reached the house, he was already handing us treasures. 'Nutmeg

[*Myristica fragrans*]', he said, passing us the freshly harvested spice, its outer shell still encasing the vibrant red mace inside. A bag of them would be a parting gift, he told us, but not before making us taste one fresh. The warm, heady aroma was unlike the dried nutmeg I had tasted back home.

A tour of his back garden revealed a deeply familiar yet entirely new way of gardening. Every inch of space was used, packed with layers of edible plants, from towering jackfruit trees (*Artocarpus heterophyllus*) to pepper vines (*Piper nigrum*) winding their way up trunks. We plucked fresh mangoes (*Mangifera indica*), chewed on just-picked peppercorns, rubbed turmeric roots (*Curcuma longa*) between our fingers and crushed lemongrass (*Cymbopogon citratus*) to release its citrusy scent. It wasn't a large garden, but what it lacked in space it made up for in abundance.

We stayed for lunch, sharing a meal with his family – a spread that showcased the richness of his food forest. There was *chena mezhukkupuratti*, a spicy yam stir-fry made from elephant foot yam (*Amorphophallus paeoniifolius*) harvested just moments before, alongside a simple but deeply flavourful moong dal, finishing with a steaming cup of tulsi (*Ocimum tenuiflorum*) tea, all infused with the warmth of homegrown ingredients.

I later learned just how deeply embedded this type of growing is in Kerala's culture. Unlike in the West, where food gardens and ornamental gardens are often seen as separate entities, in Kerala every garden is an edible garden. Food and medicine come from the land around you – it is not an extra or an afterthought, but the foundation of daily life. The tradition of home gardens in Kerala dates back thousands of years, a system that has evolved through generations to be incredibly resilient, low-maintenance and regenerative.[2] These gardens don't just feed families; they nurture biodiversity, provide shade and offer medicinal plants that have been used for centuries in Ayurveda. In many ways, they are a perfect example of relocalised, regenerative agriculture – thriving on polycultures, perennial crops and closed-loop systems where nothing is wasted.

It's in the spirit of these age-old practices that today's forest garden pioneers have found their inspiration. The same principles – layering, multifunctionality, resilience – continue to inspire growers across the world. Jerome Osentowski of the Central Rocky Mountain Permaculture Institute (CRMPI) is one such practitioner. His work is a living example of these ideas reimagined for a very different climate – proof that forest gardens can thrive in even the most unlikely places.

The ecological layers of a forest garden – from canopy to groundcover – work together to create a resilient, self-sustaining system rich in food, habitat and beauty.

BIG IDEAS FROM REGENERATIVE GROWERS

Case Study
Agroforestry & Forest Gardens, Central Rocky Mountain Permaculture Institute & Colorado Edible Forest

JEROME OSENTOWSKI & VANESSA HARMONY

High in the Colorado's Rockies, on a slope that was once more stone than soil, Jerome Osentowski has spent decades coaxing an unlikely Eden into being. When I arrived at the Central Rocky Mountain Permaculture Institute (CRMPI) for a two-day workshop, it didn't feel like a site so much as a living ecosystem – scruffy at the edges yet relentlessly

Jerome Ostentowski, the founder of CRMPI and leading voice in permaculture practice and greenhouse design.

Gardening is a powerful community-building activity. Jerome seeks out double yields from every element at CRMPI; here, compost piles become worm farms.

EAT YOUR GARDEN

Edimentals, including hollyhocks, naturalising across the mountainside at CRMPI.

abundant at its core. Jerome introduced the place with a shrug and a grin: 'This is an evolving landscape. It's not sterile, it's not stagnant. It keeps changing from year to year, from season to season.' He's been here half a century, a buoyant, eccentric presence animated by mischievous practicality. The elevation is high – around 2,195 metres (7,200 feet) – the annual rain low (430 millimetres / 17 inches), and yet food and life spill out of every corner.

At CRMPI, the indoors and outdoors blur. We stepped from figs (*Ficus carica*) and avocados (*Persea americana*) within the greenhouse to apricots (*Prunus armeniaca*) and mulberries (*Morus* spp.) out under the sun without noticing the threshold; more than once, I realised that I'd left the greenhouse only when I was halfway through Jerome's kitchen. CRMPI is famous for growing tropical and Mediterranean fruit at altitude in climate-savvy structures, but what stands out is its resilience rather than its gadgets. Through summer nights, Jerome sleeps in the greenhouse. 'The night-blooming jasmine (*Cestrum nocturnum*) is just coming on. It's amazing in here at night.' You can feel why. The air is sweet and green, with leaves breathing all around you.

In terms of growing indoors, Jerome favours hybrid hoop houses: insulated on the cold sides with water tanks and stone for thermal mass to claw back weeks at the shoulders of the season. He's wary of magical solutions. 'Start by introducing thermal mass and water tanks. They take energy in by day and let it out at night. Everybody gets really excited about the climate battery we've developed – a network of buried pipes that stores daytime warmth in the soil and returns it at night – but it's not the silver bullet. In nature, there's not one thing.' A handful of greenhouses dot the slope, some tucked into buildings, others freestanding; all catch rain and snowmelt because here, water is gold.

Forest-garden thinking runs through everything, including the greenhouses. They aren't rigid rows; they're layered agroforestry. Grapes (*Vitis vinifera*) and pomegranate (*Punica granatum*) are trained for edible shade; biomass trees like leucaena (*Leucaena leucocephala*) are coppiced hard several times a year (grown primarily for producing organic matter used as fuel, mulch or soil-building material); a supporting cast ranges from Surinam cherry (*Eugenia uniflora*) and grapefruit (*Citrus × paradisi*) to lablab bean (*Lablab purpureus*) and the odd avocado (*Persea americana*). This is syntropic agroforestry adapted to a cold climate. Dense planting, deliberate pruning and rapid cycling of biomass speed succession and build soil. The principle is

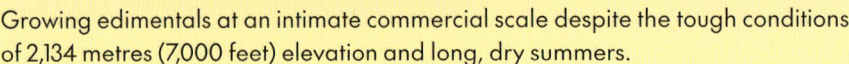

Growing edimentals at an intimate commercial scale despite the tough conditions of 2,134 metres (7,000 feet) elevation and long, dry summers.

simple and powerful: grow nutrients as well as fruit. 'You can go anywhere in the world on any kind of soil – if you have water – and grow your own mulch, your own nutrition. Chop and drop. That's what we're doing here.' Outside, the same logic applies. But instead of dealing with greenhouse glass and vents, the focus shifts to natural forces like wind, frost and sun.

Beyond the greenhouses, an acre-ish forest garden is the permanent element that Jerome has been stewarding for decades. He began by making places for soil to form – a terrace carved here, a hugelkultur mound there (a raised bed built on buried wood and organic matter that stores moisture and emits heat as it decomposes), free organic matter dragged in from town and blankets of mulch to keep soil from drying out. In building a food forest, he accidentally created a worm farm. 'You always want to keep the soil covered and keep it moist; that way, in time it becomes a worm farm.' He grins. 'Make America mulch again.' Covered soil does the heavy lifting at CRMPI.

Stand still and the layers come into focus. Most forest gardens follow the classic seven layers. The goal is to stack life vertically, so every niche is filled and every plant earns its keep. Some feed you, some feed the soil, some feed pollinators, and many do several jobs at once. At CRMPI, in one small pocket you might see a walnut (*Juglans* spp.) taking the canopy, a Siberian pea

> CRMPI has been leading education in permaculture and forest gardening for almost forty years.

shrub (*Caragana arborescens*) beneath, lilac (*Syringa vulgaris*) to one side, a patchwork of lamb's-quarters (*Chenopodium album*) and green orach (*Atriplex hortensis*) on the ground, with grapes (*Vitis vinifera*) threading through. A few steps on: elder (*Sambucus nigra*), hops (*Humulus lupulus*) and a self-seeded apricot (*Prunus armeniaca*) left 'for the bears and the birds'.

Management is steady, with a light touch. If ground turns bare, Jerome's quick to sow cover and drop a fresh comfrey (*Symphytum officinale*) cut. Where undesirable weeds seed in, he resets with a disturbance – remove, reseed, mulch. Succession is steered, not forced. Syntropic thinking, again, translated for a mountain garden: plant densely, grow biomass in place, prune hard in pulses, and let the next stage take the light. Outside in the forest garden, it means accepting that sun-loving pioneers will give way to a shadier understorey as the canopy thickens. 'It kind of keeps going on its own, for the most part – you just have to add a few elements to make sure everything works.'

There's room for other lives, too. One winter, a crab apple (*Malus* spp.) left unpicked 'became a bird feeder. They were eating the fermented applesauce for weeks.' Not all wildlife impact has been favourable. For decades,

> Jerome and CRMPI are world-renowned for pioneering 'climate battery' technology to heat greenhouses and grow tropical food forests.

BIG IDEAS FROM REGENERATIVE GROWERS

bears came at night, tearing down trees and eating everything. Eventually, Jerome brought in livestock guardian dogs and this natural deterrent solved the problem. 'It's not so much that they bark or do anything beyond lying around and getting attention – just their smell and presence is enough.'

Soil health is the engine beneath it all. Years of adding organic matter, keeping soil covered and cycling biomass in place have built a sponge that holds moisture through dry summers. The comfrey (*Symphytum × uplandicum*) patch that keeps giving, the leaf bags scrounged in town, the coffee grounds from the local café – none of it glamorous, all of it compounding.

People constantly thread through CRMPI. It's been a classroom for decades, and you can hear it in Jerome's voice: half instruction, half provocation. Ask what to do with an apricot (*Prunus armeniaca*) pit and he deadpans, 'You put it in a bucket and you plant it, duh.' Alumni have carried the pattern outward: Eric Toensmeier interned here before writing on edible forest gardens and carbon farming; Mark Shepard took his design course before stewarding a large agroforestry farm; even the public park down the road holds a forest garden designed by a past student and is now managed by the town. The point isn't a list of names; it's the way an idea seeds itself in people and place, and keeps travelling.

One of those people is Vanessa Harmony. Warm, practical and full of energy, she moved from a cubicle job to a life with plants, deciding after a permaculture design course to design her life and career, too. An apprenticeship at Stone Barns in New York gave her the courage to leave the desk, seasons at CRMPI (including co-running Jerome's nursery) sharpened the craft, and then she stepped out on her own. Colorado Edible Forest, her nursery near Glenwood Springs, specialises in hardy edible perennials for mountain gardeners. 'In our region, there aren't any other nurseries focusing on edible perennial plants. My motto is, "To grow food, build soil and nurture nature",' she says. Vanessa has translated the CRMPI pattern, adapting to a slightly different microclimate and bringing these ideas to people at an everyday garden scale.

Her shortlist of plants for small gardens is practical: plums (*Prunus domestica*) for reliability; currants (*Ribes* spp.) or gooseberries (*Ribes uva-crispa*) for tight spaces; raspberries (*Rubus idaeus*) along sunny edges; asparagus (*Asparagus officinalis*) for low-effort abundance – stitched together with insectary herbs and a strawberry

Vanessa Harmony, Colorado Edible Forest.

Vanessa's beautiful nursery set in the dramatic Colorado landscape.

(*Fragaria × ananassa*) groundcover. Then a blanket of leaves or wood mulch compost to make the worms feel at home.

Walk her nursery and you see why people return: immaculate stock is coupled with an infectious love for the wildlife that moves through the place. There are no sprays and no grand attempts to keep animals out; where some might feel locked in a battle against nature, Vanessa thanks the birds and squirrels for 'planting' trees and shrubs in her pots even if, occasionally, a berry bush is the casualty. Her relationship with CRMPI loops back here, too: Jerome now sources plants from her and has talked about trialling honeyberries (*Lonicera caerulea*) from Vanessa in one of the greenhouses.

My time on Jerome's hillside and among Vanessa's nursery rows left me hopeful. The work isn't unobtainable; it's ordinary and rhythmic. Every time Jerome hacked back a biomass tree or carved a terrace edge, I felt how replicable it is. Read your microclimates. Layer your planting and think in time as well as space. Grow biomass as well as food and keep the ground covered. Cycle energy so nothing dead ends. The rest is attention and tempo – chop, drop, mulch, seed, harvest, repeat. On a tough slope in Colorado, a forest garden hums, inside and out. Down the road, a nursery spreads the power of edibles and edimentals through the valley – and the idea keeps travelling through people who've been here and carried it home. CRMPI is already bigger than its birthplace – and perhaps the most contagious lesson Jerome continues to impart is simply to begin: plant something, pay attention and let nature play out.

Sid Hill and Chris Hull's edible meadow at the 'Microbiome Garden', RHS Chelsea Flower Show, 2024.

Discovering Edible Meadows

From Jerome's mountain food forests and greenhouses of CRMPI, we've seen how layering, diversity and a focus on soil health can transform even the toughest conditions into an abundant landscape. Yet these principles don't only apply to forests – they can reshape open landscapes just as powerfully. One of the most exciting expressions of this is the edible meadow.

For years, I had been working with wildflower meadows in various contexts – incorporating them into urban settings (as we saw with The Lodge green roof in chapter 3) and managing them in larger landscapes to boost biodiversity. At the same time, my practice had roots in food growing and enhancing productivity in the gardens we design. Strangely, I hadn't yet put the two together.

Meadows have long captured the imagination in the UK, but, across the Atlantic, prairies hold a similar place in people's hearts. UK meadows are managed ecosystems, shaped by centuries of grazing and cutting that steadily reduce nutrients and create the lean soils native UK wildflowers need. Prairies, by contrast, evolved as vast, self-sustaining grasslands on deep, often fertile soils, maintained by fire, roaming bison and deep-rooted perennials. Many staples of naturalistic planting – and several edimentals, from wild bergamot (*Monarda fistulosa*) to Jerusalem artichoke (*Helianthus tuberosus*) – originate in these prairie systems, where they thrive in rich soils that would quickly overwhelm more delicate UK wildflowers.

Enter Sid Hill – a fellow designer, teacher and now a good friend – who has been pioneering edible meadows in the UK. Seeing his work was a lightbulb moment for me. Here was a planting style that took the structure and biodiversity of a meadow but replaced some of the wildflower species with edimentals – plants that not only support pollinators and wildlife but also offer a harvest for humans. They can be adapted to any scale, from large rural landscapes to compact urban gardens. The principles remain the same: create a dynamic, low-maintenance, self-sustaining system where plants can coexist, self-seed and thrive with minimal intervention.

Sid's 'Microbiome Garden', designed for the RHS Chelsea Flower Show, is a beautiful example of his work in this field. The garden radiated a powerful atmosphere, a living, breathing ecosystem that was vibrant, immersive and filled with food. It was a naturalistic landscape that didn't just look beautiful but had real purpose. He has been at the forefront of this movement, refining the concept and exploring how edible meadows can be integrated into different landscapes.

Case Study
Edible Meadows
SID HILL

I've had the great pleasure of getting to know Sid Hill over the years as we've both navigated our way through the wonderful world of horticulture, connected by shared passions for food, landscape and bringing people closer to nature.

Sid has never followed the conventional path. His innovative approach to designed edible meadows emerged naturally from an upbringing on permaculture farms and smallholdings, and later, a degree in landscape design from the Eden Project. He admired the naturalistic planting styles championed by Nigel Dunnett and James Hitchmough at Sheffield University – inspired by their vibrant, ecological

Sid Hill, designer, teacher and permaculturalist.

A beautiful scene from one of Sid's designs in Cornwall, UK. Edible musk mallow spills over the artistic pathway made from local and salvaged materials.

Sid has been pioneering edible meadows as a way to create low-input, productive plantings. Here, a handful of edible leaves and flowers, including mallow, violet and cornflower, are gathered fresh from the meadow.

landscapes. Yet Sid, guided by his permaculture background, sensed untapped potential, 'Their planting was beautiful and ecological, but I thought, "Why not integrate edible plants? Why can't we have beauty, biodiversity and food all in one landscape?"'

He soon discovered that edible meadows hold unique emotional resonance. 'Meadows capture people's imagination,' he reflects. 'They move us deeply, pulling us into nature. When you add edible plants, it becomes personal. It's not just beautiful – it's interactive. People taste plants, hear their stories and build relationships. It's incredibly powerful.'

For smaller gardens and urban spaces, he recommends planting rather than seeding for greater control. 'In smaller spaces, a planted edible meadow lets you balance grasses and edible perennials more intentionally, creating calm and cohesion.' For larger spaces or tighter budgets, he suggests another practical option: 'Take a ready-made wildflower seed mix and enhance it by integrating edible species. It keeps things manageable and cost-effective. You can enrich the diversity over time.' Sid also highlights prairie species for gardens, noting their ability to dramatically extend seasonal interest, though he advises careful selection to ensure suitability for local climates.

He passionately advocates thoughtful ecological management, stressing human intervention's essential role in sustaining an edible meadow. In gardens, we rarely have the natural forces – herbivores, fires or natural disturbances – that shape prairies and meadows. 'You need to become the herbivore,' Sid explains with a laugh. 'Meadows are dynamic, living systems needing our interaction to thrive. Actively weeding, harvesting and planting ensure the ecosystem succeeds in the long term.' He also suggests incorporating quick-growing annual vegetables like radishes and turnips into newly established meadows, cleverly utilising the initial soil disturbance for a productive 'catch-crop' approach – a fast-maturing crop grown between or alongside main crops – before the meadow fully establishes.

When pressed to choose his top three edimentals, Sid landed on camassia (*Camassia quamash*) for its striking beauty and nutty bulbs, common bistort (*Persicaria bistorta*) for tender leaves and sweet cicely (*Myrrhis odorata*) for its sweet, aniseed fragrance.

Traditional Systems, Allotments & Kitchen Gardens

Allotments, kitchen gardens, community garden plots and smallholdings still form the backbone of homegrown food culture across much of the temperate world, and I love them for it. As we've seen, my own allotment weaves together the two worlds, albeit with a focus on edimentals.

For centuries, food and beauty have shared the same beds. Across cultures and time periods, people have found joy in growing plants that nourish both body and soul, as we explored in chapter 2. And you don't need edimentals to appreciate the beauty of traditional crops: the ruby stems of Swiss chard (*Beta vulgaris* subsp. *cicla* var. *flavescens*), the spirals of romanesco broccoli (*Brassica oleracea* var. *botrytis* 'Romanesco'), the fresh lime-green flush of mustard leaves (*Brassica juncea*). Even the most practical veg patch often has nasturtiums (*Tropaeolum majus*) or calendula (*Calendula officinalis*) woven in as pollinator plants or simply for their beauty.

Mallow, fennel, Babington's leek, love-in-a-mist and lavender growing in harmony beneath a pear tree at my allotment.

Bringing edimentals into these spaces takes that a step further. As with all the practices we've explored – from agroforestry to edible meadows – it helps to think in layers. Bringing in fruit trees can provide shade, blossom and harvest, while the ground beneath can be stitched together with meadow-style mixes that combine pollinator plants and productive edimentals. In annual beds, work in Babington's leeks (*Allium ampeloprasum* var. *babingtonii*) alongside later crops like squash, which sprawl during the leek's summer dormancy. Let herbs like lovage (*Levisticum officinale*) self-seed to add structure and scent. Use edimentals to extend the harvest across the year: alexanders (*Smyrnium olusatrum*) for early shoots, red-veined sorrel (*Rumex sanguineus*) in cooler months and skirret (*Sium sisarum*) for long-term yields once established.

These additions don't just look good – they fill gaps, feed pollinators, and offer easy, low-maintenance harvests across the season. You're not starting from scratch; you're layering in, adding resilience and richness with each season.

Allotments in the UK (community garden plots in the US) play an important role in localised food production and community building.

Case Study
No-Dig Pioneer
CHARLES DOWDING

Charles Dowding has done more than anyone to bring the no-dig growing method into mainstream awareness, showing that food can be grown simply, beautifully and in harmony with the soil.

We met at the RHS Chelsea Flower Show in 2023. Charles wandered into our 'School Food Matters Garden' and was instantly taken by the edible planting – the textures, colours and structure of the scheme. It sparked a warm conversation, and he later invited me to visit Homeacres, his market garden in Somerset. When I finally made it down for a weekend, Charles was just as joyful as I had remembered. He's a cheerful, eccentric figure with a cheeky, knowing grin – a carrot and pea-pod brooch pinned to his jacket and a stitched kohlrabi adorning his jumper. He wears his love for vegetables proudly. But beneath the charm lies over forty years of deep, practical knowledge. Charles understands soil, vegetables and seasonal rhythms better than anyone I've met. His passion is infectious. Spend even an hour with him and you'll find yourself scheming how to carve out space for a veg patch of your own.

Wandering through Homeacres is spellbinding. Tucked off an unassuming village lane in rural Somerset, around half an acre of intensive cropping sits within one and a half acres of land, bordered by thick, biodiverse hedgerows that teem with life. The beds are immaculate, lined with vegetables of all shapes, sizes and colours, and punctuated by flowering plants, fruit trees and an array of edimentals. It's productive, yes, but also deeply peaceful. The whole place hums with harmony, and there's a palpable feeling of joy. The vegetables almost seem to sing.

At the heart of this thriving system is 'no-dig'. Charles doesn't till or disturb the soil. Instead, he nurtures it from the top down, layering compost and letting biology do the work. The paths are mulched with woodchip; the beds are enriched each autumn with just 2.5 centimetres (1 inch) of compost. There are no raised beds, no rigid rotations, no chemical inputs – just consistent attention and care. When discussing how to start out on the no-dig journey, Charles says, 'Start small. Small is beautiful.' And

Charles Dowding enjoying the bounty of annual vegetables at Homeacres.

BIG IDEAS FROM REGENERATIVE GROWERS

Charles's work is a showcase of the great beauty and innate satisfaction found in neat rows of perfectly grown vegetables.

while half an acre of cropping may not sound small to most, Homeacres has grown gradually over time, shaped by what was manageable, affordable and right in that moment. Today, Charles produces over 3 tonnes of vegetables each year – all of it sold within a 4-mile radius. It's localised food production at its finest, a system that works with nature, feeds the community and proves that resilience begins at the soil level.

But what's most striking at Homeacres is not just the productivity, it's the joy. Charles doesn't just grow food – he grows it with love. 'Green fingers are really your desire,' he told me. 'You're giving your plants the energy.' That energy flows through every bed. You see it in the upright rows of chicory (*Cichorium intybus* [Palla Rossa Group] '506TT'), the ruby stems of beetroot (*Beta vulgaris*) and the proud towers of sprouting broccoli (*Brassica oleracea* [Italica Group] 'Claret'). Mustard greens (*Brassica juncea* 'Pizzo') glow lime against deep purple lettuces (*Lactuca sativa* 'Batavian Red'); red-veined leaves catch the light like stained glass. Even among the onions (*Allium cepa*) and Chinese cabbages (*Brassica rapa* [Pekinensis Group] 'Yuki'), there's always a flicker of surprise – calendula (*Calendula officinalis*) edging a path, or marigolds (*Tagetes patula*) brightening a bare corner. Beauty isn't an afterthought here – it's embedded in the rhythm of the garden.

Edimentals and flowering plants are woven throughout the traditional crops and rows at Homeacres.

Edimentals are scattered throughout the site. Some are grown as main crops such as rhubarb (*Rheum × hybridum*), asparagus (*Asparagus officinalis*) and globe artichokes (*Cynara cardunculus* Scolymus Group). Others, like sedums (*Hylotelephium* spp.), daylilies (*Hemerocallis* spp.) and violas (*Viola tricolor*), are threaded in for colour, habitat and pollinator support, regardless of their edible qualities. You'll find them flanking the polytunnels, dotting the borders or tucked among the herbs: rosemary (*Salvia rosmarinus*), wild rocket (*Diplotaxis tenuifolia*), fennel (*Foeniculum vulgare*), lupins (*Lupinus* spp.) and salad burnet (*Sanguisorba minor*). Juneberries (*Amelanchier* spp.) anchor the corners with their spring blossom and subtle fruit. Some are grown simply for the joy they bring. 'Vegetables can sometimes be quite flat,' Charles said as we wandered. 'There's often not much vertical structure, so having edimentals makes the space feel more uplifting.'

Charles places many of his perennial crops and low-maintenance edimentals farther from the house – out on the fringes, where they can thrive with minimal input. 'You can shove a globe artichoke in the corner and forget about it,' he said, laughing. These plants, often tucked into wilder areas or layered into borders, help strike a balance. Even in Charles's mature no-dig system, which reduces weeding, watering and the need for feeding beyond compost, annual veg still requires regular attention. Sowing, planting, protecting, harvesting – it's a hands-on process. Edimentals offer another rhythm. They don't need constant tending. Once established, they subtly contribute, feeding pollinators, offering harvests and adding resilience to the system. It's a practical approach that spreads labour and reward more evenly across the year.

At the end of each bed, Charles plants an edimental or flowering plant, bringing a splash of colour, a boost for biodiversity and a sense of harmony. Although edimentals are woven throughout, his heart lies with annuals. When you produce 3 tonnes of organic veg every year, edimentals have little room to compete as staples. He finds deep satisfaction in their cycles, their pace, their generosity and their beauty. 'Those leeks,' he gestured as we walked the rows, 'the colour on them, the structure of the leaves, the height they bring – they're stunningly beautiful. The snag is, I get reluctant to harvest them!'

Charles and I are coming at a shared message from different angles. His heart lies with the beauty of rows of lettuce and towering leeks, and he's built a life around the magic of annual vegetables. *Eat Your Garden*, meanwhile, champions edimentals – beauty, resilience and nourishment in a wilder, layered way. But underneath it all is the same truth: food and beauty don't need to be separated. In fact, they never should be. And that's exactly what Homeacres shows us. It's a garden that proves what's possible when power, love, beauty and abundance meet intention – and compost.

A variety of winter salad crops intermingle with garlic in one of Charles's polytunnels.

BIG IDEAS FROM REGENERATIVE GROWERS

Chapter 5

Understanding Your Garden

Before diving into the creative excitement of designing an edimental scheme, the single most important step is to truly understand your site. Every garden is different, shaped by unique conditions that dictate what will thrive or struggle within it. Working with these conditions, rather than battling against them, not only ensures greater success but saves considerable time, money and frustration in the long run.

Begin by building a foundational knowledge of your plot. Ask yourself simple yet essential questions that will help you think about different aspects of your garden. Consider the soil beneath your feet. Is it sticky, heavy clay that holds moisture tightly, such as the iconic London clay, or perhaps the sandy, free-draining soil characteristic of Nebraska's Sandhills? Does sunlight drench your plot generously throughout the day, or is it shaded beneath mature trees or overshadowed by neighbouring buildings? Reflect on rainfall patterns: do you benefit from consistent moisture or have more seasonal patterns? Feel the

Assessing your soil should be a sensory-driven process.

wind and observe how it interacts with your site: is your garden regularly buffeted by strong winds, or is it tucked comfortably into a sheltered microclimate?

Within every garden exist numerous microclimates, created by varying combinations of sun, shade, structures and topography. These pockets of unique conditions offer valuable planting opportunities. Beyond these subtle variations, consider if your garden faces specific conditions such as salty coastal winds or the stress of urban pollution. Also, reflect on the practicalities of your site. Are you planting directly into the earth, or is your garden on a rooftop, balcony or podium landscape, requiring everything to be grown in pots or containers? Each scenario brings with it specific quirks and considerations that will directly influence your design choices and plant selections.

Crucially, consider your ultimate vision and goals for the garden and how your environmental conditions will shape or influence them. By taking all these elements into account, you lay down the essential groundwork for creating a resilient, thriving edimental landscape.

Time & Observation

One of the most valuable skills a gardener or designer can cultivate is the art of observation. After years spent working closely with gardens, I've honed my ability to swiftly assess and understand a new space. Yet each new plot I encounter continues to offer fresh lessons. Every garden and landscape reflect their unique personalities, and uncovering that personality takes patience, curiosity and mindful attention.

Time becomes your greatest ally here. Gardens are living, dynamic spaces, continually evolving through days, seasons and years. When my wife and I first took on our eight acres in Wales, the temptation to immediately dive into designing and planting was strong, but circumstances held us back – a constraint I'm now deeply grateful for. Having this enforced pause offered the precious opportunity to slow down, to watch the land quietly and carefully. Observing these gentle transformations has helped me build a deeper connection with the place, noticing details I might otherwise have overlooked: the way sunlight shifts subtly across the hills throughout the day, the ebb and flow of moisture levels, and how different winds might influence plant growth or highlight sheltered areas.

This kind of attentive practice can be cultivated in countless ways. In both my own garden and in clients' spaces, I find it useful to walk the perimeter boundaries at different times of day and in different seasons. It helps to gain vantage points and a variety of perspectives, enabling

you to experience firsthand how the site changes and responds to its environmental conditions. I've found that something as simple as closing my eyes to listen to birdsong, buzzing insects or wind gently rustling the trees deepens my understanding of the ecosystem's unique character. Journaling, sketching or maintaining photographic records can capture a garden's unfolding story, highlighting seasonal shifts, emerging patterns and subtle changes that might otherwise pass unnoticed.

Taking time to notice the subtleties of your garden is an invaluable process.

Drawing or painting your garden is another useful practice, whether you're skilled with a pencil or not. Beyond being creatively fulfilling, it sharpens observational skills, encouraging a closer connection and deeper focus on textures, forms and the spatial context of your garden. Technology can also play a useful role; it is commonplace to use computer-aided design (CAD) software as a designer, and it has helped me gain new perspectives on my land in Wales. If you are not familiar with CAD software, then online mapping systems can also be a helpful tool to see your plot from a new perspective.

Even if eagerness or practical necessity means you must get started immediately, pausing to observe your site will prove invaluable. If you're able to take your time, or perhaps you are forced to by budget constraints or circumstance, embrace it as a rare and valuable gift. The better you know your land, the more beautifully, abundantly and effortlessly your garden will evolve.

Environmental Conditions

Understanding your environmental conditions is central to knowing your site and designing a successful edimental garden. These conditions are the external influences that shape your garden's personality – soil, sunlight, water, wind, microclimates and biodiversity – and your approach to design should work in harmony with them.

Location

Begin by reflecting on your garden's broader location. Is it rural and remote, nestled among fields and forests, or does it lie within the urban bustle, influenced by the urban heat island effect, or perhaps sheltered by surrounding buildings? Your wider geographic context influences everything that grows naturally there. Take time to observe plants thriving in local natural spaces, hedgerows or parks and look for wild edibles flourishing effortlessly – these all offer clues to what could thrive in your garden, too.

Soil

Of all the factors influencing a healthy garden and a successful edimental scheme, soil may well be the most vital. Soil isn't simply a passive backdrop to your plants – it's a vibrant ecosystem teeming with life, underpinning virtually every form of terrestrial life, including us. Without soil, terrestrial ecosystems as we know them simply wouldn't exist. Yet, soil around the world faces immense pressures. In 2014, the UN issued a stark warning that globally we might have fewer than 60 harvests left if current practices continue, largely due to topsoil erosion and poor soil management.[1] As gardeners, we have an important role in protecting and regenerating soil health, particularly through practices like mulching and planting diverse edimental schemes. These simple interventions help protect against erosion, particularly on sloping sites and during storm events or heavy rainfall.

Far too often, I see soil neglected, even in mature and established gardens. Whether through compaction caused by machinery during garden work or simply by walking over wet, heavy clay soil to weed or harvest, careless treatment damages the structure and life within the soil. On heavy soils, it's especially important to minimise foot traffic when wet and to treat soil as a valuable, living resource during garden builds.

In almost all cases, you should embrace the soil you already have rather than resorting to wholesale replacement or intensive amelioration. If you are concerned about your soil health, you can no doubt improve it over time through applying homemade compost, planting diversely and minimising disturbance or digging. Occasionally, though, major interventions are unavoidable. On one project I designed in central London, contamination was so severe that the planning authorities mandated the complete removal and replacement of all topsoil on site. Often, soils in new build developments also require extensive work. I experienced this firsthand in my sister's garden, where the developers had stripped away the fertile topsoil, leaving behind a compacted clay subsoil that took considerable effort to restore.

WHAT EXACTLY IS 'GOOD' SOIL?

The idea of 'good' soil is quite subjective – it entirely depends on what you wish to grow. If you're dedicated to abundant annual vegetable harvests, good soil might mean nutrient-rich, free-draining loam. But someone cultivating a Mediterranean herb garden may find that lean, gravelly, low-nutrient soils are ideal. There's no single perfect soil – the key is understanding what you've got, nurturing it appropriately and choosing edimentals suited to thrive in those conditions.

UNDERSTANDING YOUR SOIL

Getting familiar with soil begins by recognising its layers or horizons. Digging a 40-centimetre deep × 30-centimetre wide (16-inch × 12-inch) hole or test pit in your garden will usually reveal a few distinct soil layers. At the top, you'll find a thin layer of humus, which is rich organic matter. Below that is a layer of topsoil, a darker, crumbly layer with comparatively high levels of organic matter and biological life. This layer is typically around 15–30 centimetres (6–12 inches) deep, though its depth can vary depending on your site and its history. Beneath that layer lies the subsoil, often lighter in colour and lower in organic content, but still important for retaining moisture and providing essential minerals. If you dig deeper still, you may reach the parent material or bedrock, which differs widely from place to place. It might be chalky limestone in parts of southern

Wildflowers thriving in dry stony soil in Turkey. Lean and mean conditions often produce the most diverse plant communities.

UNDERSTANDING YOUR GARDEN

England, reddish sandstone in Wales, or volcanic rock in the Pacific Northwest of the US. Each layer significantly influences drainage, nutrient availability and the types of plants your garden can support.

After observing your soil's layers, the next step is determining its type. Soils are made up of three main particle types – sand, clay and

Soil is built in layers over time – from surface humus and fertile topsoil to the deeper subsoil, parent material and bedrock that anchor the landscape.

silt – and are categorised as such. Each has its own distinct characteristics. Sandy soil drains quickly but retains fewer nutrients. Clay soil retains nutrients and moisture well but can compact easily and drain slowly. Silt sits somewhere in between, with smoother particles that retain water more effectively than sand yet still drain reasonably well.

Another term you've likely encountered is 'loam', often celebrated as the gardener's ideal. Loam isn't a separate particle type itself, but rather a balanced blend of sand, clay and silt, combining the beneficial qualities of each: good drainage, nutrient retention and ease of cultivation. In reality, soils exist along a wide spectrum, and yours will likely fall somewhere uniquely between these three simplified categories.

Another critical element of soil health is acidity or alkalinity, measured by pH on a scale from 0–14. A pH of 7 is neutral; below 7 is acidic, and above 7 is alkaline. Most garden plants, including many edimentals, prefer a slightly acidic-to-neutral soil, generally in the range of pH 6–7.5. However, certain edimentals require more extreme conditions. For instance, blueberries (*Vaccinium* spp.) and cranberries (*Vaccinium macrocarpon*) flourish exclusively in acidic soils below pH 6, whereas sea kale (*Crambe maritima*) thrives naturally in alkaline coastal soils. Understanding your soil's pH helps you select plants that will naturally flourish, minimising the need for extensive intervention.

ASSESSING YOUR SOIL AT HOME

The best way to get to know your soil is through direct, hands-on contact. Get your hands in the earth, grab a

Different soil textures – clay, silt, sand and loam – determine how well soil holds water, drains and supports plant life.

UNDERSTANDING YOUR GARDEN

handful, feel its texture, give it a smell – healthy, well-structured soil typically smells earthy and pleasantly sweet. If you're feeling particularly adventurous, consider exploring the soils in friends' or family members' gardens, although I recommend getting permission before plunging your hands enthusiastically into their borders.

A simple 'finger test' helps determine your soil texture. Dampen a small amount of soil and roll it gently between your fingers. Clay-rich soil forms a sticky, cohesive ball easily; sandy soil crumbles quickly; silty soil feels smooth and silky but doesn't hold shape as strongly as clay; loam generally holds its shape loosely but breaks apart easily when pressed. In that same 40-centimetre × 30-centimetre (16-inch × 12-inch) test pit, you'll see distinct soil layers, observe worms and other soil life, and you can test drainage by filling the pit with water and observing how quickly it empties. For assessing soil pH, affordable home test kits provide useful initial information. However, if you're planning extensive planting or adjustments, sending samples off to a lab for detailed analyses and recommendations can be worthwhile.

SOIL VARIABILITY

Even modest-sized gardens can display surprising variability in soil type and pH. A four-acre project I designed several years ago vividly illustrated this. Mature hydrangea shrubs (*Hydrangea macrophylla*) scattered across the garden indicated dramatic variations in pH, blooming pink in alkaline zones and vivid blue in acidic areas. When we commissioned a detailed soil survey, it confirmed a remarkable patchwork of soil conditions throughout the plot. Don't assume uniformity simply because one area behaves in a certain way, although most smaller gardens generally display more consistency within a specific range.

SOIL MOISTURE

Soil moisture also varies significantly between gardens and is heavily influenced by your soil type. Beyond this, you may notice distinct moisture patterns throughout your garden influenced by topography or structures. On my land in Wales, there's an area that appears perfectly solid and dry in summer, but after heavy winter rains it transforms into a hidden bog, once dramatically claiming one of my Wellington boots. On the other hand, rain shadows created by walls, fences or buildings similarly create persistently dry patches. At home in Bristol, my garden is surrounded by old stone walls with deep footings. A combination of both the rain shadow effect and the wall absorbing moisture makes the soil particularly dry along their bases.

THE MAGIC OF ORGANIC MATTER

If there's one universal remedy for improving soil conditions, it's adding organic matter. Well-managed garden soils typically contain 5–10 per cent organic matter, whereas intensively farmed agricultural soils commonly have less than 1 per cent. Mature permaculture systems, organic allotments or market gardens can build organic matter levels up to 10–20 per cent.[2] This was certainly the case with Charles Dowding's no-dig system, which had an impressive 18 per cent organic matter! The magic of organic matter is that it enhances drainage in clay soils, boosts moisture and nutrient retention in sandy soils, reduces compaction and feeds beneficial microbial life. Homemade compost is by far the most sustainable, cost-effective and satisfying way to build organic matter – the benefits far outweigh purchasing carbon-intensive compost in plastic bags.

SOIL AS A LIVING ECOSYSTEM

Beneath our feet lies a hidden universe teeming with life. It's often said that just one teaspoon of healthy garden soil contains more living organisms – bacteria, fungi, viruses, protozoa – than there are humans on Earth.[3] Among these microscopic allies, mycorrhizal fungi form vital symbiotic partnerships with plant roots, exchanging nutrients and water in mutually beneficial relationships. Nurturing this underground ecosystem creates robust, resilient gardens producing abundant, nutritious crops.

LEAN & MEAN

In my garden in Bristol, I took a different approach. Where mostly clay subsoil – and little topsoil – existed, I used crushed rubble, sand and

Making your own compost at home is a cost-effective and deeply gratifying way to create organic matter from recycled garden and kitchen waste, closing the loop and feeding the soil that feeds us in turn.

various waste materials from the garden works and house renovations in place of importing new topsoil. Inspired by the pioneering work of horticulturalists John Little, in the UK, and Peter Korn, in Sweden, this created a lean, resilient environment with a range of substrates – from topsoil rich to sand heavy and deep rubble – all ideal for drought-tolerant plants and certain edimentals. Not all plants want rich loam; indeed, many thrive in what appear to be harsh or challenging conditions. Where previously I might have thought to import new topsoil at great expense, this process presents a sustainable, low-cost way of growing. Whatever your soil, the key is to know what you have and match your edimental planting to it.

A few examples of edimentals for various soil situations include moisture-loving water mint (*Mentha aquatica*), drought-tolerant rosemary (*Salvia rosmarinus*) and sandy soil specialist wild thyme (*Thymus polytrichus*).

Sun & Shade

Sunlight influences your garden in more ways than you might initially consider. Even a perfectly south-facing garden is likely to have pockets of shade cast by trees, hedges, structures or neighbouring buildings. Similarly, north-facing gardens, although typically more shaded, often surprise us with sunny pockets tucked in unexpected places. To experience this firsthand, stand at the end of a long north-facing garden and turn to face the house. You'll probably feel sunlight warming your face, illuminating areas that otherwise seemed destined for permanent shade. I have a similar situation in Bristol, where my garden is north-facing and set into a steep hill. By simply climbing a few metres up some steps, I reach the main garden elevated at first-floor level, and it is a sun trap. It's bathed in intense sunlight that spills generously over the house's roof throughout much of the day and year. Closely observing and understanding how sunlight moves across your garden, shifting subtly yet significantly each day and season, is fundamental to successful planting.

Gardening books often categorise plants as needing set light conditions. The three basic categories you'll often see are 'full sun', 'partial shade' or 'deep shade'. These terms can be helpful guidelines, although it's worth remembering that gardens rarely fit neatly into these categories. There is a spectrum of light conditions and

Some robust edimentals and ornamentals growing out of rubble in my garden in Bristol. Edimentals like sea buckthorn, Turkish rocket and red valerian share beds with toxic plants like spurges and foxgloves.

UNDERSTANDING YOUR GARDEN

subtle variations within each garden, meaning your exact conditions might not fit perfectly into these definitions. However, as a starting point, 'full sun' typically means around 6 or more hours of direct sunlight daily, usually during the peak growing season. 'Partial shade' generally refers to 3–6 hours of direct sun, often accompanied by filtered or dappled light the rest of the day. Finally, 'deep shade' usually describes conditions with less than 2–3 hours of direct sunlight, or perhaps no direct sun at all, as found beneath dense tree canopies, in narrow courtyards or on the northern side of walls or buildings.

Mapping sunlight patterns in your garden is a valuable exercise. You can easily chart this by carefully observing sunny and shaded areas at various times of day and throughout the seasons, marking your observations on a simple garden plan or sketch. CAD tools can also offer powerful digital simulations of how sunlight shifts throughout the year, though these typically require professional assistance.

Alongside soil, matching your plants to available light conditions is essential for a thriving, productive garden. Traditional annual vegetables, such as tomatoes (*Solanum lycopersicum*) or cucumbers (*Cucumis sativus*), generally need abundant sunlight, something not always readily available in home gardens. However, edimentals originate from diverse ecosystems, and, being perennial, many are naturally adapted to thrive comfortably with less sun.

Water

Water availability is a defining factor in the establishment and evolution of all gardens. It shapes not just what you plant, but how your garden thrives throughout the year. Even temperate climates, known for their relatively reliable rainfall, experience significant variation. Some regions enjoy consistent moisture year-round, while others face starkly seasonal patterns, sudden flooding or frustratingly erratic rainfall just when

The ostrich fern is a delicious edimental for moist soil conditions and for naturalising along the edges of water features.

traditional crops might need it most. Whether you live in an area with predictable rain or frequent droughts, understanding how water moves through your garden – and how best to capture and use it – is a useful process. As a starting point, your local meteorological station should be able to provide you with historic data on the annual rainfall for your area.

When thinking about how water will influence your edimental garden, begin by mapping the movement of water through the space. Observe where rainfall collects, where run-off occurs during storms and how water might flow from your rooftops, terraces or paved surfaces. Consider other sources, too, like irrigation water from hoses or pipes, or even grey water from your house or outbuildings. By carefully watching and mapping these patterns, you can design to maximise every drop, either guiding water towards your plants or capturing it effectively for future use.

To ensure a reliable supply during dry periods, storing water strategically within your garden is essential. On my allotment, a large water butt or barrel connected to the shed's downpipe provides precious water during dry spells, although even this reserve can quickly run dry without summer rain to refill it. In larger or more ambitious gardens, underground tanks can store substantial volumes of water, which we sometimes install in clients' gardens to help irrigate newly planted trees or shrubs until fully established.

For larger gardens or those with slopes and varied terrain, like we have in Wales, land-forming techniques such as bioswales – shallow,

Chamomile, well known for its calming qualities as a herbal tea, makes an excellent drought-tolerant lawn alternative in free-draining soils.

gently sloping ditches running along contours – can be invaluable. Bioswales slow down runoff, encouraging water to gently soak into the soil rather than rush off the land's surface and create a gradient of moisture conditions.[4]

Even in smaller gardens, creating a pond or a small water retention feature is hugely beneficial, not only providing critical moisture reserves during dry spells but also boosting local biodiversity by attracting wildlife. Rain gardens offer another fantastic way of managing water and creating diverse environments for edimentals, particularly for urban or suburban settings. These specially designed depressions capture runoff from roofs and hard surfaces, diverting water away from overloaded drainage systems and allowing it to infiltrate back into the soil naturally.[5] Similarly to bioswales, rain gardens create a mosaic of moisture gradients, from standing water at their base through moist areas around the edges to drier conditions on banks. This diversity of moisture conditions within a small space provides an excellent opportunity to grow a wide variety of edimentals adapted to varying water levels.

Wind & Exposure

The influence of wind on a garden is often underestimated, yet it shapes everything from plant growth and pollination success to the comfort and enjoyment of the garden itself. How windy or sheltered your garden feels largely depends on your location, landscape features and existing planting or structures. An exposed, windy site can pose considerable challenges. It can make pollination difficult for fruit trees, slow or even prevent young plants from establishing and cause physical damage by snapping branches or toppling woody plants.

Observing wind patterns throughout different times of year is a wise investment of your time. While prevailing winds often dominate, seasonal variations can dramatically alter conditions in your garden. Here in the UK, the prevailing wind typically blows from the warm southwest, a gentle influence moderated by the Gulf Stream. Yet during winter in Wales, we frequently experience harsh, bitterly cold easterly winds that whip fiercely through the Wye Valley, shaping how and where I plan to introduce shelterbelts and protective planting. In the US, similar phenomena occur, such as the powerful, drying Santa Ana winds of southern California or the intense, northerly winter winds sweeping across the Great Plains, with each demanding a thoughtful gardening approach.

Designing shelter within your garden can dramatically improve conditions, turning challenging wind exposure into opportunities for productive planting. Windbreaks or shelterbelts are groups of trees and shrubs deliberately planted to deflect, slow and diffuse wind. Planting shelterbelts early is crucial as they take several years to mature and provide optimal protection, so, if your site is exposed, they are one of your first considerations. The ideal shelterbelt isn't solid, rather it's about 50 per cent permeable. Planting achieves this well and gently filters wind, avoiding the turbulence that solid barriers can create. Positioning windbreaks at a right angle to the prevailing wind direction maximises their effectiveness.[6]

Microclimates

Microclimates – small, distinct climatic conditions within your garden – offer opportunities once you know how to spot them. A microclimate could range in scale from entire counties to a single square metre, each presenting unique conditions shaped by subtle variations in sun, shade, temperature, moisture, frost and wind exposure. They're everywhere once you start looking. From frost pockets at the bottom of a slope to the warmer, sun-drenched side of a wall or the wind-buffered corner behind a shed. Altitude also plays a role. Even modest changes in elevation within or around your garden can affect temperature and wind exposure. As a rough rule, the temperature drops by around 1°C for every 100 metres (about 3.5°F for every 1,000 feet) of elevation gain, something to keep in mind when siting tender plants in hilly or upland gardens.[7]

Identifying microclimates is a rewarding and tactile experience. Using your body and senses reveals fascinating insights – feeling

Hop trefoil taking advantage of the microclimate created at the top of this drystone wall in Turkey.

differences in temperature as you walk through your garden, noting where frost lingers longest on cold mornings or observing variations in plant flowering times. After a snowfall, watch the tapestry of patterns that evolve across the landscape as snow and frost begin to thaw, often chasing the sun's path as it rises in the morning sky. These subtle shifts map out sunny, sheltered spots versus colder, shaded ones often more vividly than any instrument could. You may notice the same plant flowering at slightly different times depending on where it's planted. A sunbaked corner might coax earlier blooms, but it may also bring an earlier end if the plant becomes heat-stressed. A more shaded spot might delay flowering, reduce bloom quantity or prolong the season altogether.

Microclimates are often overlooked, but they profoundly impact plant productivity and resilience. Fruit trees positioned carelessly atop an exposed hill, blasted by harsh winds, may struggle, whereas the same trees sheltered downslope could flourish. It's our role as gardeners to identify existing microclimates and enhance or create new ones through thoughtful design choices and planting schemes.

Specialist Conditions

Certain gardens or locations face especially unique or challenging conditions, such as coastal gardens exposed to salty air and strong winds, or urban gardens dealing with city stresses like air pollution or reflected

heat. These specialist conditions profoundly influence all other environmental factors, too, from soil type – often sandy and low-nutrient in coastal areas – to moisture availability and wind exposure.

However specific or challenging your garden conditions might seem, there are always edimentals adapted to thrive. I was keen to include edimentals on a development project of new homes along the UK's exposed south coast. Despite fierce winds, salty air and intense sunlight, we successfully established European hackberry (*Celtis australis*), strawberry tree (*Arbutus unedo*) and ginkgo (*Ginkgo biloba*) among other edible trees and shrubs, creating a resilient, attractive and productive landscape for residents to enjoy and harvest from. Whatever your scenario, don't feel disheartened – do your research, trust your instincts and experiment boldly.

Some of my favourite edimentals that excel in coastal conditions include saltbush (*Atriplex halimus*), with its silvery, edible leaves; the striking caper bush (*Capparis spinosa*), known for its pickled flower buds and sprawling form; Scots lovage (*Ligustrum scoticum*), a hardy, coastal perennial with a celery-like flavour; red valerian (*Centranthus ruber*), which self-seeds readily; and biennial seacoast angelica (*Angelica lucida*), a bold, architectural umbel with a long history of coastal use.

Biodiversity

Observing and nurturing biodiversity within your garden is not merely mutually beneficial – it's essential. Healthy ecosystems are resilient, productive and full of life, and the same holds true at a garden scale. Paying attention to which plant communities and wildlife already thrive on your site, or nearby, is a powerful way to assess your conditions.

Certain plants act as indicators, vividly demonstrating specific soil types, pH, moisture levels or climatic influences. As we've discussed earlier, hydrangeas (*Hydrangea macrophylla*) blooming pink or blue can signal variations in soil pH across your garden. There are many indicator plants out there, and they vary depending on your local environment. In the UK, nettles (*Urtica dioica*) flourish in nutrient-rich soils, and yarrow (*Achillea millefolium*) and sheep's sorrel (*Rumex acetosella*) thrive in poor, free-draining ground.[8] In the US, species like big bluestem (*Andropogon gerardii*) can point to rich prairie soils, while cheatgrass (*Bromus tectorum*) often colonises disturbed, low-nutrient areas.[9]

Plants at the extremes of your garden, the ones that look especially vigorous or particularly stressed, can tell a story, too. Ask yourself what's thriving, what's struggling and why? These observations provide clues about underlying conditions like light, drainage, nutrient availability or exposure. Over time, you'll begin to read your garden like a living map.

Beyond plants, wildlife tells a story, too. Birds, mammals, insects and amphibians all provide clues to your garden's health and resilience. Some species, like ladybirds feeding on aphids, actively support your garden through pest control. Others, like hedgehogs or song thrushes, may suggest the presence of healthy invertebrate populations. In some cases, wildlife can pose challenges, too: gophers burrowing around roots, for example, can be a common issue in certain US gardens.

Encouraging biodiversity begins with diverse planting schemes, creating structural complexity and supporting numerous microhabitats. If you want to go deeper, conducting a biodiversity baseline assessment is a brilliant way to track how your planting and landscape choices affect local wildlife over time. We're doing this in Wales, aiming to gain real data on how an evolving edible landscape impacts a site that was previously grazed by sheep. While formal ecological assessments can be complex or costly, there are plenty of accessible ways to get involved. From citizen science projects to wildlife ID apps on your phone, many tools exist to help you monitor and connect with the life in your garden. Whatever level of engagement suits you, the key is simply to observe and understand your garden's wildlife – appreciating how it helps support an edimental garden and considering ways you might encourage beneficial wildlife populations into the space.

By taking the time to understand your garden's conditions – from soil and water to sunlight, wind, microclimates and biodiversity – you lay the foundation for an edimental landscape that collaborates with nature. Observation, patience and curiosity turn a plot of land into a living partner, revealing what will thrive and how best to nurture it. With this knowledge in hand, you're ready to design a garden that is not only productive and resilient, but also deeply connected to its place.

Chapter 6

Designing with Edimentals

I'd like to invite you into an imagined garden, a space where food growing, ecological resilience and beautiful design come together in harmony. It's around the average size of a suburban garden (16 × 12 metres or 52 × 40 feet), but far from a typical UK or US garden of sweeping lawn and narrow ornamental borders. While that style still holds appeal for many, it often feels like the only option. The Edimental Garden offers an alternative, an immersive, productive, biodiverse oasis that provides beauty, sustenance and ecological health. Drawing on the core principles explored throughout this book, this imagined space distils big ideas into garden form and shows how even a modest urban or suburban plot can be transformed into a magical, edible landscape.

Edimentals aside, it's important to design places to pause – spaces to sit back, watch wildlife and soak in the surroundings. Even in compact gardens, seating can be immersed in planting for a richly sensory experience.

Design Features

The following elements bring The Edimental Garden to life. Any one of these ideas – or a combination – can be adapted to suit your site and conditions, offering practical ways to transition your garden into a resilient, edible landscape.

A Agroforestry

Trees introduce height and structure, making the modest space feel larger than it is. Planted throughout the garden rather than confined to the edges, they create layered views that draw the eye deeper into the space. This composition adds depth, interest and a sense of intrigue, inviting you to look again and discover more.

A mini orchard occupies a central, sunlit spot and is underplanted with productive shrubs and low-growing edimentals. It creates microclimates, providing shade and harvests throughout the year while encouraging beneficial insects and wildlife.

Along the garden's rear perimeter, an edible hedge of productive plants like hazelnuts (*Corylus avellana* var. *maxima*), elder (*Sambucus nigra*) and blackthorn or sloes (*Prunus spinosa*) forms a windbreak that also provides berries, blossom and habitat. Planted at right angles to the prevailing wind, it gently shelters the garden.

B Boundaries

The edible hedge defines the garden's rear, while the side boundaries are softened with edimental climbers trained up stone walls. Espaliered fruit trees enrich the vertical space, adding seasonal interest and yield. By covering hard edges in greenery, the garden perimeter seems to dissolve, making the space feel larger, lusher and more immersive.

C Composting

Making good use of a shady north-facing corner, a composting area transforms garden waste and kitchen scraps into valuable organic matter, supporting soil fertility and structure. Different methods are used, from worm compost bins to leaf mould piles, traditional compost heaps to Japanese Bokashi fermentation composting, creating an effective and reciprocal closed-loop system.

D Forest Garden

A small forest garden enjoys shelter from the edible hedge. It's layered with edible, medicinal and craft plants, bringing a holistic richness to the space. From canopy trees to groundcovers, every layer serves a purpose: providing food, materials and biodiversity. It also helps

buffer wind and create a gentler microclimate for features closer to the house. A wilder, more immersive pocket of the garden, it's rich with texture, scent and seasonal interest.

E Meandering Deck

A gently winding deck meanders through the planting, inviting exploration and offering intimate encounters with edimentals. Constructed from sustainably sourced local timber, it draws on biophilic design principles and enhances the garden's mystery and intrigue.

F Sculptural Habitat

Sculptural elements such as log piles and bee posts are designed habitats that invite wildlife into the garden while providing visual interest and personal character.

G Edible Meadow

An open, sunny edible meadow provides void and breathing space for both pollinators and people to enjoy. Wildflowers intermingle with edimentals to create a vibrant, productive and low-maintenance planting. The edible meadow extends to the green roof where drought-tolerant and shallow-rooting edimentals grow in 12cm (5in) of substrate, making use of otherwise unused space.

H Traditional Vegetables

The sunniest spot is dedicated to polycultures of annual vegetables, where permaculture principles are used to maximise the productivity

of this small space. A greenhouse adjoins the dining terrace and extends the growing season, allowing warmth-loving crops like tomatoes (*Solanum lycopersicum*), chillies (*Capsicum annuum*) and basil (*Ocimum basilicum*) to flourish even in cooler climates.

🟢 Containers

Two oversized pots anchor the terrace by the rear of the house, simple and sculptural. Each container is planted with layered edimentals, combining structure, scent and seasonal interest. By using a single large pot rather than many small ones, the design feels bold and intentional, while still productive and full of life.

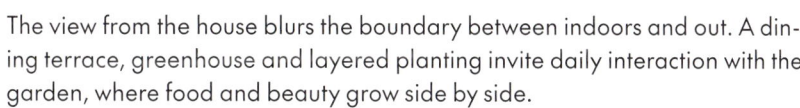

A meandering deck leads through fruit trees and diverse planting, creating mystery, rhythm and discovery. Layers of edimentals, shrubs and groundcovers blend orchard-style planting with the intimacy of a small-scale forest garden within an urban/suburban space.

The view from the house blurs the boundary between indoors and out. A dining terrace, greenhouse and layered planting invite daily interaction with the garden, where food and beauty grow side by side.

DESIGNING WITH EDIMENTALS

At the heart of the garden, a naturalistic pond gathers rainwater from the greenhouse and green roof, sustaining a rich community of plants and wildlife that thrive across its many moisture gradients – from standing water to saturated soil and drier edges.

Rain Garden & Pond

Rainwater is harvested from the house's green roof and greenhouse, feeding a small, naturalistic pond and surrounding rain garden. This captures runoff, replenishes groundwater and provides diverse habitats for an array of edimentals to thrive.

Planting Design: An Ecological Approach

Planting design is, undeniably, a vast and intricate topic. But here we'll aim to keep it simple, practical and approachable. Together, we'll focus on key principles and ideas, helping you build a foundational understanding of an ecologically inspired design approach.

So often, people make garden planting decisions impulsively, choosing whatever catches the eye in the garden centre. We've all been there – enticed by colourful displays in oversized pots, usually sold at their peak. The approach I'll share here is fundamentally different. Instead, we'll carefully plan our planting to align with natural plant communities, selecting plants based on ecological considerations as well as aesthetics, sometimes choosing species that may not reach their prime for months or even seasons to come. It's a way of designing for long-term success.

From a deep understanding of your site emerges one of gardening's most enduring principles – 'right plant, right place'. Although this phrase has been around in horticultural circles for decades, it remains timeless for good reason. This simple idea helps us step away from traditional planting schemes of old that prioritised individual plants solely for their ornamental appeal, often creating beautiful but incredibly high-maintenance gardens. By choosing plants suited to your specific

conditions, you set yourself up for a garden that thrives naturally, requiring far less intervention.

Ecological Niches

One of the most fundamental concepts in planting design is the idea of ecological niches. It's a term that might sound technical at first, but in reality it's incredibly simple. Every plant (and animal) has a role to play, a space to fill, a particular set of conditions in which it thrives and an ecological function it performs. When we design with this in mind, rather than forcing plants into positions they're not suited for, we create resilient, low-input planting schemes that are not only beautiful but also aligned with nature.

Diversity in a plant community is, in many ways, a reflection of how many ecological niches have been filled. If you look at a wild meadow, a woodland edge or an area of unmanaged scrubland, you'll notice that every available space is occupied by something. Plants of different heights and forms, growing at different times of the year, interact in an ever-evolving dance of competition and cooperation. These plant communities are everywhere: in the fringes of local parks, hedgerows, brownfield sites and the more untouched corners of gardens.

The term 'plant community' has come up a lot in this book, and you may be wondering exactly what it means. Put simply, a plant community is a group of plants growing together in a particular place, interacting with one another and with their environment. You don't have to venture into pristine wilderness to find these communities in action. Some of the most fascinating plant communities I've encountered have been in unexpected places – from brownfield sites in east London to scrubby roadside verges and urban canal edges. Sometimes, though, it takes stepping away from the

Ferns growing from walls illustrate how plants adapt to even the narrowest ecological niches, thriving where moisture, shelter and a foothold align to create challenging yet exploitable conditions.

DESIGNING WITH EDIMENTALS

landscapes we're familiar with to truly sharpen our ability to see them. I remember standing among meadows in southern Turkey, surrounded by layers of flowering plants and edimentals, all interwoven in a tapestry of abundance. It was a moment of complete awe, and yet, as I looked closer, the patterns were familiar. The same fundamental principles are at play in the woodlands, meadows and coastal landscapes I'd grown up with in the UK.

Within any plant community, no two species can occupy exactly the same niche indefinitely. One will inevitably outcompete the other. This is how ecosystems self-regulate, how they settle into a jostling, shifting equilibrium where plants carve out their own roles. If every possible niche is filled, bare soil disappears, and, with it, the risk of invasion by weeds. The soil stays shaded and cool, reducing evaporation and stress on the plants. In other cases, when conditions are just right for one particular species, that species will dominate, expanding aggressively and taking over.[1] You see this in stands of nettles (*Urtica dioica*) on nitrogen- and phosphorus-rich ground, or in dense swathes of Canadian goldenrod (*Solidago canadensis*), pushing out more delicate competitors. Wetlands are a great example where a few species can often dominate. Certain edimentals, such as sweet flag (*Acorus calamus*), thrive in these conditions of abundance, spreading relentlessly across boggy ground.

Ecological niches exist in every dimension: above ground, below ground and in the way plants interact with their surroundings. Some plants shoot up tall and upright, while others stay low and sprawling. Some leaf out early in spring, racing to capture light before taller plants take over, while others wait, emerging late and filling the gaps left behind. Some flower in spring, others in summer and others still in the fading warmth of autumn.

Sweet flag establishing in a pond and soon to form an extensive colony.

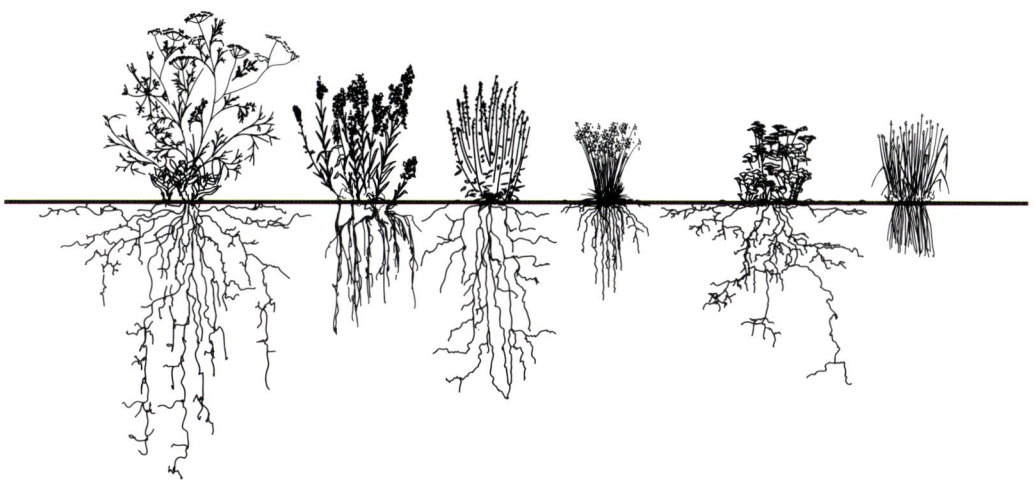

Plant niches extend both above and below ground. A thriving plant community makes full use of these varied spaces, with roots and shoots occupying every available layer to share light, water and nutrients efficiently.

Below ground, the variety is just as intricate. Deep-rooted edimentals like black salsify (*Scorzonera hispanica*) mine moisture from far beneath the surface, while shallow-rooted groundcovers like wild strawberries (*Fragaria vesca*) knit together the top layer, preventing erosion and suppressing weeds. Tap-rooted plants anchor themselves firmly, while bulbs like wild garlic (*Allium ursinum*) lurk beneath the soil, waiting to push up fresh growth in early spring before disappearing again. In any well-functioning plant community, these differences allow plants to coexist, each drawing from slightly different resources, each playing a distinct role in the ecosystem.

Plants are constantly competing, but they're also working together. Nitrogen-fixers, such as clover (*Trifolium* spp.) and sea buckthorn (*Hippophae rhamnoides*), draw nitrogen from the air and store it in their roots, naturally enriching the soil for their neighbours. Many share nutrients through mycorrhizal networks, forming underground relationships with fungi that connect them to a vast, unseen exchange system. Others, like fennel (*Foeniculum vulgare*), release chemicals that suppress competing plants, creating space around them in a phenomenon known as allelopathy.[2] Understanding these relationships allows for smarter plant choices, ones that work with, rather than against, the system you're creating.

Some species have incredibly narrow niches, finely tuned to a specific set of conditions or a particular relationship with another species. But many species are generalists, able to adapt and survive across a wide range of environments. In Wales, I have hawthorns (*Crataegus monogyna*) growing in full sun, blasted by wind and others thriving in the deep shade of a mature woodland.

Tuning into how plant communities function takes time. At first, it's easy to see gardens as a set of separate plants rather than a woven, interconnected whole. But once you start observing how plants arrange themselves in the wild, everything shifts. A patch of scrubland on the side of the road isn't just a mess of weeds, it's a dynamic, evolving ecosystem. A woodland isn't just a collection of trees, but a layered and deeply interconnected community. The best way to understand this is to immerse yourself in it.

Layers

My childhood spent running wild around Barton Hills saw me emerging from the cathedral-like beech (*Fagus sylvatica*) woodlands into the rolling chalk downlands beyond. These transitions between ecosystems were like portals – abrupt shifts in plant life where one landscape gave way to another. Though I wasn't consciously analysing why these changes occurred, I was instinctively drawn to them. There was something about the way plants arranged themselves, how layers of growth built upon each other, how everything slotted into place to create a living, breathing whole. Long before I had the language for it, I was absorbing one of nature's most fundamental design principles.

Layers are the natural extension of ecological niches. In any thriving plant community, plants organise themselves in a vertical structure, making use of every available resource. In a woodland (or forest garden), towering canopy trees provide shelter for an understorey of smaller shrubs and saplings, beneath which perennials, groundcovers and mosses knit together the forest floor. An edible meadow, though more open, follows the same principle: grasses and tall flowering perennials (or forbs) forming the structural framework, mid-height perennials rising and falling through the seasons and low-growing plants filling the spaces in between.

Designing with edimentals of different growth habits, flowering periods, environmental preferences, and edible uses is essentially a process of designing with layers. In the wild, plant communities naturally find ways to coexist over time. In a designed garden, however, we usually don't have the luxury of waiting decades for those relationships to unfold unless we're taking a true rewilding approach. Instead, we begin with intention. At the most basic level, we want to create a scheme that suits the site, meets the needs of the gardener, and supports local ecology. That means considering the ecological layers we want to represent from the outset and accelerating natural processes by introducing the right plants to the right conditions. Thinking about where a plant fits within a layered structure offers a practical framework for building a planting scheme and for shaping a resilient, self-sustaining community.

A beautiful example of layering in action can be seen in the UK's beech woodlands. Bluebells (*Hyacinthoides* spp.) thrive in these environments because they time their growth to make the most of seasonal light shifts. Before the beech canopy comes into full leaf, bluebells burst into flower, taking advantage of the brief window of sunlight before the forest floor is cast into deep shade. It's a reminder that layers are not just physical, they are temporal, changing throughout the seasons, one wave of growth giving way to the next.

Thinking in layers transforms the way we approach planting design. We create plantings that function more like natural ecosystems. Instead of isolated plants spaced apart in empty soil, we build a multidimensional structure where plants support and complement one another.

As we saw when looking at food forests in chapter 4, plant communities can be broken down into seven distinct layers (with the eight in food forests being fungi). For most design purposes, I

Bluebells under beech trees are a magical sight and celebration of spring.

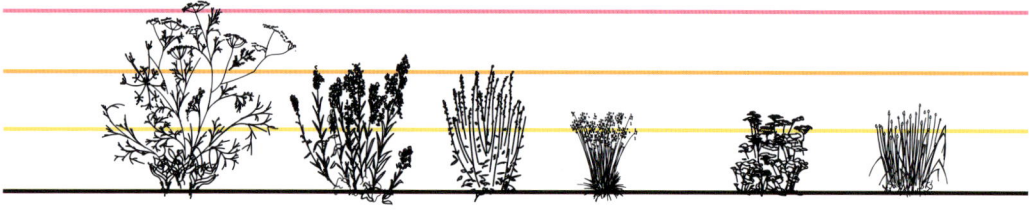

The three essential layers: structural or emergent species for height and form, a mid-layer of long-season interest, and a low groundcover layer that knits the planting together.

simplify this to a few essential layers that provide a practical framework for creating balanced, resilient and ecologically rich planting schemes.

STRUCTURAL / EMERGENT

At the uppermost level is the structural or emergent layer, typically forming around 5–15 per cent of the planting. These plants provide the backbone of the scheme, making it legible and easy to read. They are the rhythm-setters, guiding the eye through the space and offering structure across the seasons. While many are taller species, typically exceeding 1.2 metres (4 feet), height alone doesn't define this role. Structural plants can also be those with a strong form or architectural presence. They are plants with enough character to anchor the planting, often used individually or in small groups, and which wouldn't work as well planted en masse. Whether through bold verticality, striking foliage or sheer mass, these plants hold space confidently. They are used sparingly to avoid overwhelming the planting, particularly in smaller gardens, but they are essential in giving the design a sense of intent and cohesion. Many persist through winter, ensuring the scheme has a presence beyond the growing season. This layer can include trees and shrubs, although these are placed consciously on a planting plan rather than being included in the percentage mix.

MID-LAYER & SEASONAL HITS

Beneath this sits the mid-layer and seasonal hits, making up around 30–40 per cent of the planting and typically around 40 centimetres–1.2 metres (16 inches–4 feet) in height. This is the main visual impression of the planting at any one time, the shifting, dynamic body of the scheme. Plants in this layer rise and fall with the seasons, forming waves of texture and colour. As one set of plant combinations fades, another emerges, creating a continuous flow of interest. The balance of species in this layer dictates the overall mood of the planting – whether soft and naturalistic, wild and exuberant or more restrained and controlled.

LOW / GROUNDCOVER

The most expansive layer is the low and groundcover layer, typically accounting for around 50 per cent of the planting and often including plenty of grasses. These plants are the glue that holds everything together, suppressing weeds, stabilising the soil and creating a textural base from which other layers emerge. As a guide, they are generally 40 centimetres (16 inches) and below in height. Unlike the mid-layer, they are not designed to be the stars of the show; rather, they provide a continuous presence that enhances the resilience of the scheme. Some are evergreen, ensuring year-round structure, while others retreat underground seasonally. Many of these plants need to cope with shifting light levels, enjoying full sun early in the season before taller layers grow up around them, casting shade. Mass plantings of bulbs and geophytes can further enhance this layer, their dense root networks minimising weed invasion while delivering bursts of early interest.

DOTS & FILLERS

Scattered throughout these three essential layers are the dots and fillers, making up roughly 5–10 per cent of the planting. These ephemeral species – short-lived perennials, biennials and annuals – bring an initial flush of visual impact, often dominating the first year or two while the main body of the planting establishes. Over time, many of these plants naturally fade, but some persist through self-seeding, filling in gaps and adapting to changes in the planting. This acts as a kind of self-healing mechanism, with a natural seed bank forming in the soil, ready to germinate when bare soil appears and conditions allow. It's best to avoid heavy self-seeders here to ensure they do not outcompete the main body of your planting, particularly during the establishment phases.

Beyond these core layers, other elements can be incorporated to add further complexity and function. Climbers play an essential role, extending the planting beyond ground level to cover walls, boundaries and other structures, adding vertical interest and increasing productivity in small spaces. A top edimental example includes the chocolate vine (*Akebia quinata*) – fast-growing and producing edible and medicinal fruits. Another layer that can be woven in is the carpet layer – species that thrive beneath the groundcover, minimising weed invasion in deep shade. Plants like bugle (*Ajuga reptans*) and wood sorrel (*Oxalis acetosella*) form dense mats, providing an extra layer of resilience.

You may be wondering how to determine which layer a plant belongs to. The height ranges given here are only guidelines. What is considered a mid-layer in one planting might be a structural plant in another. You may be designing a scheme where the tallest plants reach just 75 centimetres (30 inches), in which case your layers would adjust accordingly. The key is to observe how plants grow, how they relate to one another and how they integrate within a community. Looking at botanical drawings, or even sketching plants yourself, can be an invaluable way to understand their form and presence within a design. There are no rigid rules. Everything depends on the overall goals and conditions of the planting.

I haven't invented this way of thinking. The concept of layers in planting design has been shaped by ecologists, horticulturists and designers for decades. From books such as Richard Hansen and Friedrich Stahl's *Perennials and Their Garden Habitats* to Nigel Dunnett's *Naturalistic Planting Design: The Essential Guide*, or *Planting in a Post-Wild World* by Thomas Rainer and Claudia West, many leading voices have explored and refined these principles, each bringing their own terminology and perspective. What I present here is simply how I have distilled these ideas into something practical – an approach that works for me and, hopefully, a foundation for you to build upon and adapt to your own creative process.

Constraints

Andrew Wilson, an old mentor of mine and co-founder of the London College of Garden Design, taught me the value of constraints in planting design, and I've never looked back. A master plantsman with

Bugle makes a great shade-tolerant carpet layer with minor edible qualities.

decades of experience, he understood something fundamental: creativity flourishes within limits. Without clear parameters, the sheer volume of choice can be overwhelming. In my early design career, I would zip through plant catalogues, scribble endless lists in notebooks and wander around nurseries getting overly excited about all the plants I loved. It was exhilarating but lacked structure. As we've seen, there are thousands of edimentals that can be grown in a temperate climate, so where do you even begin? How do you whittle that down to fifteen to thirty for a mix? If you love plants, it's easy to get caught up in the sheer abundance of possibilities. But without a clear framework, designing a coherent, effective planting scheme becomes nearly impossible.

Start by identifying your core constraints – the key filters through which every plant choice must pass. These parameters reflect your project's goals and help narrow the overwhelming list of possibilities into a focused, coherent scheme. Common constraint categories include:

- **Aesthetic vision:** for example, a palette of soft textures and pinks and yellows immediately rules out bold, architectural plants and flowers of different colours.
- **Environmental conditions:** for example, drought-prone soil, deep shade, maritime exposure, or poor drainage will limit your selection to species that can truly thrive on site.
- **Site constraints:** for example, desirable and undesirable views, which may dictate the height or density of your planting or the need for screening versus openness.
- **Practical needs of the client:** such as low maintenance requirements, child-safe planting, or year-round edibility.
- **Big idea:** Andrew always layered in a broader concept of constraint – a theme or atmosphere to unify the planting. It could be practical, like 'edible abundance', or playful, like 'let's party'. This overarching idea helps shape the feel of the garden and ties the scheme together.

If a plant doesn't meet your criteria, don't force it – there will always be a better fit. Defining your constraints from the outset makes selection far more efficient and ensures that every plant earns its place. Constraints aren't about restriction; they bring clarity, cohesion and intention. They focus your creativity, not limit it. They are liberating.

Successional Planting

At its core, successional planting is the art of layering seasonal highlights, ensuring that as one species fades, another rises to take its place. Just as ecological niches are arranged spatially, they also play out temporally. A well-designed planting scheme isn't a static composition but a dynamic and ever-changing system, where different plants step into the spotlight at different points in the year. Considering the season of interest is critical to this process: Which times of year does the planting need to shine? Will it peak in early summer or are you hoping for a winter display?

For smaller gardens, the temptation is often to aim for year-round perfection, to try to create a space that looks good in every season. But this leads to compromise, resulting in something passable throughout the year but never truly spectacular. Instead, it's more effective to focus on key moments of peak interest. I aim to make my gardens sing from late spring through early autumn. A gentle start with bulbs that push through in the cold months that give way to three distinct waves of perennials from early summer to early autumn. This approach ensures there is always a moment of intensity, where the garden feels at its fullest and most alive, rather than an attempt to maintain a constant but muted presence.

For larger spaces, a different approach can be taken, dedicating specific areas to shine at particular times. A woodland edge that bursts into life in spring, a prairie-style meadow that reaches its peak in late summer, a border that carries rich autumn tones as the year fades. Rather than expecting every part of a garden to deliver at all times, this allows for a more naturalistic ebb and flow, extending the overall impact of the space.

Beyond aesthetics, successional planting plays a fundamental role in ecological function. By designing in layers of time, you provide continuous resources for pollinators and wildlife throughout the year. Early nectar sources from bulbs and spring perennials sustain emerging bees while late-flowering species support insects long into autumn. Meanwhile, structural elements left standing over winter provide shelter and food sources for countless species, turning a garden into a functioning habitat rather than a purely ornamental space.

Diversity

As we saw in Stephen Barstow's garden in chapter 1, a truly resilient, low-input planting scheme thrives on diversity. The more diverse a planting is, the more ecological niches it fills, and the more stable, abundant and self-sustaining it becomes. But diversity isn't about cramming in as many species as possible for the sake of variety. It's about finding the right balance between ecological complexity and aesthetic clarity. Are you working with shrubs and perennials? A mix of grasses

My Bristol garden demonstrates successional planting, with edimentals thriving in shallow, rubble-rich soil. Sea kale, garlic cress and stringy stonecrop mingle with red valerian and yarrow. While many are edible, some, like spurges, are toxic – a reminder that, even in an edimental garden, it's vital to exercise caution and be certain of any plant before you eat it.

and perennials? Understanding the plant categories you're working within helps structure the scheme.

The level of diversity needed depends on multiple factors, from the style of planting and available space to environmental conditions of your site and design intent. In food forests or highly experimental edimental gardens, diversity can be vast, as experienced in Stephen Barstow's astonishing two thousand edimentals. But in most designed planting schemes, a sweet spot lies somewhere between fifteen and thirty different species per planting mix. This range is enough to create ecological richness while maintaining legibility, structure and repetition – essential for a planting to feel intentional rather than chaotic.

A planting mix is, in essence, a designed plant community, a combination of species selected to work together within a particular set of conditions. Within a garden, multiple mixes will likely be present, responding to variations in sun, shade, moisture levels and soil type. But these mixes don't exist in isolation. There is always an interplay between them, an intermingling at the edges where species cross over and connect.

This crossover is essential for coherence. If a garden contains, for example, three distinct planting mixes, I always ensure that several plants span across them all, creating unity and flow throughout the space. Without this, when each mix contains its own unique set of species, a garden can become visually fragmented. A mid-sized garden with three different mixes and seventy-five separate species, each sparsely appearing, will feel disjointed, whereas a well-planned scheme with repetition and distribution of key plants will hold together as a whole. Fewer species throughout the entire planting can have a greater impact than an overwhelming number of different plants competing for attention.

Edibility

Does every plant in an edimental planting scheme need to be edible? Absolutely not. While the focus is on creating beautiful, food-producing landscapes, there's no need to be dogmatic about it. A garden made up entirely of edible plants might seem like the logical conclusion of an edimental approach, but in reality it's rarely the best or most sustainable option. Even in the 'School Food Matters Garden' at the RHS Chelsea Flower Show, which was designed to showcase the potential of edimentals, around 80 per cent of the plants were edible. The remaining 20 per cent played just as crucial a role, bringing biodiversity benefits, structural interest and aesthetic value to the planting.

Within edimentals, there are two broad categories. Some plants are first and foremost food sources, but happen to be visually striking, like globe artichokes (*Cynara cardunculus* Scolymus Group) with their dramatic silvery foliage and chives (*Allium schoenoprasum*) with their neat clumps of grassy leaves and bursts of pink blooms. Others are primarily ornamental plants but have edible parts, whether that's flowers, seeds, young shoots or roots, including bistort (*Persicaria bistorta*), with its elegant pink flower spikes and edible young leaves, and king's spear (*Asphodeline lutea*), whose roots can be harvested and cooked. A balanced planting includes a mix of both: high-quality, productive edibles that provide a reliable harvest and more subtle, multipurpose species that contribute to the scheme's overall function and beauty.

As mentioned earlier, the ground layer (as well as other layers) of a planting scheme often contains a high proportion of grasses, and in many cases these aren't edible. For me, grasses are an essential component of naturalistic planting. They bring texture, cohesion and

In the 'School Food Matters Garden', ornamental species were woven among edibles to provide structure, texture and vital habitat.

movement, offering a sense of structure even in the most dynamic, free-flowing plantings. Some grasses do have edible qualities, such as Indian ricegrass (*Achnatherum hymenoides*) or foxtail barley (*Hordeum jubatum*), but realistically very few gardeners are going to harvest, process and use them in their kitchens. That doesn't mean they shouldn't be included. Their role in the ecosystem, their aesthetic contribution and their ability to bind a planting together make them indispensable, regardless of their edibility.

Finding the right balance is key. The essence of edimentals is all about that sweet spot where beauty and food exist in harmony. Zoom out from an individual edimental to a whole planting scheme, a garden or an entire edible landscape, and that balance still needs to hold. A harmony between food production and visual appeal, structure with spontaneity and ecological function with human enjoyment.

Aesthetic Considerations

You might be wondering how we've got this far into a section on planting design without yet diving into aesthetics. It's an essential part of the process, but aesthetics alone won't carry a planting. You can create the most visually stunning scheme, but if it isn't suited to the site or the environmental conditions it will struggle. On the other hand, if you design a planting that works ecologically – one that's suited to the soil, the microclimate and the way plants naturally grow together – but it doesn't look good, then it's just as likely to fail. If a planting doesn't

This garden applies forest garden principles to a small suburban space, layering edimentals through a design that remains primarily recreational. Roses soften the boundaries while hazel, crab apple and juneberry provide height and structure. Rosemary, mint and wild strawberries weave through the lower layers.

Sketching a planting scheme in elevation (side view) can help to process your thinking and work towards a desired design.

connect with people, whether that's you, a client or the gardener responsible for its care, it risks being neglected, undervalued or even eventually removed. A planting must have an emotional pull, something that draws us in and makes us want to engage with it, to nurture it, to ensure it thrives in the long term. Beauty isn't just a superficial consideration, it's a fundamental part of what makes a garden thrive.

There are, however, some fundamental aesthetic considerations that help bring a planting together. Size is an obvious one: how large a plant will grow, how it spreads and how it fits within the overall composition. Setting a maximum and minimum height ensures a balanced composition and prevents plants from overwhelming one another. Understanding plant form is just as crucial. A planting with nothing but upright, vertical accents can feel static, just as a mix of only billowing, arching plants can lack definition. Texture is important as well: Is the planting frothy, light and airy, or more defined with bold forms, strong outlines, or large architectural foliage? The best schemes balance these different forms, mounding plants against vertical spikes, and loose, airy textures alongside bold, architectural statements.

Foliage plays a huge role in a planting's character. It's not just about whether a plant is evergreen or deciduous but about its texture, colour and reflectivity. Large, glossy leaves absorb and throw back light differently than fine, feathery ones. Glaucous blues and silvers create an entirely different feel than verdant greens. A garden where no thought has been given to foliage variation can feel flat, even when it's full of flowers.

Flower colour is often the first thing people consider, and the key is to see how colours work together in combination as opposed to looking at individual plants alone. Are they harmonious, blending into one another in subtle gradients, or are they intentionally clashing, creating energy and contrast? Different shades of the same colour can bring cohesion – a planting filled with multiple shades of one or two colours feels vastly different from one packed with a riot of hot pinks, oranges and yellows.

Then there's flower shape. A mix of spikes, umbels, daisy-like forms and ball-shaped flower heads creates contrast and visual rhythm. Too much of the same shape can feel monotonous, too much variation can feel chaotic. It's all about finding the balance between contrast and unity, tension and cohesion.

One of the best ways to develop a planting's aesthetic is to sketch it out, whether on paper or in your mind's eye. Imagine the composition in layers, thinking about form, colour, movement and rhythm. Where will the eye be drawn? Are there moments of repetition that help create cohesion? Is there enough contrast to keep things interesting? Play with ideas, go bold and get creative. The more you experiment, the more you'll refine your own visual language.

Planting Design: A Step-by-Step Process

In this section, I'll walk through the step-by-step process I use when approaching planting design. I'll use the edible meadow in The Edimental Garden as a working example to bring it to life and show how these principles translate into a real planting scheme.

Research Plants & Develop Long List

Once constraints and design considerations are all thought through and in place, the first step is researching plants and developing a long list. At this point, it's about exploring possibilities, discovering new species and assembling a palette of plants that fit the brief.

The key at this stage is not to start with personal favourites. It's tempting to lean on plants you already love and know well, but the goal is to keep it fresh and original. This is where in-depth research comes in – digging into books, exploring online databases, checking nursery catalogues and seeking out specialist growers who stock

Plant palettes are a great visual aid that assist with the shortlisting process.

unusual edimentals. Over the years, I've built up a library of go-to suppliers, whose deep knowledge and niche selections have shaped many of my designs.

Short List Plants

With a long list of potential plants in place, the next step is refining it into a cohesive shortlist. This is where the planting mix starts to take shape, as you narrow down the selection to around fifteen to thirty species. While this number serves as a useful guideline, it's not a rigid rule – some schemes might benefit from more diversity, while others work best with a tighter, more controlled palette. The key is to balance variety with clarity, ensuring the mix feels intentional rather than chaotic.

At this stage, it's not just about ticking off plants that meet the constraints, it's about experimenting, making choices and understanding how different species will interact. This is where visualisation tools come in. Gathering images into a plant palette, whether digitally or printed, helps to see how the colours, textures and forms work together. Organising plants by layers or by colour palettes can reveal whether the scheme feels balanced or if certain elements are overpowering. Sketching is another invaluable tool, whether it's quick hand-drawn elevations or more detailed perspectives, allowing you to explore composition, rhythm and structure.

Collate Your Information

At this stage, I gather key information about each plant, looking at traits such as height and spread, flowering months, form, foliage texture, edible qualities, drought tolerance and any specific requirements. Information on a plant often varies across sources, as different climates, soils

Table 6.1. Edible Meadow Plant Mix

BOTANICAL NAME	COMMON NAME	SIZE Spread × Height (mm)	QUALITY	EDIBLE	ORIGIN
Trees & Shrubs					
Punica granatum	Pomegranate	2,000×4,000	Central tree; gnarled	Yes	Europe, Asia
Structural / Emergent					
Salvia rosmarinus 'Miss Jessopp's Upright'	Rosemary	700×1200	Vertical punctuation	Yes	Mediterranean
Foeniculum vulgare	Fennel	400×1500	Tall; umbels; hazy	Yes	Mediterranean
Cynara cardunculus Scolymus Group	Globe artichoke	1,000×1500	Tall; spiky; bulky	Yes	Mediterranean
Crambe maritima	Sea kale	600×800	Course texture	Yes	UK
Mid-Layer & Seasonal Hits					
Asparagus officinalis	Asparagus	450×1,200	Feathery	Yes	Mediterranean
Deschampsia cespitosa 'Goldtau'	Tufted hairgrass	500×750	Hazy	No	UK
Asphodeline lutea	King's spear	500×900	Spiky	Yes	Mediterranean; North Africa
Hesperis matronalis & H. matronalis var. albiflora	Dame's rocket	450×900	Soft; emergent	Yes	Europe
Salvia nemorosa 'Caradonna'	Balkan clary	300×500	Spiky	No	Europe; West Asia
Achillea millefolium 'Terracotta'	'Terracotta' yarrow	400×600	Umbels	Yes – as tea	UK
Hylotelephium spectabile	Sedum	400×500	Lower body	Yes	China, Korea

Monthly colour blocks indicate either foliage or flower colour. Foliage is coded as green, glaucous or autumnal, but when a plant is in flower the flower colour takes precedence and is shown instead. If no colour appears in a given month, the plant is dormant, with no visible foliage or bloom. O marks months when edible parts of the plant are available.

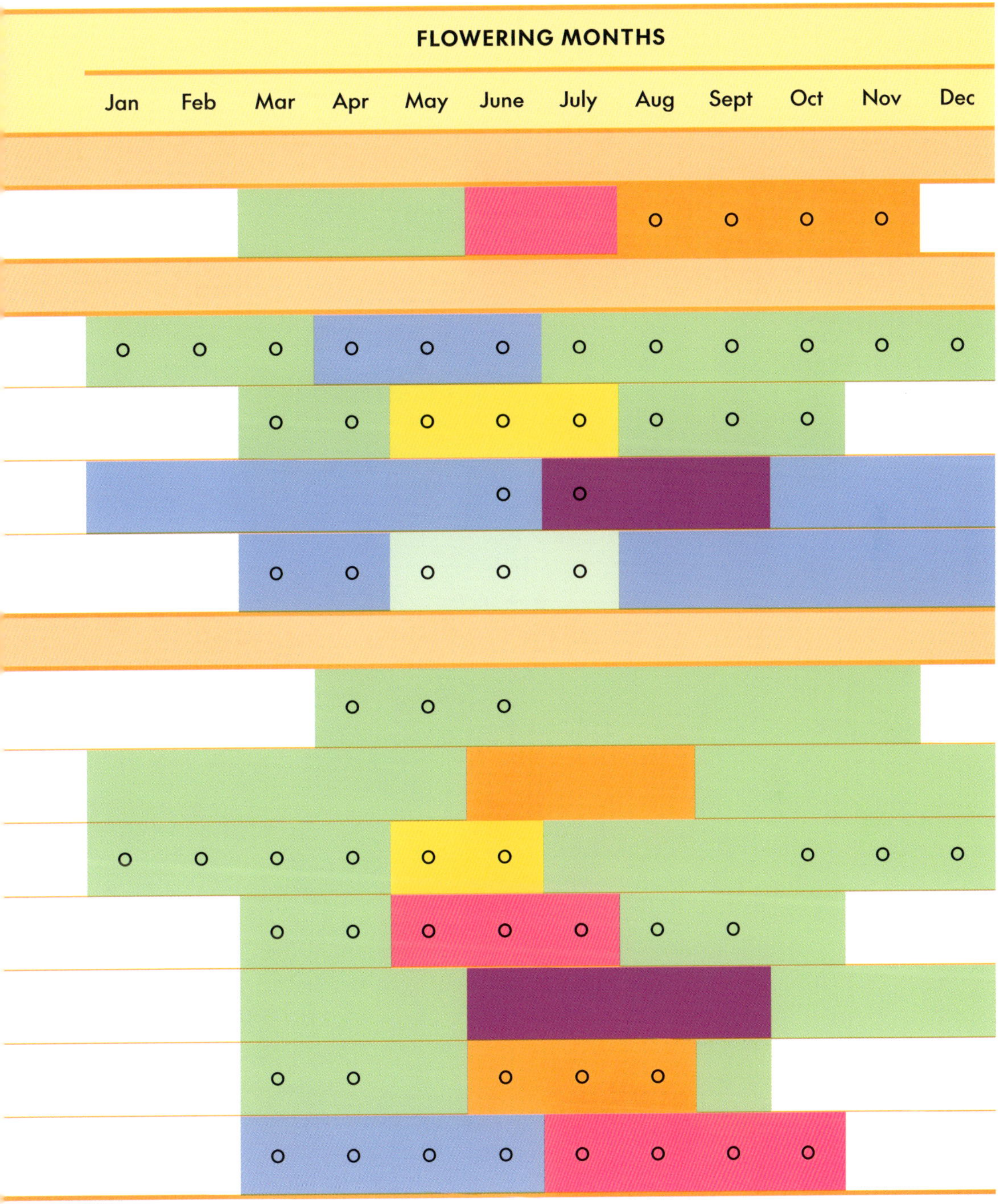

FLOWERING MONTHS

Jan	Feb	Mar	Apr	May	June	July	Aug	Sept	Oct	Nov	Dec

DESIGNING WITH EDIMENTALS

Table 6.1. Edible Meadow Plant Mix (*continued*)

BOTANICAL NAME	COMMON NAME	SIZE Spread × Height (mm)	QUALITY	EDIBLE	ORIGIN
Low / Groundcover					
Briza media	Quaking grass	400×600	Soft; bobbing	No	UK
Achillea millefolium 'New Vintage White'	'New Vintage White' yarrow	300×400	Umbels	Yes – as tea	UK
Geranium × johnsonii 'Johnson's Blue'	'Johnson's Blue' cranesbill	600×450	Lower colour; cup-shaped flowers	No	Europe
Silene vulgaris	Bladder campion	300×600	Soft haze	Yes	UK
Allium schoenoprasum	Chives	450×450	Lower colour; ball-shaped flowers	Yes	Europe, Asia
Dots & Fillers					
Allium ampeloprasum var. *Babingtonii*	Babington's leek	150×1200	Tall spires	Yes	Mediterranean; naturalised in UK
Eschscholzia californica	Californian poppy	300×300	Vibrant, lower colour	Yes – in moderation	North America

and conditions influence growth, so, rather than getting fixated on exact figures, I take an average and use it as a guide. Some projects require deep technical research, particularly for long-term, large-scale landscapes. When working on a section of the Shuttleworth Botanic Garden on the Isle of Man, for instance, we conducted extensive research, the level required for a scientifically driven project. But for many other projects, a more intuitive approach works well. The key is to reach a level of familiarity where you feel confident in how each species will perform.

To keep things organised, I compile all this information into a simple table. Some designers use high-tech spreadsheets, others prefer handwritten notes – whichever format works best for you is fine. For me, the key is to create something that allows for easy comparison and quick reference. A good table visually displays all plants organised by layers and gives a sense of the overall structure of the mix. Which plants will be in flower at the same time, how the balance of colour shifts across the seasons, how heights and forms interact and when different

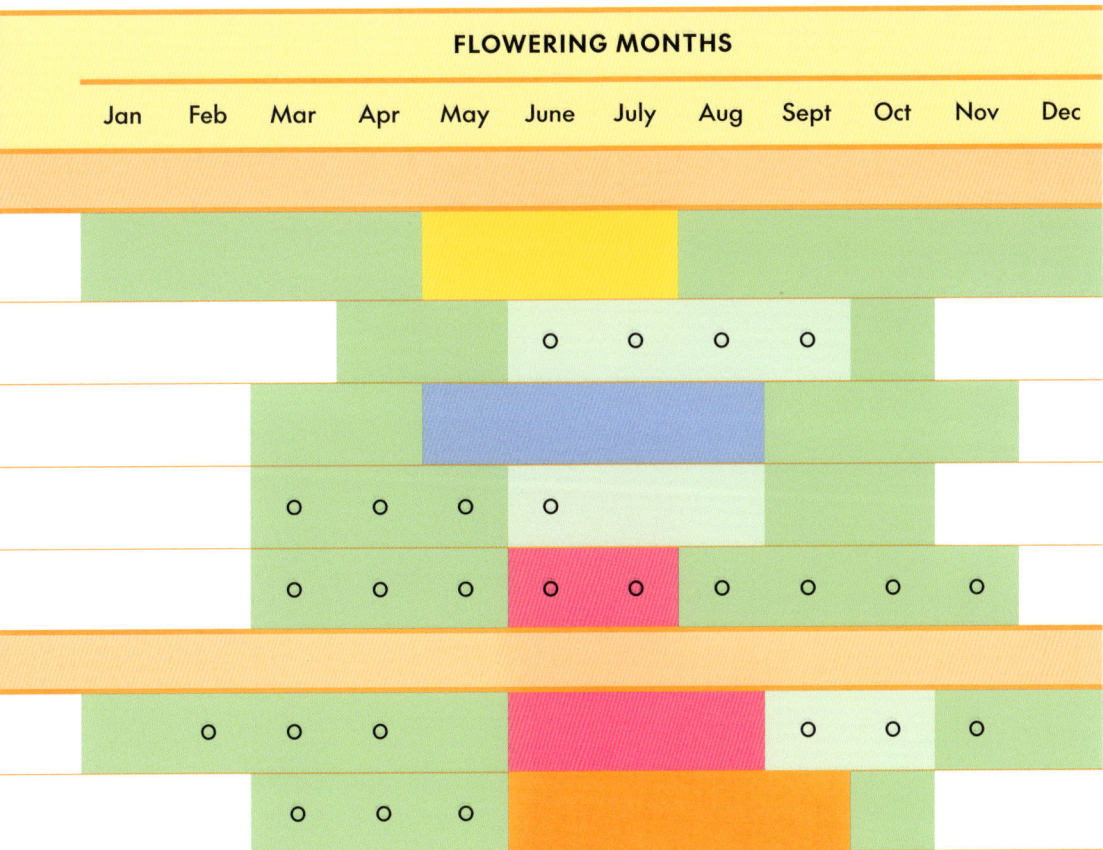

edible elements will be ready for harvest. I often also include plant origins. While not essential, this can help create a coherent aesthetic, particularly when drawing inspiration from specific natural ecosystems.

Percentages

With the plant list refined and research in place, the next step is to assign a percentage to each species. To do this effectively, each one is grouped into a planting layer, as outlined above. Seeing the plants set out in this format allows you to analyse the structure of the scheme to determine whether it has a strong enough framework, whether there's continuity of seasonal interest and whether the balance between food-producing and ornamental elements is right.

Deciding on what percentage to attribute to each layer and species isn't an exact science. There are no hard rules dictating how much of each layer should be present or how much of a species should appear. The key is to analyse the composition and make adjustments based on

DESIGNING WITH EDIMENTALS

Table 6.2. Edible Meadow Plant Mix

PERCENTAGE	DENSITY (Plants/m²)	BOTANICAL NAME
		Trees & Shrubs
N/A	N/A	*Punica granatum*
10%		**Structural / Emergent**
3.5	3	*Salvia rosmarinus* 'Miss Jessopp's Upright'
4.5	5	*Foeniculum vulgare*
1	1	*Cynara cardunculus* Scolymus Group
1	3	*Crambe maritima*
40%		**Mid-Layer & Seasonal Hits**
3	7	*Asparagus officinalis*
6	6	*Deschampsia cespitosa* 'Goldtau'
6	8	*Asphodeline lutea*
9	7	*Hesperis matronalis* & *H. matronalis* var. *albiflora*
5	8	*Salvia nemorosa* 'Caradonna'
7	7	*Achillea millefolium* 'Terracotta'
4	7	*Hylotelephium spectabile*
45%		**Low / Groundcover**
15	7	*Briza media*
5	8	*Achillea millefolium* 'New Vintage White'
6	8	*Geranium* × *johnsonii* 'Johnson's Blue'
9	8	*Silene vulgaris*
10	10	*Allium schoenoprasum*
5%		**Dots & Fillers**
2	5	*Allium ampeloprasum* var. *Babingtonii*
3	9	*Eschscholzia californica*

the intended effect. Some gardens call for a stronger structural presence; others might need a more meadow-like feel with a lighter touch on emergent elements.

This process of refining layers and species percentages is where visual aids are also useful. Sketching out the composition, playing with proportions and laying out plants on paper (or digitally) allows you to see how the planting will come together before it's in the ground. It's a chance to step back and assess: Are the seasonal waves distributed well? Does the planting hold interest year-round? Is there enough structure to guide the eye? These are the questions that help shape the final design before moving on to the next phase: calculating plant densities and preparing for planting.

Calculating Plant Densities, Areas and Quantities

The next step is to calculate how many plants you need. This is where design meets numbers, translating ideas into practical, tangible quantities.

The first thing to determine is the planting density for each species. Different plants require different spacing. For example, you might plant 12 chives per square metre (about 12 square feet) but only a single artichoke in the same space. Finding the right densities requires a mix of research and experience – books and online resources will provide guidelines, while observing plant growth in real-world settings will refine your understanding over time.

As a general guide for naturalistic planting, I often work to around 7–9 plants per square metre (about 12 square feet). But this will flex depending on soil conditions and plant vigour. In leaner, low-nutrient soils or stressful environments, plants grow more slowly and remain compact, so you may need to increase your densities to achieve a full, cohesive planting. In richer soils, plants bulk up quickly, so give them more space to avoid overcrowding and allow them to mature naturally.

Once you've set your densities, you're ready to calculate how many plants of each species you'll need. Let's walk through an example step by step using an imagined border.

STEP 1: CALCULATE THE AREA

Imagine a border that's 10 metres (33 feet) long and 3 metres (10 feet) wide. Multiply the length by the width to get the total planting area.

$$10m \times 3m = 30m^2 \text{ (or } 33ft \times 10ft = 330ft^2)$$

STEP 2: DEFINE THE PERCENTAGE DISTRIBUTION AND PLANTING DENSITY FOR EACH PLANT

Now decide what percentage of the overall mix each species will make up, and at what density it will be planted. These are decisions made

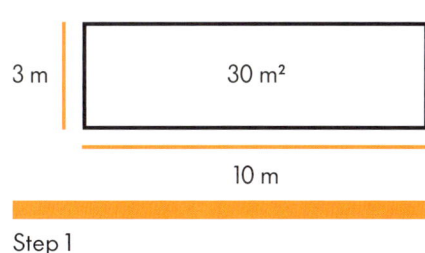

Step 1

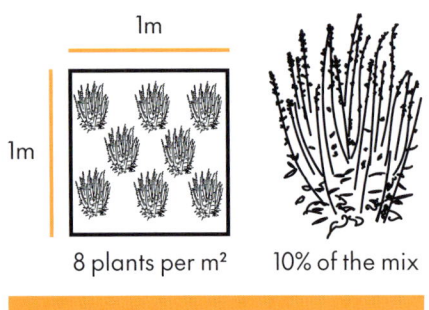

Step 2

earlier during the design process we've been working through, including assigning plants to layers, balancing percentages, and considering structure, seasonality and texture.

In this example, our chosen plant makes up 10 per cent of the total mix and will be planted at a density of 8 plants per square metre (about 12 square feet).

STEP 3: CALCULATE THE QUANTITY

Now that the area, density and plant percentage are in place, it's time to calculate the number of plants needed.

Formula:

Planting Area × Plant Density × Plant Percentage

Example:

30 × 8 × 10 per cent = 24 plants

This simple formula can be run on a phone calculator or in a spreadsheet. On a calculator, don't forget to include the % symbol; entering '10' instead of '10%' will result in 2,400 plants rather than 24.

For those using a spreadsheet and formulas, it would look like:

=30*8*10%

Spreadsheets offer a useful way to keep track of multiple species and their quantities, especially when working on larger schemes or more complex plant mixes.

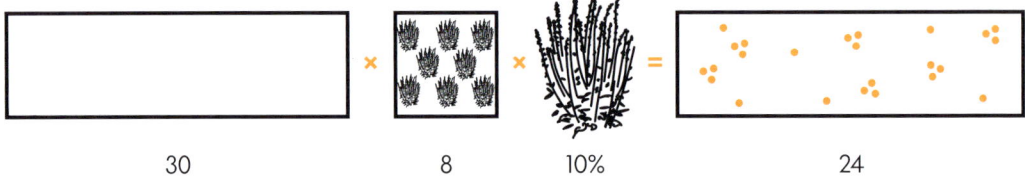

Step 3

STEP 4: REPEAT FOR THE WHOLE MIX

We now know we need 24 of our example plant. These will be arranged throughout the border according to the design intent (more on layout and rhythm in the next section).

Repeat the same calculation for each species in the mix using its unique percentage and density. This builds a full plant list with precise quantities for ordering and planting.

These calculations provide a framework, but they are not rigid rules. Sometimes, percentages and densities are adjusted based on availability, budget or desired aesthetics. A planting mix should feel dynamic and natural, not forced into rigid mathematical precision. However, having these numbers in place ensures the planting is balanced, structured and set up for long-term success.

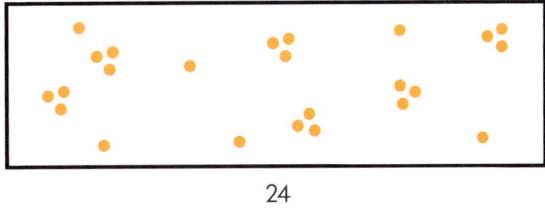

Twenty-four of our plants are laid out in a naturalistic fashion throughout our example border.

Sourcing

Now that you have established the quantity of plants you need for your plant mix, you can draft a list of the plants. In the horticulture industry, this stage is formalised as a plant schedule, a document listing each species, the required quantity and the preferred pot size or root type.

One key consideration is plant size. Smaller plants such as P9 pots, which measure 9cm (similar in size to a US 'quart' / 4-inch pot)), or bare-root perennials are often the best option, particularly for naturalistic plantings. They are more budget-friendly, have a lower carbon footprint due to reduced transport and production impact and tend to establish more successfully. Smaller plants adapt more quickly to their new environment, sending out strong root systems without the setbacks of transplant shock. As Charles Dowding says, 'You don't want the plant to know it's been planted!' In contrast, larger 2-litre pots (just under a US #1 pot, or trade gallon of approx. 2.8L), 3-litre (also close to a US #1 pot) or 5-litre (about a US #2 pot, or trade 2-gallon of approx. 5.7L) pots can be useful for structural species that need immediate presence but require more resources to establish.

Sourcing plants depends on availability and location. Local nurseries, specialist growers and online suppliers all play a role in finding the right species. Where possible, sourcing locally has significant advantages, since plants are already adapted to regional conditions. Buying from independent growers also reduces the footprint of those plants and supports local specialist knowledge. However, in the UK and many other countries, it is challenging to source locally and most plants are imported. Some rare or unusual edimentals may only be found through niche suppliers or grown from seed yourself. Growing from seed can be a rewarding route, offering access to a broader plant palette while reducing costs. Many edimentals are easy to grow this way, though it requires patience as your scheme will take longer to establish.

The sourcing phase is about balancing practicality, availability and vision. Whether selecting plants from a nursery, sourcing specialist varieties from a grower or raising them from seed, this stage bridges the gap between design and implementation, ensuring that the right plants arrive in the right numbers at the right time.

Setting Out & Planting

Setting out the plants is the moment where the design finally takes physical form. With all the plants on-site, grouped by species, the process begins. I find it most effective to set out by layer, starting with the structural or emergent plants, then moving through the mid-layer and seasonal hits, before placing the low / groundcover and dots and fillers last. This method allows for the conscious placement of key structural elements, ensuring rhythm, repetition and a natural flow throughout the planting. I like to create drifts and punctuations, allowing the eye to move through the space in an intuitive way, balancing moments of density with areas of openness.

Depending on the time of year, setting out plants can be either a highly visual process or one that requires a bit more imagination. If you're planting in spring or summer, many plants will already be in growth, making it easier to see their structure and how they interact in the space. However, if setting out in late autumn or winter, a time in most temperate climates that is ideal for planting, many perennials will be dormant, leaving you placing pots of bare soil with little indication of their eventual form. This can make it harder to visualise the final composition, requiring trust in the process and an understanding of how each plant will develop.

In all but the coldest climates, autumn planting is often the best choice, as it gives plants time to start establishing root systems over winter, ensuring they hit the ground running in spring. It also allows for bulbs to be planted at the same time. I would generally advise against planting in summer unless absolutely essential. Often, additional irrigation is required, and there is a higher risk of plant failure due to heat stress. For a deeper dive

A wild, free-flowing mix of edimentals, where structure comes from trees, shrubs and hard landscaping rather than overly manicured borders.

into the art of setting out plants, Nigel Dunnett's *Naturalistic Planting Design* provides an excellent breakdown of his technique.

Order vs Disorder

Every gardener or designer sits somewhere on the spectrum between order and disorder. Some crave structure while others delight in a wilder, more free-flowing aesthetic where plants intermingle and self-seed with abandon. Even in an ecologically driven, naturalistic planting scheme, a sense of order can be embedded. The key is in designing strong structural bones, anchoring the garden with key structural plants that provide rhythm and repetition.

Beyond that, how plants are arranged can lean towards either extreme of the spectrum. A completely random and sporadic layout

can result in a wilder aesthetic, while a highly structured approach – grouping plants in strict clusters – can create a more controlled and deliberate feel. A middle ground is often where the most dynamic and engaging schemes sit. Here, the structural framework is carefully composed, and seasonal hits of colour and texture are consciously distributed to create flow, rhythm and repetition. The remaining bulk of plants – those that form the mass and ground layer – can then be set out more loosely, interweaving naturally to add softness and dynamism.

Planting Design Example 1: Food Forest

I want to introduce two new planting designs taken from areas of The Edimental Garden we explored earlier in this chapter, the first of which is for a forest garden. These examples will highlight how the same core principles can be adapted to different styles and conditions, demonstrating the flexibility of the approach.

Environmental Conditions

Unlike the sunny, south-facing edible meadow, the forest garden mix is designed for shadier, more sheltered conditions. Set in the north-east-facing area of The Edimental Garden, it is framed by an edible hedge, canopy trees and boundaries that filter the light. The tree and shrub layer is deliberately planted in an open way, allowing sunlight to reach the lower layers and support productivity. Within the garden, moisture conditions vary. Drier, deeper shade pockets occur near walls and hedges, while wetter, more open conditions exist around the pond and rain garden margins. Overall, the soil is a free-draining loam, enriched with homemade compost, and the wind is softened by the protective hedgerow and tree layers.

Constraints

Edibility is a primary driver, as most plants are selected for their edible or medicinal value. Height is carefully managed across the different layers, ensuring a clear vertical hierarchy from canopy to ground. The scheme has a range of plant types from nitrogen-fixing canopy trees to creeping carpet species. Seasonality is well-considered, with visual and edible interest sustained throughout the warmer months but peaking in early summer. The colour palette leans towards soft, calming tones such as pinks, whites and lilacs with small

Muted tones and lush green textures bring visual interest to the forest garden mix.

pops of vibrant yellow. Texture is essential: fine, feathery ferns and grasses are set against coarser, bolder foliage, creating rich visual contrasts. The overall mood is calm and reflective, offering a restorative, layered space.

Layers & Percentages

Trees & Shrubs: A nitrogen-fixing canopy tree provides dappled light and wind protection, while understorey shrubs offer multi-stem forms, spring flowers and edible fruit. Trees and shrubs are positioned on the planting plan as key structural elements. Since they form the framework, they are consciously placed and not included in the broader percentage mix.

Structural / Emergent (5 per cent): Tall or structural perennials punctuate the planting sparingly, adding rhythm and contrast without overwhelming the space, since trees already provide much of the structure.

Mid Layer & Seasonal Hits (35 per cent): This layer brings shifting seasonal waves of edible flowers, stems and foliage, with species chosen for their shade tolerance and visual interplay.

Low / Groundcover (45 per cent): A dense, shade-adapted low layer knits the planting together, offering long-lasting edible and textural interest.

Carpet (10 per cent): Creeping plants weave through the base, suppressing weeds and thriving in the deepest shade.

Dots & Fillers (5 per cent): Short-lived perennials and self-seeders create moments of spontaneity, particularly in the early years.

Climbers: Climbing plants harness walls, trees and habitat structures, maximising vertical space for yield and visual intrigue.

DESIGNING WITH EDIMENTALS

Table 6.3. Forest Garden Plant Mix

PERCENTAGE	DENSITY (Plants/m2)	BOTANICAL NAME	COMMON NAME	SIZE Spread × Height (mm)	QUALITY
			Trees and Shrubs		
N/A	N/A	Alnus cordata	Italian alder	5,000×2,0000	Canopy; nitrogen-fixer; wind break
N/A	N/A	Cornus mas	Cornelian cherry	3,000×5,000	Understorey; fruits; winter flowers
N/A	N/A	Amelanchier alnifolia	Saskatoon	2,500×4,000	Understorey; berries; summer flowers
5%			Structural / Emergent		
2	6	Polygonatum biflorum	Solomon's seal	600×1,000	Arching stems; bell flowers
3	6	Valeriana officinalis	Valerian	450×1,500	Emergent; umbels
35%			Mid Layer & Seasonal Hits		
7	6	Deschampsia cespitosa 'Goldtau'	Tufted hairgrass	500×750	Hazy
4	5	Matteuccia struthiopteris	Ostrich fern	600×1,000	Lush fronds
6	7	Bistorta officinalis	Bistort	600×600	Coarse foliage; spiky; flowers
5	6	Myrrhis odorata	Sweet cicely	750×1,500	Umbels; fern-like foliage
6	7	Hemerocallis citrina	Citron daylily	600×1,000	Trumpet flowers; strappy foliage
7	7	Monarda fistulosa	Wild bergamot	500×1,000	Tubular flowers; aromatic

Monthly colour blocks indicate either foliage or flower colour. Foliage is coded as green, glaucous or autumnal, but when a plant is in flower the flower colour takes precedence and is shown instead. If no colour appears in a given month, the plant is dormant, with no visible foliage or bloom. O marks months when edible parts of the plant are available.

EDIBLE	ORIGIN	FLOWERING MONTHS											
		Jan	Feb	Mar	Apr	May	June	July	Aug	Sept	Oct	Nov	Dec
No	Europe		●										
Yes	Europe, West Asia	●	●						●	●			
Yes	North America							●					
Yes	North America			●	●								
Yes – medicinal	Europe			●	●	●	●	●	●				
No	UK						●						
Yes	Northern hemisphere			●	●								
Yes	Europe, Asia			●	●	●	●	●					
Yes	Europe					●	●	●	●	●			
Yes	Europe, Asia						●	●	●				
Yes	North America				●	●	●	●	●	●			

DESIGNING WITH EDIMENTALS

Table 6.3. Forest Garden Plant Mix (*continued*)

PERCENTAGE	DENSITY (Plants/m2)	BOTANICAL NAME	COMMON NAME	SIZE Spread × Height (mm)	QUALITY
45%			Low / Groundcover		
10	9	*Melica uniflora* f. *albida*	Wood melick	500×600	Soft grass
8	8	*Rumex sanguineus*	Red-Veined sorrel	400×500	Red veins; coarse foliage
7	9	*Galium odoratum*	Sweet woodruff	400×300	Fragrant flowers
8	6	*Hosta* 'Fortunei Hyacinthina'	Hosta	500×700	Bold foliage
12	9	*Stachys affinis*	Chinese artichoke	300×400	Spiky
10%			Carpet		
10	12	*Fragaria vesca*	Wild strawberry	300×150	Creeping mat
5%			Dots & Fillers		
5	9	*Aquilegia vulgaris*	Columbine	300×700	Bell flowers
			Climbers		
N/A	N/A	*Apios americana*	Groundnut	2,000×3,000	Pea-like flowers
N/A	N/A	*Humulus lupulus*	Hops	3,000×6,000	Fragrant; cone-like flowers

Key Highlights

This design intentionally echoes elements from the edible meadow for visual cohesion. Repeating species like tufted hairgrass (*Deschampsia cespitosa* 'Goldtau') provide textural unity, while vibrant yellow citron daylily (*Hemerocallis citrina*) ties into the meadow's colour palette despite the shadier context. Wild bergamot (*Monarda fistulosa*) and Chinese artichoke (*Stachys affinis*) reinforce this link,

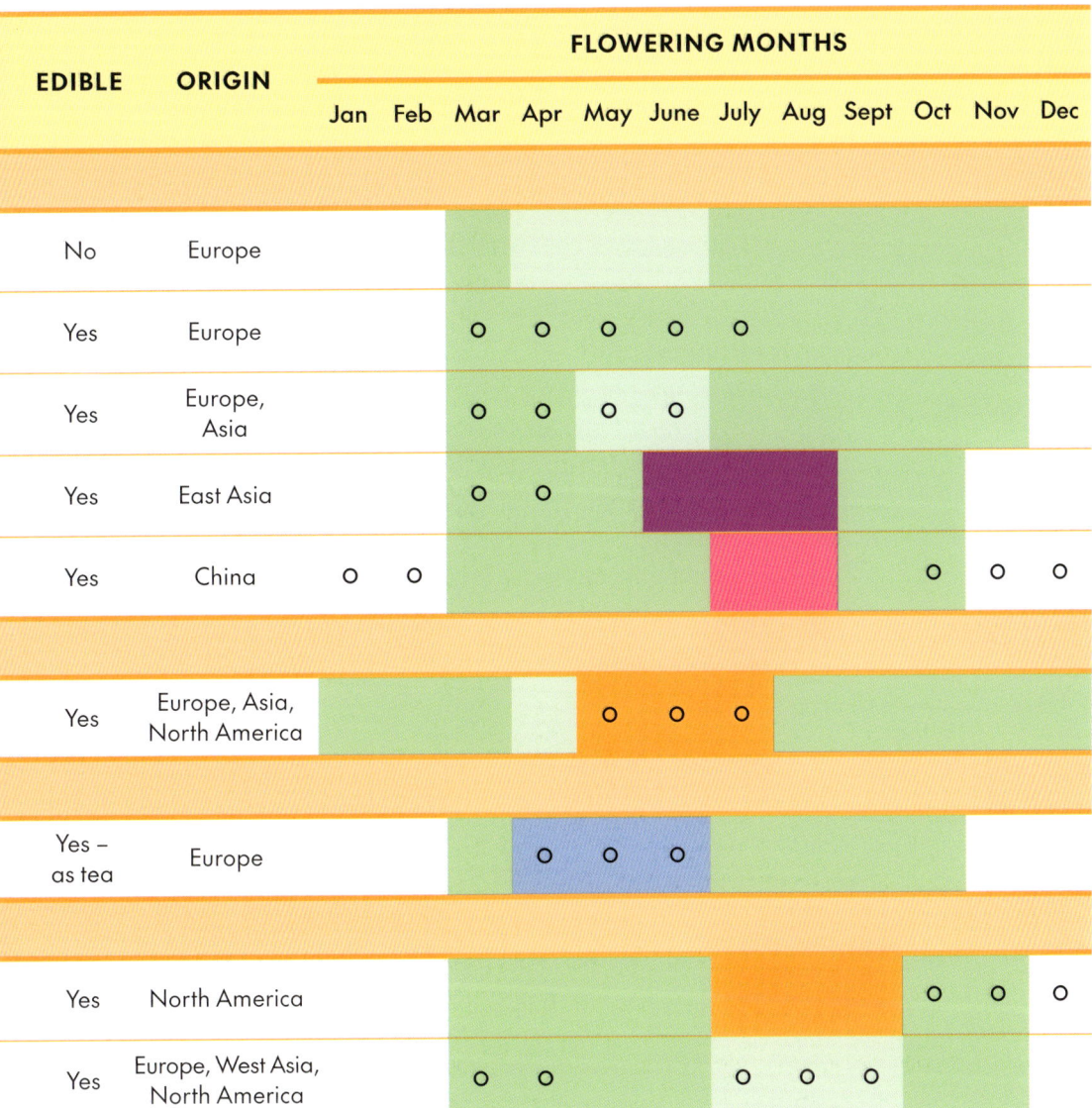

complementing the sedum (*Hylotelephium spectabile*) tones in sunnier areas. Rather than meadow style intermingling, plants are grouped in larger drifts, reflecting natural plant community patterns in shaded conditions and focusing attention on texture and form. Together, the layers create a calm, immersive space that balances productivity with woodland-inspired beauty.

Planting Design Example 2: Large Container

This second design example comes from the large container near the dining terrace in The Edimental Garden. It shows how the same planting principles can be applied at a much smaller scale, creating a layered, edible, sensory-rich scheme in a single pot.

Environmental Conditions

This layered planting sits in a large container on the sunny, south-facing dining terrace near the greenhouse, adjoining the edible meadow. The pot creates an artificial growing environment, combining free-draining topsoil with added drainage material and an annual mulch of homemade compost. Hot, dry and exposed, the pot demands drought-tolerant species to minimise maintenance. A non-porous container is essential to prevent excessive water loss (terracotta pots, for example, dry out too quickly here).

Table 6.4. Container Planting

BOTANICAL NAME	COMMON NAME	SIZE Spread × Height (mm)	QUALITY	EDIBLE	ORIGIN
Structural / Emergent					
Cydonia oblonga 'Vranja'	'Vranja' quince	3,000×4,000	Edible fruit	Yes	Turkey, Georgia, Serbia
Mid-Layer & Seasonal Hits					
Allium schoenoprasum	Chives	300×450	Lower colour; ball-shaped flowers	Yes	Europe, Asia
Origanum vulgare	Oregano	450×450	Aromatic; sprays of flowers	Yes	Europe, West Asia
Low / Groundcover					
Thymus serpyllum	Creeping thyme	300×100	Scented mat	Yes	Europe, North Africa

Monthly colour blocks indicate either foliage or flower colour. Foliage is coded as green, glaucous or autumnal, but when a plant is in flower the flower colour takes precedence and is shown instead. If no colour appears in a given month, the plant is dormant, with no visible foliage or bloom. O marks months when edible parts of the plant are available.

Constraints

The planting is designed for maximum edibility, combining fragrance and harvestable herbs right next to the dining table. The layered approach is deliberately simplified, scaling down the forest garden and meadow concepts for a compact setting. The visual interest spans the seasons, with an architectural framework providing year-round structure and a lively pop of colour in

Vibrant pinks and aromatic foliage create a sensory experience, elevated to waist height in the oversized pot.

	Jan	Feb	Mar	Apr	May	June	July	Aug	Sept	Oct	Nov	Dec
FLOWERING MONTHS												
				●	●					○	○	
			○	○	●	●	●	○	○	○	○	
			○	○	○	●	●	●	○	○	○	
	○	○	○	○	●	●	●	○	○	○	○	○

DESIGNING WITH EDIMENTALS

summer. The colour palette leans towards pink tones, supported by a focus on finer, lighter foliage. The big idea is 'sensory foragables': brushing past herbs and drinking in the scent of fresh quince fruits, all within arm's reach of the dining table.

Layers & Percentages

Structural / Emergent: One striking architectural quince (*Cydonia oblonga* 'Vranja'), delivering fruit, sculptural form and seasonal presence.

Mid Layer & Seasonal Hits: A simple, productive mix of chives (*Allium schoenoprasum*) and oregano (*Origanum vulgare*) offering contrasting textures, unified colour and continuous harvest.

Low / Groundcover: Creeping thyme (*Thymus serpyllum*) spreads at the base, retaining moisture in the soil and spilling over the pot edges, releasing scent when brushed.

Key Highlights

Repeating plants and colour waves (such as chives [*Allium schoenoprasum*] echoed from the edible meadow and oregano [*Origanum vulgare*] tying into the colour palette) create cohesion across the wider garden. The multi-stem tree echoes forms in the forest garden. Despite the small space, the layered design delivers long seasonal interest. Most importantly, the planting maximises fragrance – elevated closer to nose level, it releases scent as you brush past en route to the table.

Whether you're working with a sun-drenched meadow, a shady forest garden or a compact container, the same core principles apply: respond thoughtfully to the site, meet the needs of the brief and balance structure, seasonality and function. By adapting these ideas to your own conditions and goals, you can craft a planting scheme that is both personal and dynamic, one that evolves over time and thrives in its unique setting.

Ongoing Management & the Question of Weeds

Establishing a planting scheme is just the beginning. What follows is the ongoing relationship between you and the garden. While this book can't go into detail on the long-term maintenance of an edimental scheme, it's worth touching on how management shifts over time. You'll find that the most intensive period is the first year, when plants are settling in, roots are developing and weeds are at their most opportunistic. Newly planted gardens inevitably have areas of bare soil, and the recent disturbance from planting creates the perfect conditions for weed seeds to germinate. A weed, in essence, is a plant growing where it's not wanted. In the early years, this is particularly relevant, not because weeds are inherently bad, but because your freshly planted scheme needs a chance to establish without competition draining resources. Watering your plants is also often essential, even for drought-tolerant species. Resilience comes with deep root systems, but those roots take time to form. Your goal is to support the planting in its early years so that, in time, it becomes self-sustaining, with dense growth suppressing weeds and reducing the need for intervention.

By years two and three, you'll notice that the grip begins to loosen. As the intended plants establish and spread, covering more soil, weeds have fewer opportunities to take hold. Your management will shift from intensive intervention to a more observational approach – a process of dynamic editing. From year three onwards, this will become the primary way of engaging with the planting. You'll also notice that some plants may become overly prolific and need thinning, while others may struggle and require encouragement. A self-seeded plant appearing in a gap might not be an intruder but a welcome addition, stepping in where needed and providing a free plant. Your role transitions from active control to gentle guidance, helping the planting evolve rather than forcing it into a fixed state.

A well-designed, ecologically aligned planting should become easier for you to manage over time, requiring minimal intervention as it finds its balance. In the long run, this means less input, less weeding, less watering and less effort overall on your part. The role of the gardener mirrors natural processes: disturbance, renewal, succession. Cutting back certain plants mimics the role of grazing animals; pruning echoes the shaping effects of wind and weather; and selective removal makes space for new growth, much as seasonal dieback would in a wild ecosystem.

While pristine lawns or paving need regular mowing, weeding or pressure washing, a well-established edimental planting can thrive with little more than an annual cutback, sporadic weed management and the occasional tweak or selective thinning to guide its natural succession. For me, the most rewarding gardens are the ones that feel alive, responsive and ever-evolving – not static displays, but dynamic landscapes that continue to surprise and delight through the years.

Chapter 7

Plant Profiles

This selection brings together some of my favourite edimentals referenced throughout the book. All are garden-worthy in their own right, and some may already be growing in your borders. Organised by planting layers, these profiles are designed to support the design process explored earlier in the book.

Each profile includes details such as preferred light conditions, mature size, flower colour, flowering months and USDA hardiness zone. Flowering month is shown numerically; for example, '4–5' means April–May. USDA hardiness zones are used here because they offer a broad reference point for gardeners, particularly across the varied climates of North America, but most of these plants will grow happily in much of the UK as well.

A note on ecology and regulation: invasive status is regional and dynamic. The US spans a vast range of climates and biomes, so a species that's benign in one US state – or in the UK – may be invasive elsewhere. Where possible, I flag species that are noted as invasive or regulated in parts of the US or UK, but lists and laws change. Always check the most current local guidance before planting.

Trees & Shrubs

Trees and shrubs are the backbone of an edible garden. They're the first elements to place and plan around, setting height, shade, shelter and long-term structure that shape every other layer. They provide fruit, nuts, edible leaves and habitat, anchoring biodiversity and guiding the rest of the planting.

Saskatoon (*Amelanchier alnifolia*)

Sun or shade: Sun or partial shade
Height: 4 m (13 ft)
Spread: 3 m (10 ft)
Flower colour: White
Flowering month: 4–5
USDA hardiness zone: 4–6

DESCRIPTION

A deciduous, multi-stemmed shrub native to North America, saskatoon is found in a range of wild habitats – from the banks of streams and woodland edges to open, dry hillsides. It's a hardy and adaptable plant that thrives in cold climates and can cope with both moist and drier soils once established. In the same genus as the widely loved juneberry (*Amelanchier lamarckii*), which has graced many a European planting scheme, saskatoon is its North American cousin with arguably the best-tasting berries of them all and several large-fruited cultivars, such as 'Northline', 'Smokey' and 'Thiessen'.

SOIL

Tolerant of most soil types, including sandy, loamy and clay soils provided they're well-drained. Prefers slightly moist soils but is adaptable.

DESIGN USES

With an upright, architectural habit and naturally multi-stemmed form, saskatoon works beautifully as a stand-alone specimen, especially when left exposed to show off its branching structure. Its finely toothed, oval leaves emerge flushed with bronze in spring, turn deep green through summer and take on warm red and orange tones in autumn. White, star-shaped flowers arrive in spring, offering seasonal punctuation. It can be dotted into naturalistic meadows or woodland edges, or used to form an edible hedgerow.

EDIBLE QUALITIES

Saskatoon berries ripen around midsummer and are packed with antioxidants. The flavour is sweet and nutty, almost almond-like, and often described as having undertones of apple. Berries can be eaten fresh or dried and turned into preserves or cooked in baked goods. Young leaves can be harvested and used as a tea substitute. The seeds and leaves contain small amounts of cyanogenic glycosides – avoid consuming large amounts.

HARVEST & STORAGE

Berries are ready when fully purple and slightly soft to the touch. Birds love them,

Saskatoon (*Amelanchier alnifolia*).

Saltbush (*Atriplex halimus*).

so netting may be needed. They store for up to a week in the fridge and can also be dried or frozen.

Saltbush (*Atriplex halimus*)

Sun or shade: Full sun
Height: Up to 2 m (6 ft)
Spread: Up to 3 m (10 ft)
Flower colour: Inconspicuous
Flowering month: 7–8
USDA hardiness zone: 7–10

DESCRIPTION

A salt-tolerant evergreen shrub from southern Europe, with silvery-grey foliage and a rounded, bushy form. Often found in coastal sands and saline soils.

SOIL

Prefers well-drained, poor soils, including sandy or alkaline ground. Intolerant of winter wet and waterlogged soils.

DESIGN USES

Excellent for dry, exposed sites, coastal gardens, gravel gardens and low-nutrient substrates. It offers a mounded form and punctuating structure through a planting scheme.

EDIBILITY & HARVEST

Leaves are edible raw or cooked with a salty flavour and a variety of uses in the kitchen, much like spinach. It's harvestable year round, although harvest sparingly in winter when growth slows. The leaves are high in salt and oxalates – go easy if you're on a low-sodium or low-oxalate diet.

Sea Buckthorn (*Hippophae rhamnoides*)

Sun or shade: Full sun
Height: Up to 6 m (19 ft)
Spread: Up to 2.5 m (8 ft)
Flower colour: Yellow-green
Flowering month: 3–5
USDA hardiness zone: 3–8

DESCRIPTION

A vigorous, thorny shrub native to Europe and Asia with silvery leaves and vivid orange berries. Drought-tolerant and

Sea buckthorn (*Hippophae rhamnoides*).

PLANT PROFILES

thrives in maritime exposure. Cultivars like 'Hergo' are bred for larger fruit and fewer thorns. In the UK, it can spread inland beyond coastal habitats, and it's listed as invasive in some US states.

SOIL

Prefers dry, poor, free-draining soil, especially sandy, coastal or mountainous ground.

DESIGN USES

Can be pruned into an architectural multi-stem tree or left informal and used for hedging, windbreaks, erosion control and, as a nitrogen-fixing species, it enriches even poor soils, making it valuable in challenging sites.

EDIBILITY & HARVEST

Considered a superfood, the bright orange berries are extremely high in vitamin C. Use in juices and jams. Harvest early autumn before frost. Needs male and female plants to fruit.

Sichuan Pepper (*Zanthoxylum simulans*)

Sun or shade: Sun or partial shade
Height: Up to 4 m (13 ft)
Spread: Up to 6 m (19 ft)
Flower colour: Inconspicuous
Flowering month: 5–6
USDA hardiness zone: 5–8

DESCRIPTION

A deciduous, dioecious shrub from China with citrus-scented leaves, knobbly bark and vivid red husks.

SOIL

Prefers deep, moisture-retentive but well-drained soil.

DESIGN USES

Works well as a forest garden understorey or statement tree. Prune to reveal its sculptural, multi-stemmed form and bark, or let it grow naturally into an open shrub.

EDIBILITY & HARVEST

Dried husks (not seeds) are used in Chinese cuisine for a numbing, peppery citrus hit. Leaves offer a lesser-used lemony flavour. Harvest berries in autumn, leaves in spring; both sexes needed for fruit.

Sichuan pepper (*Zanthoxylum simulans*).

Structural / Emergent

After trees and shrubs, this layer provides the framework of the planting – the bold, characterful species that give form and coherence across the seasons. They may be tall, broad, or simply strong in presence, used sparingly to guide the eye and hold space within the design. These are the plants that define rhythm and structure, setting the tone for the layers that follow.

Udo (*Aralia cordata*)

Sun or shade: Partial or full shade
Height: Up to 2.4 m (8 ft)
Spread: Up to 1.5 m (5 ft)
Flower colour: Cream-white
Flowering month: 7–8
USDA hardiness zone: 4–9

DESCRIPTION

A dramatic, architectural herbaceous perennial from East Asia, traditionally cultivated in Japanese cuisine for its edible spring shoots. Its bold presence lends it the stature of a shrub or small tree in the landscape.

SOIL

Prefers rich, moisture-retentive loam but tolerates poorer soils once mature.

DESIGN USES

With its immense size and seasonal drama, it provides structure and impact in shaded settings. Considered and placed much like a shrub.

EDIBILITY & HARVEST

In Japan, young spring shoots are blanched and sliced for their tender texture and citrusy bite. Used green for tempura or eaten raw or lightly cooked in salads and stir-fries. Shoots must be cooked; raw shoots can be an irritant. Fruits not to be eaten.

Sea Kale (*Crambe maritima*)

Sun or shade: Full sun
Height: Up to 60 cm (2 ft)
Spread: Up to 60 cm (2 ft)
Flower colour: White
Flowering month: 5–7
USDA hardiness zone: 4–8

DESCRIPTION

A striking, salt-tolerant perennial native to European coastlines and naturalised in Oregon and California, forming low

Udo (*Aralia cordata*).

Sea kale (*Crambe maritima*).

Fennel (*Foeniculum vulgare*)

Sun or shade: Sun
Height: 1.5 m (5 ft)
Spread: 40 cm (16 in)
Flower colour: yellow
Flowering month: 7–8
USDA hardiness zone: 3–10

DESCRIPTION

One of my all-time favourite edimentals. Native to arid regions of southern Europe, this herbaceous perennial has a strongly vertical form and an abundance of delicious qualities. Its highly aromatic, feathery foliage is topped with acid-yellow, umbel-shaped flowers that emerge from fast-growing stems in summer. When grown in harsh, dry conditions, it acts as a perfect filler, seeding itself into gaps and staying relatively short and sparse. In richer soils, it takes on a taller, more statuesque form while retaining its delicate, transparent quality. *Foeniculum vulgare* is considered invasive in parts of the US (not in the UK, but it self-seeds readily), particularly in coastal and disturbed areas, so check local guidelines before planting.

SOIL

Thrives in a wide range of soil types, but well-drained soil is essential. It performs best in poorer soils where its growth remains upright and more sculptural.

DESIGN USES

A versatile plant, equally at home in drought-tolerant schemes, kitchen gardens and traditional long borders. Its

mounds of blue-green foliage with frothy white summer blooms. Once a prized Victorian vegetable.

SOIL

Thrives in well-drained, poor or sandy soil in full sun. Tolerates drought and maritime exposure.

DESIGN USES

Ideal for gravel gardens, coastal gardens or sunny edimental borders. Its architectural form and seasonal blooms add sculptural, punctuating interest at lower levels.

EDIBILITY & HARVEST

Blanched spring shoots are prized for their nutty, asparagus-like flavour. Young leaves are also edible, raw or cooked. Long-lived and low maintenance once established.

upright stems and plate-like flower heads offer striking vertical punctuation, especially when contrasted with domed or spiked forms. It is naturally ephemeral and prone to self-seeding, so avoid relying on it for permanent structure.

EDIBLE QUALITIES

All above-ground parts are edible and carry the plant's signature aniseed flavour. Leaves can be used fresh in salads, stems eaten when young and tender, and seeds harvested for flavouring dishes or brewing herbal tea. Florence fennel (*Foeniculum vulgare* var. *azoricum*) is a cultivated form that produces a bulbous base and is grown as a biennial vegetable. Avoid large quantities if pregnant.

HARVEST & STORAGE

Foliage can be picked throughout the growing season, while stems are best harvested early before they toughen. Seeds ripen in autumn and should be dried for 7–14 days before storing in airtight containers for use through winter and beyond.

Solomon's Seal (*Polygonatum biflorum*)

Sun or shade: Partial or full shade
Height: Up to 1 m (3 ft)
Spread: 60 cm (2 ft), slowly spreading via rhizomes
Flower colour: Creamy white
Flowering month: 5–6
USDA hardiness zone: 3–7

DESCRIPTION

A graceful, shade-tolerant perennial from eastern North America with arching stems and pairs of hanging, bell-like flowers.

SOIL

Prefers humus-rich, moisture-retentive but well-drained soil. Dislikes drought or excessive heat.

DESIGN USES

Elegant in naturalistic or shaded planting schemes. Its form becomes more pronounced with age. Mature clumps create visual rhythm and punctuation through naturalistic woodland plantings.

Fennel (*Foeniculum vulgare*).

Solomon's seal (*Polygonatum biflorum*).

PLANT PROFILES

Sochan (*Rudbeckia laciniata*).

EDIBILITY & HARVEST

Young and surprisingly sweet and tender spring shoots can be boiled and eaten like asparagus. Shoots must be cooked. Berries and mature parts are toxic.

Sochan (*Rudbeckia laciniata*)

Sun or shade: Sun or partial shade
Height: 2 m (6.5 ft)
Spread: 60 cm (24 in)
Flower colour: Yellow
Flowering month: 7–9
USDA hardiness zone: 3–7

DESCRIPTION

A tall, herbaceous perennial native to much of North America, sochan is a resilient plant that thrives across a range of environments. It tolerates wind and fluctuating conditions with ease and has long been valued by Indigenous communities for its edible and cultural significance, a legacy that far predates its use in ornamental gardening. It spreads by rhizomes and can form expansive colonies where conditions allow. In some regions of the US and in other countries like Japan, it is considered invasive, particularly in moist or disturbed soils, so consult local guidance before planting (not invasive in the UK). Double flowered cultivars don't spread by seed.

SOIL

Prefers moist, fertile, well-drained soils, but is highly adaptable, tolerating heavier ground and seasonal wetness.

DESIGN USES

Planted in small to mid-sized groups, sochan provides vertical punctuation and structural rhythm within layered schemes. It's a strong grower and benefits from pairing with equally vigorous companions to hold its place in balance. Consider managing its spread to maintain smaller clusters. Its soft, finely divided foliage offers a feathery contrast to broader-leaved perennials, and in late summer its tall stems push through the mid-layer, topped with loose, lemon-yellow daisies that bring vibrant colour and movement to the garden.

EDIBLE QUALITIES

Sochan has a long tradition of being foraged and eaten. The young top shoots and stems can be cooked much like leafy greens or tender stalks. They are typically boiled, stewed or sautéed. The flavour is earthy and slightly bitter, intensifying with age.

HARVEST & STORAGE

Only the youngest, most tender growth should be harvested, in early spring while shoots and stems are still supple. Best eaten fresh, although they can also be dried and stored for use later in the year.

Mid-Layer & Seasonal Hits

This is the dynamic body of the planting – the layer that shifts most visibly through the seasons. It carries the main visual rhythm, with plants that rise, flower and fade in succession to create continuous movement and change, setting the scheme's character and atmosphere from spring to autumn.

Yarrow (*Achillea millefolium* 'Terracotta')

Sun or shade: Full sun
Height: 75 cm (2.5 ft)
Spread: 60 cm (2 ft)
Flower colour: Orange
Flowering month: 6–8
USDA hardiness zone: 4–8

DESCRIPTION

A much-loved yarrow cultivar with warm-toned umbels that mellow as they age. This upright perennial is prized for its long flowering season, drought tolerance and finely cut, aromatic foliage. A magnet for bees and other pollinators.

SOIL

Tolerates most soils, thriving in dry, poor or lime-rich ground. Avoid heavy or waterlogged conditions.

DESIGN USES

One of my favourite plants for the mid-layer in naturalistic meadow-style plantings or dry gravel gardens. Its strong vertical form is punctuated with orange, plate-like flower heads that contrast beautifully with spike flower shapes.

EDIBILITY & HARVEST

I love to brew the flowers and leaves into a fragrant, bitter tea. Young leaves are also edible – raw in salads or cooked – though more of a spurious edible. Consume in small quantities and avoid in pregnancy or with anticoagulants / bleeding disorders due to potential toxicity from thujone and other alkaloids. Use in modest amounts.

King's Spear (*Asphodeline lutea*)

Sun or shade: Sun
Height: 1 m (3.3 ft)
Spread: 30 cm (12 in)
Flower colour: yellow
Flowering month: 5–7
USDA hardiness zone: 6–9

DESCRIPTION

Asphodeline is a genus with great untapped potential. Its striking beauty is apparent, yet its edible qualities remain unfamiliar to most. Native to the harsh,

'Terracotta' yarrow (*Achillea millefolium* 'Terracotta').

King's spear (*Asphodeline lutea*).

dry landscapes of southern Europe and northern Africa, it was once prized by the Ancient Greeks and cultivated as a delicacy, although it has since slipped from common use. This hardy edimental can occasionally be found in drought-tolerant schemes or sunny borders, where it offers vertical accents and a vibrant flush of yellow blooms in early- to mid-summer.

SOIL
Adaptable to most garden soils and thriving on well-draining soils. Avoid poorly drained soil.

DESIGN USES
In its native range, *Asphodeline lutea* often grows in loose-to-dense groupings on rocky hillsides and mountain slopes. Planting in similar drifts or clusters can create a striking effect in garden settings. The yellow flower spikes rise cleanly from its clumps of fine, grass-like foliage, weaving effectively through other edimentals such as yarrow, and adding both structure and texture. As the plant goes dormant in late summer, its foliage can begin to look tired, so it's best kept away from key edges or high-visibility positions where long-season interest is needed.

EDIBLE QUALITIES
The thin, fleshy roots can be roasted much like potatoes, with a rich, nutty flavour that pairs well with olive oil and salt. Young shoots can be boiled and have a mild, pleasant taste. The sweet yellow flowers can be eaten raw and make a colourful, delicate addition to summer salads.

HARVEST & STORAGE
Roots are best harvested once the plant enters dormancy, from late summer into early autumn. Unlike true root vegetables, they do not store well and should be eaten within a few weeks. Shoots can be harvested sparingly from spring through to early summer. Raw roots may irritate.

Greater Pignut (*Bunium bulbocastanum*)

Sun or shade: Full sun
Height: 60 cm (2 ft)
Spread: 30 cm (1 ft)
Flower colour: White
Flowering month: 6–7
USDA hardiness zone: 4–8

DESCRIPTION
A delicate umbellifer native to chalk grasslands across Europe, including the UK. Its small, nutty-flavoured tubers have long been foraged and enjoyed.

Greater pignut (*Bunium bulbocastanum*).

SOIL

Thrives in well-drained soils – light, loamy or heavier clays – with a wide pH tolerance from mildly acidic to very alkaline. Prefers moist conditions but resents waterlogging.

DESIGN USES

Best planted in drifts or clusters where its light, feathery foliage and lacy umbels won't be overwhelmed. Ideal for sunny meadow-style plantings and naturalistic borders.

EDIBILITY & HARVEST

The small underground tubers have a flavour reminiscent of sweet chestnuts when cooked. Leaves can be used sparingly like parsley, while the seeds and flowers bring a mild cumin-like note to dishes.

Korean Aster (*Doellingeria scabra*)

Sun or shade: Sun or partial shade
Height: 1.2 m (4 ft)
Spread: 50 cm (20 in)
Flower colour: White to pale violet-blue
Flowering month: 8–10
USDA hardiness zone: 6–9

DESCRIPTION

A late-flowering perennial native to woodland edges, thickets and clearings across Korea and Japan, Korean aster thrives in low mountain regions where summers are warm and soils remain reasonably moist. Traditionally foraged and cultivated in Korean cuisine, it's an edimental with real garden potential. It is used similarly to the North American native bigleaf aster (*Eurybia macrophylla*), forming broad clumps of coarse, ovate foliage from which tall, wiry stems emerge as the season progresses. In some parts of North

Korean aster (*Doellingeria scabra*).

America, it can naturalise readily, so check local guidance before planting.

SOIL
Performs best in well-drained, moderately fertile soils with some moisture retention. Tolerates a range of soil types but dislikes prolonged dryness.

DESIGN USES
Korean aster brings late-season height to the mid-layer, rising through earlier-flowering companions and adding fresh energy as summer fades. Its tall, branching stems carry daisy-like flowers – mostly white, sometimes tinged with pale violet-blue – that hover lightly above the foliage, catching light and movement. Plant in groups among other late-season edimentals, or weave into woodland-edge and naturalistic schemes where its upright habit adds lift without dominance.

EDIBLE QUALITIES
Widely eaten in Korea, where it's known as *chamchwi* or *chwinamul*, the young leaves are a spring delicacy. They're typically stir-fried or blanched and served as *namul*, a seasoned side dish of greens. The leaves can also be added to kimchi or rice dishes to impart a mild, herbal depth. Grown commercially, and dried leaves are available in Asian supermarkets around the world.

HARVEST & STORAGE
Harvest leaves while young and tender before they become coarse and tough. They can be eaten fresh or blanched, dried or frozen for later use.

Citron Daylily (*Hemerocallis citrina*)

Sun or shade: Full sun to light shade
Height: 80 cm (2.5 ft)
Spread: 70 cm (2.3 ft)
Flower colour: Lemon yellow
Flowering month: 6–7
USDA hardiness zone: 4–8

DESCRIPTION
A lemon-scented, evening-blooming daylily from East Asia. Its trumpet-shaped yellow flowers open at

Citron daylily (*Hemerocallis citrina*).

dusk and fade by morning, rising above strappy, grass-like foliage in midsummer.

SOIL

Thrives in most soils, including clay. Prefers moisture-retentive but well-drained ground.

DESIGN USES

Ideal for naturalistic borders or cottage-style planting. Works well in small to mid-sized groups or larger drifts. Loose form and grassy foliage pair beautifully with ornamental grasses. Plant different species of daylily for a prolonged flowering season.

EDIBILITY & HARVEST

Buds are delicious cooked like green beans and are delicious in stir-fries. Flowers can be stuffed and tempura-fried or eaten fresh. Spent flowers can be harvested and dried for use as a flavouring in winter soups. Widely used in Chinese and Southeast Asian cuisine. Some people experience mild gastrointestinal upset (nausea, vomiting, diarrhoea) from raw buds or flowers. Highly toxic to cats.

Bistort (*Bistorta officinalis*)

Sun or shade: Full sun or light shade
Height: 50 cm (1.6 ft)
Spread: 50 cm (1.6 ft)
Flower colour: Pink
Flowering month: 6–10
USDA hardiness zone: 4–7

DESCRIPTION

A moisture-loving perennial with upright pink spires above large, spoon-shaped leaves. Native to damp meadows across

Bistort (*Bistorta officinali*).

Europe and Asia, it spreads slowly by rhizome to form tidy clumps.

SOIL

Thrives in moist or damp soil. Tolerates a wide range of pH and soil types, including heavy clay.

DESIGN USES

Best planted in generous groups and drifts near features such as ponds and rain gardens or within moist borders. In wet meadow-style planting, smaller groupings offer contrast through bold foliage and flower spikes.

EDIBILITY & HARVEST

Young leaves are edible raw or cooked (used traditionally in northern England to make the Easter ledge pudding). Flowers can be sprinkled on salads. Use in moderation due to oxalic acid content – a natural compound in many leafy greens that binds calcium and can contribute to kidney stones. Large raw portions may irritate the mouth or stomach. Blanch or cook to reduce levels, and people with a history of kidney stones or kidney disease should limit intake. Sap can irritate sensitive skin; peel under water or wear gloves.

Black Salsify (*Scorzonera hispanica*)

Sun or shade: Full sun
Height: Up to 90 cm (3 ft)
Spread: 40 cm (1.3 ft)
Flower colour: Yellow
Flowering month: 6–8
USDA hardiness zone: 5–8

DESCRIPTION

A hardy perennial often grown as an annual or biennial for its long, tapering

Black salsify (*Scorzonera hispanica*).

black-skinned roots. If left unharvested, lumps of narrow, grass-like foliage give rise to bright yellow, daisy-like flowers in summer.

SOIL

Prefers deep, loose, well-drained soil free of stones to allow straight root growth. Avoid waterlogged sites.

DESIGN USES

Use in small groups or drifts, interwoven with grasses in meadow-style planting. Best not overcrowded by other bold edimentals.

EDIBILITY & HARVEST

Roots, harvested from October to spring, have a mild, oyster-like flavour. Young shoots can be eaten like asparagus and

the flowers, flower stems or buds can be added to salads.

Lamb's Ear (*Stachys byzantina*)

Sun or shade: Full sun
Height: 50 cm (20 in)
Spread: 60 cm (24 in)
Colour: Pink to purple
Flowering month: 6–8
USDA hardiness zone: 4–9

DESCRIPTION

This soft-textured ornamental has proven to be much more than a highly prized garden plant. Native to the dry, rocky hills of western Asia – particularly Turkey, Iran and Armenia – lamb's ear has long been grown for its striking silver foliage. It's cultivated worldwide and has naturalised in many temperate regions, including parts of the UK and US. In the right conditions, it spreads readily through creeping roots and stems. Drought-tolerant and hardy, it copes well with cold winters, though it often sheds its leaves in prolonged frost.

SOIL

Requires free-draining soil and thrives in poor, sandy or gravelly substrates. Dislikes winter wet and benefits from good air circulation to prevent rot.

DESIGN USES

Lamb's ear is most often used as a low edging or groundcover plant, its

Lamb's ear (*Stachys byzantina*).

velvety, silver foliage forming a reflective carpet that pairs well with upright or green-leaved companions. While typically grown for texture alone, its tall pink-purple flower spikes bring added vertical interest and work well in loose, naturalistic schemes. Cultivars vary in height, flower production and foliage tone.

EDIBLE QUALITIES

In Brazil, the young leaves are dipped in batter and fried to make *peixinho da horta*, a dish whose name ('little garden fish') refers to their shape and texture rather than taste. The tender leaves can also be used in stir-fries, rice dishes and salads or brewed into herbal teas. Nutritionally, they are rich in fibre, protein and minerals, with notable antioxidant content.

HARVEST & STORAGE

Harvest the youngest leaves in spring or early summer. They are best eaten fresh, but they can also be blanched or dried for later use.

Society Garlic (*Tulbaghia violacea*)

Sun or shade: Full sun
Height: 50 cm (1.6 ft)
Spread: 30 cm (1 ft)
Flower colour: Purple
Flowering month: 5–9
USDA hardiness zone: 7–11

DESCRIPTION

An evergreen perennial from South Africa with strappy, grass-like foliage and lilac flower umbels held above. The whole plant carries a light garlic scent.

SOIL

Prefers well-drained soil in full sun. Tolerates clay, sand and dry conditions once established.

DESIGN USES

Ideal for edging sunny borders, gravel gardens or containers. Neat, clumping habit suits both more formal and naturalistic schemes.

EDIBILITY & HARVEST

Leaves and flowers offer a mild garlic flavour. Use raw in salads or cooked like chives. Harvestable year-round in frost-free areas.

Society garlic (*Tulbaghia violacea*).

Low / Groundcover

This layer binds the planting together. It protects the soil, suppresses weeds and creates a continuous base for the layers above. These plants weave between others, filling gaps, softening edges and ensuring the scheme remains resilient and cohesive year-round.

Chives (*Allium schoenoprasum*)

Sun or shade: Full sun or light shade
Height: 40 cm (1.3 ft)
Spread: 30 cm (1 ft)
Flower colour: Pink
Flowering month: 5–7
USDA hardiness zone: 3–11

DESCRIPTION

One of the most popular herbs and a favourite edimental. A compact, clump-forming perennial with hollow, grass-like leaves and globe-shaped pink flowers.

SOIL

Moist, well-drained soil. Tolerates heavy clay and a pH range, including alkaline soils.

DESIGN USES

Excellent for edging naturalistic borders, green roofs or containers. Resents competition so avoid overcrowding.

EDIBILITY & HARVEST

Leaves and flowers have a mild onion flavour. Use fresh in salads, soups or as a garnish. Harvest from late winter to autumn. Toxic to cats and dogs.

Purple Poppy-Mallow (*Callirhoe involucrata*)

Sun or shade: Full sun
Height: 30 cm (12 in)
Spread: 60 cm (24 in)
Flower colour: Bright pink to magenta
Flowering month: 5–7
USDA hardiness zone: 4–9

DESCRIPTION

Native to the southern and central US, purple poppy-mallow grows in dry, open habitats, such as meadows, prairies, roadsides and rocky banks – typically where vegetation is sparse and sun exposure is high. It has a long history of use by Indigenous communities and early European colonists, valued for both its culinary and medicinal properties. Slugs are particularly drawn to it, so be mindful when planting in slug-prone areas.

Chives (*Allium schoenoprasum*).

Purple poppy-mallow (*Callirhoe involucrata*).

SOIL

Thrives in well-drained, light soils – sandy, gravelly or stony substrates are ideal. Avoid heavy or moisture-retentive soils. Once established, it is tolerant of drought and low fertility.

DESIGN USES

Its low, mat-forming habit makes it ideal for edging borders or weaving through gravel gardens and dry, nutrient-poor planting schemes. It thrives in tough, exposed spots and serves well as an edible groundcover in water-scarce environments. The finely divided foliage is reminiscent of hardy geraniums and contrasts beautifully with broader-leaved companions. From late spring into early summer, its luminous bright pink-magenta flowers add a vivid splash of colour – often associated with late summer – early in the season.

EDIBLE QUALITIES

While somewhat spurious in its edible qualities, the fleshy taproot can be cooked and eaten, offering a sweet, nutty flavour similar to sweet potato. Cooked leaves also make a useful edible, with a mild, mucilaginous texture ideal for thickening soups and stews.

HARVEST & STORAGE

As the plant dislikes disturbance, harvest roots only from mature clumps where a portion can be removed without sacrificing the whole. Uplift roots in late autumn or winter when dormant. Use fresh, or slice and dry for storage. Pick leaves when young and actively growing.

Wild Strawberry (*Fragaria vesca*)

Sun or shade: Full sun or shade
Height: 30 cm (1 ft)
Spread: 30 cm (1 ft)
Flower colour: White
Flowering month: 5–7
USDA hardiness zone: 4–8

DESCRIPTION

A low-growing, clump-forming perennial with trifoliate leaves and delicate white flowers, followed by intensely flavoured, bite-sized red fruits. Native to woodland edges across Europe and Asia.

SOIL

Moist, well-drained soil. Tolerates clay and a range of pH levels.

DESIGN USES

Great for groundcover in herbaceous borders and woodland edge schemes. Also ideal for pots, path edges and between stepping stones.

EDIBILITY & HARVEST

Fruits are delicious fresh or in desserts and jams. Plants produce highest yields in full sun. Young leaves can be eaten raw or

Wild strawberries make an excellent shade-tolerant groundcover, preventing weeds and producing delightful fruits.

brewed into tea. Harvest from early summer to autumn. Strawberry allergy is uncommon but recognised. It can cause mild oral irritation in sensitive individuals, especially those allergic to birch pollen.

Sweet Woodruff (*Galium odoratum*)

Sun or shade: Partial to full shade
Height: 20 cm (8 in)
Spread: 50 cm (1 ft 8 in)
Flower colour: White
Flowering month: 5–7
USDA hardiness zone: 5–9

DESCRIPTION

A spreading woodland perennial with whorled, lance-shaped leaves and clusters of starry white flowers in late spring. It forms a soft, low carpet ideal for shady environments.

SOIL

Prefers moist, humus-rich soil but copes well with dry shade and a wide pH range.

DESIGN USES

Excellent groundcover and weed suppressant beneath trees and among bulbs and shade-loving plants. Perfect for naturalistic, woodland-style planting.

EDIBILITY & HARVEST

An edimental with more spurious edible qualities. Dried leaves have a sweet, hay-like scent and almond-vanilla flavour. Use sparingly to flavour drinks, cordials, teas or desserts. Flowers can garnish salads. Harvest leaves and flowers in spring to early summer. Contains coumarin (a fragrant compound that can affect liver and blood function). Use in small quantities and avoid in pregnancy or with anticoagulant medication.

Hosta (*Hosta* 'Fortunei Hyacinthina')

Sun or shade: Partial to full shade
Height: 40 cm (16 in)
Spread: 60 cm (24 in)
Flower colour: Pale lavender
Flowering month: 7–8
USDA hardiness zone: 3–8

DESCRIPTION

Hostas are herbaceous perennials native to damp woodlands, riverbanks and forest edges in East Asia – particularly

Sweet woodruff (*Galium odoratum*).

Hosta (*Hosta* 'Fortunei Hyacinthina').

Japan, Korea and China. They thrive in cool, shaded habitats with rich soils and consistent moisture. Now cultivated worldwide, they've become staples of shade planting schemes. Like all hostas, *Hosta* 'Fortunei Hyacinthina' is vulnerable to slug damage and may require protection in slug-prone environments.

SOIL

Prefers moist, humus-rich soil with good drainage. Benefits from consistent moisture and spring mulching to conserve water and support strong growth.

DESIGN USES

Hostas are ideal where texture, foliage and form take precedence. While many cultivars feature bold variegation or exaggerated leaf shapes, *Hosta* 'Fortunei Hyacinthina' stands out for its simplicity. Its refined, mid-green leaves and compact habit offer understated elegance – perfect for the low / ground layer in shade. Mounds of foliage contrast beautifully with finely divided ferns, such as the edimental ostrich fern (*Matteuccia struthiopteris*). Slender, pale lavender flower spikes appear in midsummer, adding gentle vertical lift. Plant in small- to mid-sized groups to create rhythm through a scheme. Hostas come in a vast range of forms, from compact cultivars to large, structural varieties that can punctuate a planting with mass and scale.

EDIBLE QUALITIES

Young shoots are harvested in spring and cooked like asparagus. In Japan, hostas are widely foraged and farmed, especially for their spring-blanched shoots, known as icicles, which are often eaten raw with a sesame oil and soy sauce dip. They're also used in stir-fries, soups and stews. Larger varieties, such as *Hosta sieboldiana*, are preferred for their yield, but all are worth exploring. Toxic to dogs and cats.

HARVEST & STORAGE

Harvest young shoots as they emerge, although older unfurled leaves can still be cooked. Flowers can also be picked and eaten raw or sautéed.

Bladder Campion (*Silene vulgaris*)

Sun or shade: Full sun
Height: 50 cm (1.6 ft)
Spread: 30 cm (1 ft)
Flower colour: Pale pink to white
Flowering month: 5–8
USDA hardiness zone: 5–9

DESCRIPTION

A soft, mounding perennial with inflated, bladder-like calyxes and delicate pale flowers. Common in dry meadows and grassy verges, it spreads gently by seed and root.

SOIL

Prefers well-drained, light loam but is fairly tolerant.

DESIGN USES

Weave through naturalistic borders or meadow-style plantings to add seasonal texture and lower-layer interest.

EDIBILITY & HARVEST

Young shoots and leaves can be eaten raw or cooked – best before flowering. Sweet, pea-like flavour. Blanch to reduce bitterness. Use sparingly due to natural saponins. Harvest in spring and early summer. Contains saponins (natural plant compounds that can irritate the gut if eaten raw). Use in moderation and preferably cooked.

Chinese Artichoke (*Stachys affinis*)

Sun or shade: Full sun to partial shade
Height: 30–45 cm (12–18 in)
Spread: 30 cm (12 in) and gradually expanding
Flower colour: Purple-pink
Flowering month: 7–8
USDA hardiness zone: 4–8

DESCRIPTION

A hardy, herbaceous perennial in the mint family, Chinese artichoke is grown primarily for its crisp, edible tubers.

Bladder campion (*Silene vulgaris*).

Native to northern China and long cultivated in both China and Japan, it has been used for centuries in food and traditional medicine. In Japan, it's known as *chorogi* and is traditionally served pickled with shiso (*Perilla frutescens*) leaves as part of New Year celebrations. The plant spreads via rhizomes, forming a gradually expanding, dense mat of foliage. Wild artichoke (*Stachys floridana*) is very similar and grown in warmer climates.

SOIL

Thrives in moist, well-drained soil rich in organic matter. Prefers lighter soils but tolerates heavier ground if improved. Can

Chinese artichoke (*Stachys affinis*).

withstand occasional waterlogging in winter, but it needs consistent moisture through the growing season for good tuber production.

DESIGN USES

Well suited as an edible groundcover in sunny or lightly shaded borders. Its dense foliage creates a weed-suppressing carpet that works well in drifts or mid– to large-sized groups. While top growth dies back with frost, the tubers overwinter well in the soil, and the plant reliably returns each year. In warmer seasons, it sends up slender purple-pink flower spikes, adding subtle seasonal interest without overwhelming the surrounding planting.

EDIBLE QUALITIES

Tubers are crisp, white and mildly nutty, and excellent raw, roasted or pickled. Their unique, knobbly shape adds visual interest and texture, especially in salads or as a garnish.

HARVEST & STORAGE

Begin harvesting in late autumn and lift as needed. Tubers store best in the ground – dig them up only when required. Avoid peeling to retain flavour and nutrients and to reduce discolouration. Always replant a few tubers to maintain your patch.

Creeping Thyme (*Thymus serpyllum*)

Sun or shade: Full sun
Height: 10 cm (4 in)
Spread: 30 cm (1 ft)
Flower colour: Pink
Flowering month: 5–7
USDA hardiness zone: 5–9

DESCRIPTION

A kitchen favourite, wild thyme is a low-growing, mat-forming sub-shrub with tiny aromatic leaves and clusters of pink flowers. It's wind-tolerant and highly resilient.

SOIL

Thrives in light, well-drained soil – even in poor, low-nutrient conditions. Prefers alkaline or neutral pH.

DESIGN USES

Ideal for dry, sunny spots. Spreads well between stepping stones, along path edges or in gravel gardens. Tolerates drought and light foot traffic.

EDIBILITY & HARVEST

Leaves add deep flavour to dishes and teas, raw or cooked. For best aroma, harvest in spring to early summer before flowering.

Creeping thyme (*Thymus serpyllum*).

Dots & Fillers

This layer is made up of plants that bring brief but memorable moments. Often ephemeral bulbs, short-lived perennials, biennials or annuals, they thread through the main planting, appearing for a season before retreating underground or fading as other plants outcompete them. Used sparingly, they add spontaneity, depth and dynamism.

Persian Shallots (*Allium stipitatum*)

Sun or shade: Full sun
Height: 1.5 m (5 ft)
Spread: 20 cm (8 in)
Flower colour: Purple
Flowering month: 5–6
USDA hardiness zone: 4–9

Persian shallots (*Allium stipitatum*).

DESCRIPTION
A tall, dramatic allium with globe-shaped purple blooms and broad, strap-like leaves. Native to Iran and Central Asia, it thrives in hot, dry conditions.

SOIL
Requires light, well-drained soil in full sun. Dislikes winter wet.

DESIGN USES
Ideal for adding architectural flower form and height to sunny borders. Intermingle in drifts for a naturalistic effect. As a bulb, it is naturally ephemeral in the aesthetic qualities it brings to a scheme.

EDIBILITY & HARVEST
Bulbs are used as a shallot substitute in cooked dishes and are commercially cultivated in Iran, where they're sliced, dried and distributed to supermarkets worldwide. Leaves and flowers are also edible – young leaves can be eaten raw. Harvest bulbs in mid- to late summer. As with all alliums, toxic to cats and dogs.

Cuckoo Flower (*Cardamine pratensis*)

Sun or shade: Full sun or partial shade
Height: 50 cm (1 ft 8 in)
Spread: 30 cm (1 ft)
Flower colour: Pale lilac to white
Flowering month: 4–6
USDA hardiness zone: 4–8

DESCRIPTION
A graceful clump-forming perennial with finely divided leaves and lilac-white flowers. Found in damp meadows, along streams, and spring grasslands.

Cuckoo flower (*Cardamine pratensis*).

SOIL

Thrives in moist to wet loam or clay. Tolerates a wide pH range.

DESIGN USES

Naturalise through meadow-style borders or plant near ponds and streams for a soft, understated spring display.

EDIBILITY & HARVEST

Young leaves and shoots have a strong, cress-like flavour and can be eaten raw or cooked. Flowers and buds are peppery and pretty in salads. Harvest in early spring and use sparingly. Contains mustard oils – use modestly if sensitive to brassicas.

Colombia Lily (*Lilium columbianum*)

Sun or shade: Sun to partial shade
Height: Up to 120 cm (4 ft)
Spread: 30 cm (12 in)
Flower colour: Orange with dark spots
Flowering month: 7–8
USDA hardiness zone: 5–10

DESCRIPTION

A striking lily native to the Pacific Northwest and the western slopes of North

staple. Plant bulbs 10–15 centimetres (4–6 inches) deep in early autumn.

SOIL

Prefers moist, loamy, well-drained soils. Slightly acidic to neutral conditions are ideal.

DESIGN USES

I like to use this lily as an ephemeral summer presence. Its vivid blooms punctuate a border, with vertical stems rising into the mid-layer to add fleeting colour and height. As the top growth dies back soon after flowering, it's best used as a filler in naturalistic meadow-style or woodland-edge schemes, where other plants can step in to cover the gap. Avoid relying on it for long-term structure.

EDIBLE QUALITIES

The bulbs are rich in starch and can be roasted, boiled or stir-fried much like potatoes. When cooked, they have a sweet, chestnut-like flavour with a slight bitterness. Though technically edible raw, cooking improves both taste and digestibility. Highly toxic to cats.

HARVEST & STORAGE

Lift bulbs in late autumn to early winter once the foliage has fully died back. Only harvest mature bulbs from well-established clumps, and always replant a portion to sustain the patch.

Colombia lily (*Lilium columbianum*).

America, Colombia lily thrives in moist mountain meadows, light woodlands and forest margins. It grows from an underground bulb, producing slender stems topped with nodding, tiger-like orange blooms in mid to late summer. Indigenous communities traditionally harvested the bulbs as a starchy food source and valued them as a seasonal

Climbers

Climbers extend the planting vertically, softening boundaries and adding another productive layer. They make use of walls, fences, trees and structures to create height and enclosure, while offering edible leaves, flowers or fruits. In small spaces especially, they're an efficient way to increase abundance without taking up valuable ground area.

Hardy Kiwi (*Actinidia arguta* 'Issai')

Sun or shade: Full sun or partial shade
Height: 6 m (20 ft)
Spread: 4 m (13 ft)
Flower colour: White
Flowering month: 6–7
USDA hardiness zone: 4–8

DESCRIPTION

A vigorous, deciduous climber from East Asia. The self-fertile 'Issai' produces fragrant white flowers followed by smooth, grape-sized fruits. Emerging invasive in parts of the Northeastern US. Site carefully and don't allow escape into woodlands.

SOIL

Moist, well-drained soil preferred, though it tolerates dry soil when established.

DESIGN USES

Ideal for sunny walls, structures or growing into trees. Needs strong support and space to ramble.

EDIBILITY & HARVEST

Fruits are sweet, vitamin-rich, and eaten whole – no peeling needed. Harvest in autumn once fully soft. Prune in winter to manage growth and improve yield.

Groundnut (*Apios americana*)

Sun or shade: Full sun to partial shade
Height: 2.5 m (8 ft)
Spread: 1.5 m (5 ft)
Flower colour: Pink-maroon
Flowering month: 6–9
USDA hardiness zone: 3–9

DESCRIPTION

A vigorous, nitrogen-fixing climber with violet-scented flowers and edible tubers. Native to eastern North America, it thrives in damp, partly shaded sites. Spreads by tubers and can be invasive in parts of the US.

SOIL

Prefers moist, well-drained soil; tolerates acidity.

DESIGN USES

Enjoy its beautiful foliage and scented flowers grown over boundaries and walls. Or grow up trees in

Hardy kiwi (*Actinidia arguta* 'Issai').

Groundnut (*Apios americana*).

Caucasian spinach (*Hablitzia tamnoides*).

forest gardens and in patches where digging to harvest tubers is possible.

EDIBILITY & HARVEST

Tubers are rich in protein and taste delicious. Treat them much like potatoes and roast, boil or mash. Harvest in autumn from the second year onwards.

Caucasian Spinach (*Hablitzia tamnoides*)

Sun or shade: Full shade to partial sun
Height: Up to 3 m (10 ft)
Spread: 60 cm (24 in)
Flower colour: Pale green-white
Flowering month: 5–7
USDA hardiness zone: 3–9

DESCRIPTION

A remarkable perennial climber from the Caucasus Mountains, where Europe meets Asia, *Hablitzia tamnoides* thrives in moist, shady woodlands, ravines and riverbanks. With its scrambling growth and cold-hardiness, it's one of the few perennial leafy greens suited to deep shade. It emerges early in spring and can grow fast if given support, with heart-shaped green leaves and pale, starry flowers. It's enjoying a surge of interest over recent years as a leafy staple among forest gardeners and perennial veg growers. The plant dies back entirely in winter, returning each year from a hardy crown and deep taproots.

SOIL

Tolerant of most soils but prefers rich, moist, well-drained ground with plenty of organic matter. Grows in light, medium or relatively heavy soils.

DESIGN USES

Albeit not the most attractive with regards to foliage or striking flowers, it brings lushness to tricky, low-light areas such as shady corners, north-facing walls, woodland edges and forest gardens – especially where vertical space is

Hops (*Humulus lupulus*).

HARVEST & STORAGE

Begin harvesting shoots in early spring as they emerge. Pick regularly to promote new growth. Leaves can be used fresh or blanched and frozen for later use.

Hops (*Humulus lupulus*)

Sun or shade: Full sun to partial shade
Height: 6 m (20 ft)
Spread: 2 m (6.5 ft)
Flower colour: Green-yellow
Flowering month: 7–8
USDA hardiness zone: 5–7

DESCRIPTION

A vigorous, herbaceous climber with aromatic foliage and cone-like female flowers. Native to hedgerows and woodlands of Europe and western Asia, it's valued for brewing and edible shoots. May cause skin irritation in sensitive individuals. Spent hops are highly toxic to dogs – never compost where dogs could access.

SOIL

Prefers deep, fertile soil; tolerates drought once established.

DESIGN USES

Grow up architectural structures or supports for visual impact or allow to scramble over boundaries and up trees in forest gardens.

EDIBILITY & HARVEST

Young shoots are a spring delicacy – blanch them briefly and serve warm or cold. Female flowers flavour beer and herbal teas. Best grown in polycultures due to pest issues in monoculture.

underused. Grow it up trees, wire supports, boundary fences or purpose-built structures. Use it in a natural way, allowing it to scramble, or in more designed architectural ways, training it up supports to add a sculptural quality to planting borders.

EDIBLE QUALITIES

Young leaves and tender shoots are mild, spinach-like and highly versatile – delicious raw in salads or lightly cooked in soups, stir-fries, curries or savoury bakes. Their gentle flavour blends easily with a range of ingredients.

Aquatic

Plants for water and saturated soils – lakes, ponds, rills, rain gardens and wet margins. They add bold texture, support wildlife, and can deliver edible leaves, stems or tubers. Match species to water depth and flow, and use baskets or containers for control where required.

Water Chestnuts (*Eleocharis dulcis*)

Sun or shade: Full sun
Height: 1 m (3.3 ft)
Spread: 40 cm (1.3 ft)
Flower colour: White (inconspicuous)
Flowering month: 7–8
USDA hardiness zone: 9–12

DESCRIPTION

An aquatic, frost-tender perennial grown for its crisp, sweet tubers. Native to Asia and Australia, it thrives in shallow water or flooded containers, and is best suited to warmer temperate zones.

SOIL

Prefers fertile, slightly acidic, wet soil. Grows in 10–30 centimetres (4–12 inches) of standing water.

DESIGN USES

Use in ponds, bog gardens or stream edges, where its fine, grassy foliage contrasts well with bold, coarse-leaved plants.

EDIBILITY & HARVEST

Tubers are crunchy and sweet, eaten raw or cooked. Popular in Chinese cuisine. Harvest in late summer after foliage yellows. Needs seven frost-free months to crop. Grow in containers in cooler climates.

Water chestnuts (*Eleocharis dulcis*).

Himalayan Water Creeper (*Houttuynia cordata*)

Sun or shade: Partial or full shade
Height: 40 cm (1.3 ft)
Spread: 1 m (3 ft 3 in)
Flower colour: White
Flowering month: 6–8
USDA hardiness zone: 5–10

DESCRIPTION

A vigorous, aromatic plant from East and Southeast Asia with heart-shaped leaves and a bold citrus-coriander scent and unique flavour. Invasive in parts of the US and can spread aggressively in UK gardens – plant with care, contain roots and consider planting within pots.

SOIL

Moist or wet soils in shade or partial shade; grows well in shallow water.

DESIGN USES

Perfect for naturalising around ponds and wet areas in forest gardens. Spreads to form low groundcover and contrasts well with grasses or large-leafed aquatics.

EDIBILITY & HARVEST

Harvest leaves and shoots in spring. Eat raw or cooked – distinctive and divisive in flavour. Traditionally used in tinctures for antiviral and antihistamine properties. The long white rhizomes are also edible and good in stir-fries. Avoid during pregnancy.

Arrowhead (*Sagittaria latifolia*)

Sun or shade: Full sun
Height: Up to 120 cm (4 ft)
Spread: 30–60 cm (12–24 in)
Flower colour: White with yellow centres
Flowering month: 7–9
USDA hardiness zone: 6–9

DESCRIPTION

Native to wetlands and riparian zones across much of North America, arrowhead thrives in the margins of slow-moving rivers, ponds, ditches and marshes. It has long been a valued food

Arrowhead (*Sagittaria latifolia*).

plant among Indigenous communities, often growing in colonies where its tubers could be harvested seasonally. Hardy and adaptable, it tolerates freezing winters and forms a reliable perennial presence in wetland habitats. In the UK it's listed as invasive – use only in contained water features, never in the wild.

SOIL

Prefers loamy, silty or clay-rich soil that remains saturated or submerged. Best grown in still or slow-moving water 10–30 centimetres (4–12 inches) deep.

DESIGN USES

A great edimental for bog gardens, pond and stream edges, rain gardens and riparian plantings. Its striking, arrow-shaped foliage emerges from water or saturated ground, creating bold vertical lines and seasonal structure. In summer, delicate white flowers with yellow centres add lightness and pollinator value. Allow it to naturalise in colonies for the most visual impact and low-input means of growing.

EDIBLE QUALITIES

The starchy tubers are the primary edible part – delicious roasted, boiled or mashed. When cooked, they have a soft, potato-like texture and a flavour reminiscent of sweet chestnuts. Tubers form at the tips of wiry roots, often some distance from the main plant and buried deep in the substrate.

HARVEST & STORAGE

Harvest tubers from late summer into autumn, once the foliage begins to yellow and die back but while the plant's location is still visible through its withering stems. Dig carefully, as the tubers often form some distance from the parent plant and can be left behind if the tops break off. Indigenous communities traditionally boiled the tubers, sliced them thinly, and strung them on cords to dry for winter use. They can also be ground into flour or stored short-term in cool, damp conditions.

Himalayan water creeper (*Houttuynia cordata*).

Chapter 8

Eating Edimentals

If there's one key takeaway for incorporating edimentals into your diet, it's this: just give it a go. The variety of complete perennial vegetable cookbooks available is minimal, so experimentation is key. Cooking with edimentals should be a playful, enjoyable process. It's a chance to discover new flavours, challenge your expectations and work with what's right in front of you. There will be triumphs and there will be mishaps, but that's all part of the process. I used to be an outrageously experimental cook – sometimes to the horror of my wife, who comes from a family of exceptional cooks. I like to think we've balanced each other out over the years; I've become a bit more measured, and she's learned to venture outside of her comfort zone. Somewhere in the middle is the sweet spot. Ultimately, we both embrace the idea of just giving it a go.

Please remember: this book is not a foraging manual or a directive guide. Always do your own research before eating any plant. Be 100 per cent certain of identification, know which part is edible and how to prepare it, and

A spring harvest of edimentals – including alexanders, Babington's leek, sweet cicely, hosta shoots and lovage – brings diversity back into our diets.

make sure it's safe for you. Even widely eaten plants can cause allergic reactions or sensitivities in some people. Start small when trying anything new, and take extra care if you're unfamiliar with the plant.

You, Your Kitchen & Your Garden

One of the joys of growing edimentals is how it reshapes the relationship between you, your garden and your kitchen. Because they crop little and often, you're not harvesting gluts all at once. Instead, it becomes a steady, ongoing process. These mini harvests get you out into the garden at all times of the year, deepening your understanding of your site, your soil and the shifting rhythms of the space. The more you cook from the garden, the more you notice. And the more you notice, the better a grower – and cook – you become. Over time, the act of cooking starts to feel less like an indoor task and more of a blended garden-kitchen ritual. You'll find yourself hopping in and out of the garden mid-cook, scissors in hand, more often than rummaging in cupboards.

What Parts of Plants Are Edible?

When it comes to growing, harvesting and cooking with edimentals, it helps to have a sense of the different

A rosemary plant catches the evening light in a richly layered border – a garden that invites daily harvesting and deepens the rhythm between kitchen and garden.

parts of a plant. Not just the leaves and flowers, but stems, shoots, fruits, seeds, roots and bulbs, each with their own possibilities, timings and considerations. We're not getting overly botanical here – the full range of plant parts and their many variations is a whole book in itself – but it's worth stepping back and looking at the basics. If we want to make the most of what's edible in the garden, we need to pay attention to the whole plant. This is our plant-based version of nose-to-tail cooking.

The classic perennial veg rhubarb is widely known to have toxic leaves but safe and delicious stems.

Cornelian cherry is widely grown for its delicious fruits and admired for its resilience. It is a plant that thrives across a range of conditions.

A note of caution: just because a plant is listed as edible doesn't mean every part of it is safe to eat. Some are only edible at certain stages, others need cooking or processing, and a few have elements you'll want to avoid entirely. Rhubarb (*Rheum × hybridum*) is a classic example: the stalks are widely used in the kitchen, but the leaves are toxic. Same with elder (*Sambucus nigra*): the flowers and cooked berries are edible, but the leaves, stems and unripe fruit are not. It's important to be 100 per cent sure of what you're eating and what you need to do to prepare it for consumption. The Plants for a Future (www.pfaf.org) database is a brilliant resource, both online and in print, for working out what's what.

FRUITS

In botanical terms, a fruit is the mature ovary of a flower, essentially the part that carries the seeds. This includes not just the familiar apples (*Malus domestica*) and pears (*Pyrus* spp.), but also berries, stone fruits, pods and other forms. Then there are the more unusual examples, like Sichuan pepper (*Zanthoxylum simulans*), where it's the aromatic husk, not the seed, that delivers the flavour.

In a forest garden or agroforestry system, fruit tends to be abundant. With thoughtful planning, you can extend the season from early summer strawberries (*Fragaria × ananassa*) right through to winter medlars (*Mespilus germanica*) and stored apples. As we've seen, having some fruit trees is a great way to start building more layers, supporting not just long harvest windows but the vertical structure of a resilient, productive garden. Some fruits are eaten fresh, some are cooked and others need a bit of processing to be enjoyable – or even safe. It's not always straightforward. Pears, for instance, are best picked slightly under-ripe and left to ripen indoors. Medlars need to fall naturally and blet, softening until they're dark and almost mushy before becoming palatable. And fruits such as quince (*Cydonia oblonga*), while technically edible raw, only really shine once cooked. While many fruits are entirely edible, others contain stones or seeds that shouldn't be consumed, so it's important to be cautious and always check specifics.

Beyond taste, many fruits are highly nutritious. Others are particularly valuable because they thrive in tough conditions. The strawberry tree (*Arbutus unedo*), for instance, is drought-tolerant once established and produces clusters of edible red fruits in autumn.

Here are a few excellent edimental fruit crops:

Autumn olive (*Elaeagnus umbellata*): sharp, tangy red berries from a nitrogen-fixing shrub.
Cornelian cherry (*Cornus mas*): tart when raw; rich and jammy when cooked.
Saskatoon (*Amelanchier alnifolia*): sweet, nutty flavour; delicious fresh or dried.

NUTS

A nut is a hard, dry fruit that contains a single seed and doesn't split open at maturity. Hazelnuts (*Corylus* spp.) are a classic example. That said, not everything we call a nut in the kitchen is technically a nut. Almonds, cashews and Brazil nuts, for instance, are technically seeds, but we treat them as nuts in food terms because of their rich, oily seeds and hard shells. So, while the terms overlap, not all seeds are nuts, and not all nuts are truly nuts – botanically speaking.

What matters most here is that nuts are incredibly nutritious. They're compact, energy-dense and packed with fats, protein, fibre and minerals. I can't get enough of them – they're my go-to snack, and something I aim to grow a lot more of. Some, like walnuts (*Juglans regia*), store well

Nuts are among the most nutrient-dense foods we can grow; they are rich in protein, fats and minerals. A surprisingly wide variety can thrive in temperate gardens, including hazelnuts, walnuts, sweet chestnuts and heartnuts.

for months if dried properly. Others, like fresh sweet chestnuts (*Castanea sativa*), are best used soon after harvest unless processed.

Nut trees can take their time. Many won't produce a meaningful crop for several years, but they're worth the wait. In the meantime, they're often doing other jobs, too. Sweet chestnuts make excellent canopy trees in an edible woodland; hazel (*Corylus* spp.) can be coppiced for materials as well as nuts; and ginkgo (*Ginkgo biloba*), with its golden autumn colour, is a striking landscape tree even before it produces edible seeds.

Although most commercial nut production centres on a few main crops, plenty of nut-bearing species grow well in temperate climates, including several with ornamental value that deserve more attention in edimental gardens. And a final note: many nuts, especially hazelnuts (*Corylus* spp.), sweet chestnuts (*Castanea sativa*) and pecans (*Carya illinoinensis*), take on an entirely different depth of flavour when roasted. Even a quick toast in a dry pan can transform them.

Here are a few excellent edimental nut crops:

- **Heartnut (*Juglans ailantifolia* var. *cordiformis*):** a Japanese walnut with sweet, mild-flavoured nuts in heart-shaped shells.
- **Pecan (*Carya illinoinensis*):** a staple of American orchards, known for its rich, buttery flavour; hardier cultivars can also be grown in parts of the UK and Europe.
- **Yellowhorn (*Xanthoceras sorbifolium*):** ornamental Chinese tree producing oil-rich edible seeds; also drought-tolerant and pollinator-friendly.

SEEDS

Some seeds are instantly recognisable in the kitchen, like sunflower, poppy and fennel, while others, such as grains, legumes or spice seeds, aren't always considered seeds at all. In an edimental context, they're often a bonus crop. You might grow a plant for its leaves, flowers or structure and then realise its seeds bring a second wave of value.

Some are strong in flavour, like lovage (*Levisticum officinale*), whose seeds taste like celery with a deeper, more aromatic kick. Others, like sweet cicely (*Myrrhis odorata*), offer soft, green liquorice-scented seeds used in teas, baking or infusions. Seeds can be eaten fresh, dried, sprouted, toasted or ground. Some add crunch or spice, and others can be used like small grains. Many of these plants are prolific self-seeders, bringing spontaneity to the planting. Once harvested, seeds store well, an easy way to stretch the bounty of the growing season into the colder months.

Here are a few excellent edimental seed crops:

- **Angelica (*Angelica archangelica*):** a biennial with strikingly architectural seeds that can be used sparingly in desserts and liqueurs.
- **Fennel (*Foeniculum vulgare*):** both leaf and seed have a sweet, aniseed flavour; seeds used in teas, baking and spice blends.
- **Sea kale (*Crambe maritima*):** bold foliage, edible shoots and seeds that can be added to a salad raw.

Angelica seedheads are sculptural in winter and delicious to cook with in the kitchen.

FLOWERS

Edible flowers bring more than just colour to a dish – they also bring flavour. Historically, flowers were eaten prolifically and not primarily for aesthetics, but because they tasted good. Some are punchy and aromatic, others mild and sweet, and certain flowers can even be used as substantial ingredients in their own right.

There's a huge range of edimentals with edible flowers. Some are best scattered over salads or desserts, while others, like daylilies (*Hemerocallis* spp.), can be stuffed, battered or stir-fried, much like a courgette flower. And while it's completely understandable to be hesitant about eating such a beautiful part of your garden, edible flowers often contain surprising levels of nutrients and phytochemicals, especially when eaten fresh. Beyond flavour, they add texture – crisp buds, soft petals, peppery bites – and most are excellent pollinator plants. Several also cross over into herbal teas and infusions, offering another way to enjoy their character and myriad health benefits..

EATING EDIMENTALS

Edible flowers bring a new dimension of flavour and colour to a dish, and, with so many common garden flowers being edible, they offer one of the most accessible ways to start eating from your garden.

Here are a few excellent edimental flowers:

Anise hyssop (*Agastache foeniculum*): aromatic spikes with a sweet anise flavour; lovely fresh or brewed as tea.
Chives (*Allium schoenoprasum*): bright pink pom-poms with a mild onion flavour; great in salads.
Red valerian (*Centranthus ruber*): clusters of tiny pink blooms; mildly sweet and good in savoury dishes.

SHOOTS & STEMS

When we talk about shoots, we're usually referring to the young, tender growth emerging from the ground in early spring. Asparagus (*Asparagus officinalis*) is the classic example, but many other plants produce edible shoots. These growth tips are typically high in nutrients, rich in vitamins, minerals and stored energy, and their tenderness makes them ideal for stir-frying, steaming or even eating raw. Some of the best edimental shoots come from bold, architectural plants like udo (*Aralia cordata*), whose thick, juicy stems are peeled and cooked. Others, like bamboo (*Phyllostachys* spp.), offer crisp, earthy shoots that must be cooked to remove bitterness.

Asparagus is one of the most successful edimentals and perennial food sources – a great example of delicious edible shoots.

In some cases, shoots also refer to the growing tips of leafy or climbing plants such as the tender, vine-like ends of hop shoots (*Humulus lupulus*), which are prized as a seasonal delicacy in parts of Europe. By contrast, in the context we are exploring in this book, stems, the main supporting structure of the plant, are less commonly eaten. Mature stems are usually too fibrous, though some can be enjoyed when harvested young and tender.

Here are a few excellent edimental shoots:

Black salsify (*Scorzonera hispanica*): not just a root crop – spring shoots, flower stems, flower buds and flowers are also edible.
Lovage (*Levisticum officinale*): tender early stems and leaf stalks with a bold, celery-like flavour (blanch for a milder taste).
Solomon's seal (*Polygonatum* spp.): young shoots resemble asparagus (*Asparagus officinalis*); traditionally eaten cooked in Korean cuisine.

LEAVES

Leaves are among the most useful and diverse parts of many edimental plants. They range from soft and delicate to bold and punchy, bringing a wide variety of textures and flavours to the kitchen. Some are perfect eaten raw, adding freshness to salads or scattered over a dish, while others are best cooked to soften fibres or mellow stronger, more bitter

Turkish rocket has delicious bitter leaves that are versatile and can be cooked in many ways – sauteed like spinach, added to stir-fries, or blanched and dressed with olive oil and lemon.

notes. Cooking can also reduce mild oxalates and other compounds that may affect taste or digestibility in some species.

Season and maturity make a difference. Many leaves are at their best in spring – tender, mild, and full of energy, such as sorrel (*Rumex acetosa*). Others become milder in flavour as they approach flowering, such as Turkish rocket (*Bunias orientalis*). Unlike fruiting crops, many leafy edimentals tolerate partial-to-full shade well, making them useful for the shadier parts of your garden.

Here are a few excellent edimental leaves:

- **Perennial wall rocket (*Diplotaxis tenuifolia*):** peppery, mustard-like leaves with a sharp bite; excellent for adding heat and depth to salads.
- **Saltbush (*Atriplex halimus*):** silvery, succulent leaves with a naturally salty flavour; great raw or lightly cooked.
- **Sedum (*Hylotelephium* spp.):** crisp, fleshy leaves with a refreshing crunch; best used sparingly in salads or as a garnish.

ROOTS & TUBERS

Roots and tubers are underground storage organs that provide the plant with energy. Some plants form thin, fibrous root systems, while others develop thickened roots or tubers that store starches and sugars. These are typically the ones we eat. We're familiar with annual crops like potatoes (*Solanum tuberosum*), which have been bred over centuries for large, uniform yields. Many edimentals produce smaller, more irregular tubers, but they often come in greater diversity and in more resilient, perennial forms. They also tend to face fewer pest pressures than conventional root crops, making them a great low-input alternative.

Here are a few excellent edimental roots and tubers:

Chinese yam (*Dioscorea polystachya*): climbing vine with long, nutrient-dense tubers; mild flavour and mucilaginous texture when cooked.
Oca (*Oxalis tuberosa*): colourful, tangy tubers; roasted, fried or sun-cured and eaten raw.
Arrowhead (*Sagittaria latifolia*): aquatic plant with crisp, starchy tubers; excellent boiled or stir-fried.

BULBS

We all know the classic spring bulbs – daffodils, snowdrops, bluebells – but not all bulbs are just for show. Many are edible. Technically, a bulb (or more broadly, a geophyte) is an underground storage organ made up of layers of modified leaves. These structures help plants survive seasonal extremes, especially cold or drought, and burst back into growth when conditions are right. That early surge of energy is part of

Oca tubers make for a great potato alternative, with a tangy, lemony flavour and jewel-like colours that bring visual delight to the plate.

what makes them so valuable in the edible garden. Many bulbous edimentals are among the first to appear in spring, offering beauty, food and pollinator support long before the rest of the garden wakes up.

Some are grown specifically for their bulbs, while others are harvested for their edible leaves, shoots or flowers, even though they originate from bulbs underground. Many can be layered beneath taller perennials, helping to maximise all the available ecological niches.

The allium family is where bulbs really shine. Stephen Barstow (see case study The Godfather of Edimentals in chapter 1) grows an astonishing four hundred-plus varieties (over one hundred species) in his garden at the botanical garden located down the road from his house. There's huge diversity in flavour, texture and use, from sulphurous hits to gentle sweetness – and some, like Babington's leek (*Allium ampeloprasum* var. *babingtonii*), multiply naturally by bulbils year after year. And not every edible bulb tastes like an onion: camassia (*Camassia quamash*), for instance, is mild and nutty, with a completely different character.

Here are a few excellent edimental bulbs:

- **Babington's leek (*Allium ampeloprasum* var. *babingtonii*):** perennial leek with edible bulbils and flower stalks; excellent for naturalising in low-maintenance gardens.
- **Camassia (*Camassia quamash*):** sweet, nutty bulbs (must be well-cooked); historically eaten by Indigenous peoples of North America.
- **Sand leek (*Allium scorodoprasum*):** a lightly garlicky flavour with slender bulbs and purple seedheads. Long valued in European cooking, its mild flavour suits salads, sautés and pickles.

Harvesting

I'm often asked how an edimental garden works if you're harvesting from it all the time. Doesn't that spoil the ornamental effect? It's a fair concern. The short answer is that it's absolutely possible to eat your way through an edimental garden while keeping it beautiful. It

Camassia is a well-loved ornamental yet overlooked these days as a potential food source.

210   EAT YOUR GARDEN

boils down to considered design and thoughtful management. Designing for successional planting is key. When interest is layered throughout the seasons, harvesting doesn't leave gaps or make the garden feel sparse. In fact, if designed well, one layer of planting steps in as another is harvested, maintaining structure and beauty even during peak productivity.

One of the many pleasures of working with edimentals is the rhythm of their harvests. Harvesting is a skill like anything else in gardening or cooking. It takes time to learn how much to take, when to take it and what methods work best. But most plants are forgiving, and, if you do overdo it, they usually bounce back.

The key is to harvest edimentals sensitively. Selective, staggered harvesting is key – 'little and often' is the mantra. Avoid taking too much in one go. There are various ways to harvest sensitively: you might take every other shoot, remove just a third of the leaves or flowers, harvest parts of plants instead of whole ones or take small amounts from across the entire garden so that no one spot ever looks stripped bare.

Another helpful technique is to cut certain plants back for a fresh flush of growth later in the season, treating them as 'cut and come again' plants. This is similar to a 'Chelsea Chop' – the practice of pruning a perennial back by 50 per cent around the time of the RHS Chelsea Flower Show at the end of May (hence the name). It encourages bushier, more compact growth and a later second flowering, extending the garden's season of interest.

In some cases, harvesting itself can trigger vigorous regrowth. But not all edimentals resprout in the same season, so getting to know the individual habits of your plants will help a great deal. You can also mix in some self-seeding annuals by sowing directly into any bare soil that appears. This fills gaps, builds a long-term seed bank and adds a welcome sense of dynamism to the planting. Likewise, allowing some perennials to self-seed keeps the garden evolving. Over time, older, tired-looking plants are naturally replaced by their offspring, echoing the rhythms of natural ecosystems and aligning the garden with ecological processes. This creates a more resilient planting scheme, one that we, as gardeners, help to guide rather than control.

Some crops, like fruit and nuts, will come in larger flushes, and, if you've planted trees or shrubs that fruit at the same time, you might find yourself with more than you can use. Other edimentals will offer multiple edible parts across the year – leaves in spring, roots in winter – and each of those has its own window. The trick is observation, learning how to spot when something is just right. Many of us have likely seen blackberries (*Rubus fruticosus*) where one week they are ripe for the picking, only a week later to be disappointed that we missed the narrow window. But there's always next year, and some of the best lessons come from the crops that got away.

Try not to worry. If you do get a bit overzealous and eat your way through your borders, most edimental plantings will bounce back. A well-designed scheme is resilient and should be able to take what you throw at it, within reason. You'll learn as you go, and there's no fixed rule on how much to harvest, or when. It varies from garden to garden. How intensively you can harvest is also greatly influenced by your climate and soil fertility, as this determines how vigorously your plants are growing. Manage your harvest based on your needs, your taste and the unique conditions.

FRUITS, NUTS & SEEDS

For most fruits, nuts and seeds, the key is to harvest when fully ripe, but getting the timing (and the access) right can be a challenge. Fruit trees can be grafted onto dwarf rootstocks to keep them at a manageable height, and this comes with its advantages and disadvantages. Others, especially larger nut trees, can place the best of the crop well out of reach. Shaking branches, using poles or ladders, or laying nets underneath can all help with collection.

Wildlife, of course, is another factor. Many birds, squirrels and mice love these crops as much as we do. In parts of the UK with high grey squirrel populations, getting a decent nut harvest may be nearly impossible unless you've netted the tree (not easy if it's already 6 metres tall and growing). For many gardeners, the most realistic strategy is simply to plant more than you need and accept that a share will go to the local wildlife.

Seeds are usually harvested after flowering, once the pods have dried down or started to split. Some can be snipped off easily, while others may want to be shaken from the plant or collected in bags or trays. As with fruit, some seeds and nuts continue ripening off the plant if picked at the right stage, although others, like pine nuts, must be harvested just before the cone opens and drops them.

Whatever you're gathering, harvesting in dry weather helps reduce spoilage, and collecting in stages over a few days often yields better results than trying to gather everything at once. Many fruits can be eaten fresh or cooked, but also lend themselves well to preserving – frozen, dried, or made into jams and leathers. Nuts and seeds, if harvested and cured properly, can often be stored for months, giving you nourishment long after the growing season has passed. Once dried, seeds can be stored for extended periods in glass jars. Nuts vary widely

in how they need to be processed. Some, like hazelnuts, just need cracking by hand or with a simple nutcracker. Others may require heavier-duty equipment or more time-intensive work. Nuts like acorns (*Quercus* spp.) need soaking or leaching to remove tannins before they're edible, so always check what preparation is required before diving in.

Dried seeds can be kept for a long period of time and provide valuable nutrition during less fruitful months.

FLOWERS

With edible flowers, freshness is everything. Most are best harvested in the morning once the dew has dried, but before the day's heat causes wilting. Pick only what you'll use, ideally just before serving, as they often don't store well, wilting quickly and losing both flavour and visual appeal. If needed, a damp cloth-lined container in the fridge can buy you a few extra hours, but most are best enjoyed straight from the garden.

You can either harvest whole flowers or just the petals, depending on the plant and how you plan to use them. In many cases, it's actually better to take the whole flower head as this often encourages new blooms to grow, just as

Harvesting an abundance all at once gives the opportunity to dry flowers, foliage or roots and make herbal teas (as with the chamomile flowers here).

deadheading faded flowers does, too. A sharp snip down to the next bud is usually best practice. In contrast, some plant stems only flower once per season.

While it's easy to get carried away, it's worth harvesting with a light touch across the garden. Take only a few whole flower heads each from across many plants, rather than all the blooms from just one or two plants. Doing so helps preserve the garden's structure and aesthetic and keeps it feeling full and alive, even after you've gathered a bowlful. Some edible flowers also dry beautifully and can be saved for later use. Chamomile (*Chamaemelum nobile*), bee balm (*Monarda didyma*) and anise hyssop (*Agastache foeniculum*) all make great herbal teas. Dry them in a warm, dark, well-ventilated space, then store in clean glass jars for use throughout the year.

SHOOTS & STEMS

Most edible shoots are only harvestable for a window, usually early in the season, when they're still tender and packed with energy. If left too long, they become fibrous or woody, losing their appeal. Harvesting for a window also ensures the longevity of the plant. Harvesting shoots too late or for too long can weaken the plant and interrupt its seasonal cycle. A good example is asparagus (*Asparagus officinalis*), which is typically harvested only until the summer solstice. After that, it's left to grow tall and fern out, photosynthesising, restoring energy and ensuring next year's crop.

Shoots like those of bamboo (*Phyllostachys* spp.), hop (*Humulus lupulus*) or Solomon's seal (*Polygonatum* spp.) follow a similar pattern. You're aiming to catch them young, before they elongate and toughen. Use a clean, sharp knife to cut them just above soil level, or gently twist and pull if they detach easily. Some shoots, like bamboo, may need peeling, while others, such as asparagus, benefit from snapping off the fibrous base before

Bamboo shoots are a widely eaten plant in many parts of the world.

cooking or eating. Because shoots are so full of water, they're best eaten fresh. If you do need to store them, wrap them in a damp cloth or put in a breathable container in the fridge, and use them within a day or two. It's worth harvesting lightly so you don't weaken the plant long-term. A little goes a long way, and even a handful of shoots can bring a lot to a dish.

LEAVES

As a general rule, I aim to take no more than a third of the plant's total leaf mass at any one time, enough for a good handful without compromising its ability to keep growing. This works especially well if you grow small groups of the same plant, allowing you to pick lightly across many rather than heavily from a few.

As with flowers, morning is generally the best time to harvest, when leaves are still plump with moisture and haven't wilted in the heat of the day. You can snip with scissors, twist gently or pinch by hand, depending on the plant. Many edimentals respond well to a 'cut and come again' approach. Once harvested, you can give the leaves a rinse to remove any grit or insects, then spin or pat dry. Most are best used fresh, but, if you want to store them, wrap in a damp cloth or keep in a sealed container in the fridge. For longer-term storage, some edimental leaves freeze well after blanching – for example, sea kale (*Crambe maritima*), sorrel (*Rumex acetosa*) and perennial kales (*Brassica oleracea* Acephala Group). Briefly dunk them in boiling water, then plunge them into cold water to stop the cooking. Dry thoroughly, then freeze in portions for use later in the year.

ROOTS, TUBERS & BULBS

Roots and tubers can often be dug as needed through autumn and winter, especially in milder climates. In colder regions where the ground freezes, it's best to lift them earlier, before the soil hardens and access becomes difficult. Try to harvest on a dry day if possible. Wet soil clings to everything, making roots harder to clean and more prone to rot.

Some vigorous species, like Jerusalem artichoke (*Helianthus tuberosus*), are notoriously persistent; once established, they'll regrow from whatever tubers are left behind. Others benefit from a gentler touch. You might choose to lift just a section of a clump or dig up the entire plant and replant a few tubers elsewhere for the next season. Many growers treat these as 'replant perennials' – harvest, select the best and return a portion to the soil.

Bulbs are typically lifted once the above-ground foliage has died back and the plant has entered dormancy. You can take just a few, or lift the whole clump and replant a portion, depending on how prolific

Jerusalem artichokes, one of my favourite root crops, signal the coming of autumn. They are delicious in rich, velvety soups or roasted to bring out their sweet, nutty flavour.

the species is and how much of it you want to preserve. After harvest, store roots and bulbs in a cool, dark and well-ventilated place, ideally in boxes or crates. Check periodically and remove anything that shows signs of shrivelling or rot.

Some need only a rinse and a scrub before eating, while others require more effort. Camassia (*Camassia quamash*), for example, must be cooked thoroughly to make it digestible. Others, like the perennial vegetable oca (*Oxalis tuberosa*), can be eaten raw but benefit from sun-curing to improve sweetness and texture. Peeling may help with thicker-skinned types, but often the skins contain a lot of nutrient content, so I avoid peeling whenever possible. Soaking is sometimes useful to mellow bitterness or draw out tannins, depending on the species.

Practical Tips for Eating Edimentals

Learning to cook with edimentals doesn't need to be complicated. These tips are designed to help you get started and build confidence, laying strong foundations and exploring how you can weave edimentals into your everyday kitchen habits.

Edimentals as Stand-Ins

To make things easy, here are some of mine and Stephen Barstow's favourite edimentals that can be used as direct substitutes for common ingredients. These are great entry points and simple swaps that don't require any change in how you cook, just a bit of curiosity about what you grow. Most are plants not often grown for their edible qualities, but they work brilliantly as low-input, perennial alternatives to conventional annuals.

Asparagus / Lettuce ⟶ Hosta (*Hosta* spp.) Spring shoots resemble asparagus; mature yet fresh leaves can be used in place of lettuce.

Baby leeks ⟶ Bamboo (*Phyllostachys* spp. / *Bambusa* spp.) Shoots must be cooked; earthy, nutty flavour when young.

Celery ⟶ Korean celery (*Dystaenia takesimana*) Strong, aromatic flavour; use sparingly in soups, stews or salads.

Chives ⟶ Mouse garlic (*Allium angulosum*) Attractive pink pom-poms with a mild onion kick.

Chives / Garlic ⟶ Sand leek (*Allium scorodoprasum*) Dense flower heads; rich, sulphurous flavour.

Crab apple / Lemon ⟶ Japanese quince (*Chaenomeles japonica*) Aromatic, tart fruits; great in jams, jellies or slow-cooked dishes. A great cool climate citrus alternative.

Cress / Rocket ⟶ Broad-leaved cuckoo flower (*Cardamine raphanifolia*) Peppery leaves and flowers, ideal in salads, sandwiches or as a garnish.

Garlic ⟶ Wild garlic / Ramsons (*Allium ursinum*) Mild, garlicky leaves and flower buds; use fresh or wilted in place of garlic or garlic chives. Makes great pesto.

Gooseberries ⟶ Fuchsia (*Fuchsia* spp.) Tangy berries and edible flowers.

Green beans / Baby corn ⟶ Daylily (*Hemerocallis* spp.) Crisp flower buds and shoots; use stir-fried, stuffed or tempura-style.

Kale / Spinach ⟶ Sochan (*Rudbeckia laciniata*) Abundant perennial green; can be cooked like chard or kale.

Lettuce ⟶ Greater musk mallow (*Malva alcea*) Mild-flavoured leaves ideal for raw salads or steaming.

Many leafy greens can be swapped out for a variety of edimentals, such as daylily, Turkish rocket, wild garlic and mitsuba, offering alternatives to common vegetables such as spinach, lettuce or kale, while adding new flavours, textures and colours to the plate.

New potatoes ⟶ **Oca (*Oxalis tuberosa*)** Tangy, colourful tubers work well roasted, fried or cured in sun and eaten raw.

Onion ⟶ **Golden garlic (*Allium moly*)** Decorative and edible; use bulbs or flowers.

Parsley ⟶ **Alexanders (*Smyrnium olusatrum*)** Bold, slightly bitter flavour; leaves, stems and flowers all edible.

Potatoes / Jerusalem artichokes ⟶ **Dahlia (*Dahlia* spp.)** Crunchy, mildly sweet tubers.

Salsify / Parsnip ⟶ **Black salsify (*Scorzonera hispanica*)** Sweet, earthy root; good boiled, mashed or roasted.

Shallots / Spring onions ⟶ **St. John's onion (*Allium × cornutum*)** A resilient perennial with mild onion flavour and early spring greens.

Spinach ⟶ **Caucasian spinach (*Hablitzia tamnoides*)** Climbing perennial with soft, mild leaves; thrives in shade.

Spinach / Mild salad greens ⟶ **Bladder campion (*Silene vulgaris*)** Tender, mild-flavoured leaves with edible balloon-like flowers.

Salads

Edimentals offer salad options in every season and far more variety than the handful of leaves we're used to. You'll find greens that are peppery, lemony, bitter and sweet, and flowers that add crunch, colour and delicacy. Diversity is the aim. Stephen's legendary fifty-species (and occasionally over five hundred-species!) salads are a real inspiration. But most of us aren't likely to go that far, myself included. Even just five different edimentals can turn a basic salad into something entirely your own.

Cuckoo flower (*Cardamine pratensis*): Peppery, cress-like leaves and lilac-pink flowers; lovely in early spring.

Drumstick primula (*Primula denticulata*): Bold flower clusters in spring with a mild flavour and subtle floral notes.

Stephen (aka 'The Extreme Salad Man') strikes again

Few-flowered garlic (*Allium paradoxum*): Onion-flavoured shoots and mild flowers.

Giant bellflower (*Campanula latifolia*): Tender young leaves and edible flowers. Can self-seed and spread, so monitor in small gardens. Native to Europe and Asia; introduced and occasionally naturalised in parts of North America. Check local guidance and be careful not to confuse with creeping bellflower (C. rapunculoides), a different invasive species.

Oxlip (*Primula elatior*): Soft yellow blooms with a mild, sweet flavour.

Primrose (*Primula vulgaris*): Delicate edible flowers for colour and garnish.

Sorrel (*Rumex acetosa* 'Abundance'): While not the most attractive plant, you can't beat the lemony and tangy punch of sorrel. Its leaves are great raw (in moderation).

Spring beauty (*Claytonia virginica*): Succulent leaves and tiny, flowers; mild and refreshing.

Sweet cicely (*Myrrhis odorata*): Soft ferny leaves with a sweet aniseed flavour; excellent contrast to sharper greens.

Witloof chicory (*Cichorium intybus* 'Witloof'): Crisp, bitter leaves; adds texture and edge to winter salads.

Fermenting

Many edimentals lend themselves beautifully to fermentation, pickling and preserving. These techniques not only extend the season they can be eaten but also unlock entirely new flavour dimensions. They're also a brilliant way to support your gut microbiome. Many edimentals are rich in phytonutrients and

Pickling and fermenting are great ways to extend the life of edimentals and boost your gut microbiome in the process.

There are herbal teas for all occasions. Growing your own edimental teas and drying for future use is a rewarding process.

EAT YOUR GARDEN

natural sugars. The process of fermentation can increase nutrient availability and add depth, tang and complexity to everyday meals.

Here are some classic ferments with an edimental twist:

Kimchi: Korea's famous ferment. Begin with wild cabbage (*Brassica oleracea*) or combinations of leafy greens, then layer in spices, garlic, ginger and chilli for flavour and heat.
Pickles: Great for preserving individual elements like wild garlic flower buds (*Allium ursinum*), hosta shoots (*Hosta* spp.) or young gomchwi stems (*Ligularia fischeri*). Try quick vinegar pickles or long brine ferments for more probiotic benefits.
Sauerkraut: A simple fermentation using chopped perennial veg – most of the edimentals we've already explored will work well. Add salt, pack into jars and let it ferment naturally.

Teas

Being British and loving a cup of tea, herbal teas are one of the main ways I bring edimentals into everyday life. It's such a simple way to add diversity to your diet – full of flavour, easy to make and a lovely ritual in itself. A handful of leaves or flowers from the garden can become a calming brew, a digestive aid or just a moment of pause in the day.

Here are some of my favourite herbal edimentals for tea:

Bee balm (*Monarda didyma*): Minty and floral; great fresh or dried.
Goldenrod (*Solidago* spp.): Lightly spicy with a hint of honey; supportive for colds and allergies.
Lemon balm (*Melissa officinalis*): Bright and lemony with a relaxing, mellow finish.
Lemon verbena (*Aloysia citrodora*): Fresh, citrusy and calming.
Lime tree flowers (*Tilia* spp.): Sweet and soothing; a classic for calming nerves.
Yarrow (*Achillea millefolium*): Aromatic and gently bitter; traditionally used to support digestion.

Cooking with edimentals is less a set of rules and more a practice. As we've seen, a garden can become a pantry, a classroom and a daily ritual – provided we stay curious and careful with identification and preparation. Their potential, though, reaches far beyond our kitchens and even beyond our gardens. As we move to the conclusion of *Eat Your Garden*, we'll explore how this way of thinking can spill into the wider world, transforming the spaces we share and the communities we shape.

Conclusion

Beyond the Garden

We've explored how edimentals can transform how we design and plant gardens, but what happens when we take that thinking beyond the garden gate? There's enormous potential for these plants to play a wider role in our schools, on our streets and in the shared spaces that knit our communities together. In this final chapter, I want to explore what that might look like. Where do those opportunities lie? And who are the pioneers already making this happen?

Bringing Edimentals Indoors

The first opportunity takes us from the great outdoors into the comfort of our homes. It might seem an unexpected place to begin growing edible plants, but it is one of the most untapped and accessible frontiers. Not all of us are fortunate enough to have a garden or

Biophilic design principles are being embraced in my home through this oversized palm anchoring the landing and reaching toward the skylight above – a daily reminder of our innate need for and connection to nature.

outside space, so this offers a universal way for all of us to grow edimentals at home regardless of space. From lemon trees (*Citrus × limon*) in sunlit kitchens to chillies (*Capsicum annuum*) on a windowsill, or creeping vanilla orchids (*Vanilla planifolia*) trained along shelves, edible houseplants reconnect us to nature, offering food, beauty and environmental benefits even in the smallest of spaces. They add flavour, fragrance and life to our homes, while also improving air quality and well-being.

Biophilic Design & the Need for Natural Complexity

Beyond their productive benefits, edimental houseplants tap into something much deeper: our innate connection to the natural world. As humans, we evolved over hundreds of thousands of years in environments rich in sensory diversity. Whether moving through open grasslands, dense forests or along riversides, we were constantly surrounded by layers of plant life, shifting light, changing temperatures and a vast array of natural stimuli.

In those settings, our senses were fully engaged – long views across landscapes helped us spot threats and opportunities, while close-up interactions with plants, soil and water stimulated our brains in natural and essential ways. Fast-forward to today, and most of us spend our lives in spaces that strip away that richness. The modern home – a series of smooth, flat surfaces, blank walls, artificial lighting and climate-controlled air – offers security and comfort, but it removes the natural complexity that is a fundamental part of what makes us human.

This is where biophilic design comes in. It's a concept rooted in the idea that we thrive when we're surrounded by nature. By integrating natural elements into architecture, interiors and our cities, it aims to restore the complexity and sensory richness we've lost. This idea echoes the growing interest in foraging and the broader movement towards a more nature-connected lifestyle, as we explored in chapter 1. Houseplants play a key role in biophilic design. They soften spaces, introduce texture and movement and create a more dynamic, nourishing environment. In my own home, I've embraced this fully. It's filled with houseplants, many of them edimentals, and the difference is tangible. They make the space feel more alive, more human – even if my wife occasionally rolls her eyes when I'm away and she's left in charge of the watering.

A Layered Approach

Drawing on the same planting design principles we explored in chapter 6, edimentals indoors can be arranged in layers to create a rich,

The fresh scent of citrus trees brings a sensory experience to a sunny room.

CONCLUSION

immersive environment. These layers can be applied within a single container or across a whole room.

- **Tree & Shrub Layer:** Compact fruiting trees and shrubs add structure and height to indoor spaces, making them ideal centrepieces in a bright room. Consider dwarf citrus (*Citrus* spp.), pomegranate (*Punica granatum*) or coffee (*Coffea arabica*).
- **Mid-Tall Perennials:** Plants like Vietnamese coriander (*Persicaria odorata*), lemongrass (*Cymbopogon citratus*) or chillies (*Capsicum* spp.) thrive indoors, offering seasonal fruiting interest and fresh leaves year-round.
- **Low / Groundcover:** Edimentals like Cuban oregano (*Plectranthus amboinicus*) or gotu kola (*Centella asiatica*) make an excellent lower layer.
- **Climbers:** Peppercorn vines (*Piper nigrum*) or passionfruit (*Passiflora edulis*) can be trained up cupboards, shelves or along walls with wire supports, making full use of vertical space.

Rethinking How We Live with Plants

As urbanisation continues to accelerate (with nearly 70 per cent of us living in cities by 2050) and access to green space becomes more precious, the growing presence of houseplants in our homes isn't a coincidence.[1] It's a response to an increasingly disconnected world. We seek out greenery not just for decoration, but for the sense of calm and connection it brings.

A major theme in my work is blurring the boundaries between inside and outside. My clients who live in highly urban environments often feel the strains of city life and look to their living spaces as a way to reconnect with nature. Whether by integrating plants indoors, designing gardens as extensions of their home or simply ensuring there is greenery in view, this desire for a stronger link to the natural world is clear.

Edimental houseplants take this further. They invite us to reframe the role of interior plants in our daily lives. They demonstrate that food growing doesn't have to be confined to gardens or allotments but can be woven seamlessly into the spaces where we live and work. The more we bring nature into our homes, the more we restore something fundamental: our connection to growing, to seasonality and to the sensory richness that has shaped us for millennia.

Case Study
Edimentals in the Public Realm
FOODWAY, BRONX, NEW YORK

Tucked against the mouth of the Bronx River, New York City, hemmed in by three looping highways, an old concrete plant is now teeming with life. Chestnuts (*Castanea* spp.) throw dappled shade, bee balm (*Monarda* spp.) hums with pollinators, serviceberries (*Amelanchier* spp.) give architectural form and groups of children gather herbs for sun tea and tinctures. 'We're a little oasis in the centre of the three highways that surround us and the beautiful river that runs right through,' says Nathan Hunter of NYC Parks. It's an edible commons, where food and beauty act as civic glue – a public landscape that invites people back to nature through taste and community spirit.

This ground had to be reclaimed before it could be cultivated. Concrete Plant Park was literally won by its neighbours – youth protests, riverside rallies, even a papier-mâché cement truck blocking a local road all caused a stir before the site was formalised through a New York Parks and nonprofit partnership that kept community at its heart. 'This space was a grassroots, community-activated, fought-for park,' Nathan explains. Its edible theme emerged later, when the floating food forest and art installation 'SWALE' docked here in 2016–17, a barge of fruit trees and edimentals that proved what an edible public space could feel like in a city where on-land foraging is prohibited. 'Technically, you're not allowed to forage within New York City Parks,' he says, 'so this became the first place you can practise without being fearful of getting a ticket.'

Foodway at Concrete Plant Park, New York City – the first edible public park in the city – features a food forest, layered edimental planting, annual vegetable beds and a restored meadow that enhances biodiversity while inviting the public to forage and reconnect with nature.

CONCLUSION

Today, the site is a haven for food, featuring a designed forest garden that spills out into an acre of edible meadow for trained foragers, plus a modest raised-bed garden. Throughout, the plant palette is built on edimentals, and Nathan values them highly for their low-input nature, high yield and visual delight. One replicable planting combination features chestnut (*Castanea* spp.) as a canopy, witch hazel (*Hamamelis* spp.) in the understorey, and lamb's ear (*Stachys byzantina*) and violets (*Viola* spp.) knitting the ground together. Elder (*Sambucus nigra*) and chokeberry (*Aronia melanocarpa*) edge the paths while goldenrod (*Solidago* spp.), swamp milkweed (*Asclepias incarnata*) and native grasses act as pollinator magnets. With warming winters, pawpaws (*Asimina triloba*), persimmons (*Diospyros* spp.) and figs (*Ficus carica*) are becoming staples. 'For years, we didn't have squirrels, skunks or raccoons.' Nathan smiles. 'Now the park is filled with them. That tells you the system's working.'

The gardens are host to a weekly and seasonal rhythm of community sessions. On Tuesdays and Fridays, stewardship groups

Edimentals, medicinal plants, traditional annual vegetables and ornamentals are woven together in a tapestry of beautiful plantings across the park.

open with light training and harvesting in the morning, then shift into making in the afternoon: bundling smudge sticks, blending teas, drying leaves for syrups. A DJ might be playing tunes as jars of sun tea line a table and children prune with guidance and learn how to shape plants with care. 'Consistent community activities have always focused on exercise and wellness,' Nathan says. 'During those sessions, foraging is a constant theme.' Resident herbalists lead medicine-making workshops, focusing in on edimentals and teaching about their cultural and medicinal uses. 'It's a great training ground,' Nathan explains, 'especially for young entrepreneurs, often single mums, to practise without retribution from the New York foraging laws.' Local chefs and foragers co-lead, too – paid where budgets allow, supported in kind when they don't. 'We're building a small-business directory,' Nathan adds, 'so this becomes a platform for economic opportunity.'

Seasonal events are aligned with key moments in the gardening calendar. In spring, the Mugwort Celebration flips an invasive 'problem' plant into a beloved tradition. The event ends with mugwort mochi (a

A vibrant example of community agency, the Bronx River Foodway shows the power of people coming together through food, beauty and shared stewardship. It redefines public space as a place of nourishment, culture and ecological restoration.

Korean sticky rice cake flavoured with wild herbs) shared alongside tea and stories. In autumn, the Community Banquet is a highlight – a bustling event with chefs cooking Foodway harvests, local vendors setting up shop and nature-based art made from fallen twigs and seedheads. This isn't a programme delivered to the community – it's built by them. Foodway's ethos is to try things, see what works and repeat what resonates.

That rhythm of participation is made possible by practical infrastructure. Bindweed (*Calystegia* spp.) has to be pulled again and again. Invasive weeds become teaching moments. Mulching is consistent, with 18-metre (20-yard) woodchip drops from NYC arborist operations and compost made on-site used to cover soil and suppress weeds. 'Consider the practicalities of maintenance when you're establishing a community garden. Where's your water source? Where do trucks drop mulch? A 3-foot, accessible path changes everything,' Nathan advises. 'Wheel-friendly paths, hose access and a pad for pop-up shelters turn occasional visitors into dedicated stewards. There are some days we have over fifty volunteers helping with seasonal tasks, and well-designed infrastructure makes all of that possible.'

The Bronx River Foodway wouldn't be possible without a strong and well-organised governance pattern that shares power. It's a big part of why the project endures. Day-to-day care is led by the project coordinator, Nathan, and a seasonal gardener, working hand-in-hand with the Bronx River Alliance staff and members of local 'Friends of Concrete Plant Park' groups. Strategy and programming run through the open Foodway Team, with elected co-chairs and a wide support base. 'Anyone can pop into our monthly meeting to see what's going on and how to support,' Nathan explains. 'I'm watching people and cultivating the next co-chairs. We have an election every February, followed by time to train them. Then they hit the ground running.' Mini-grants and micro-honoraria are used to recognise labour when funding allows. When budgets are tight, reciprocity keeps things moving – whether through space, introductions, shared tools or plants. The outcome is a place shaped with, not delivered to, its community.

'The social impact is best told through people,' Nathan says. He shares the story of

CONCLUSION

Journei Bimwala, who has lived locally since her teens and, in the past decade, found the Foodway. She began showing up to steward the site; Nathan encouraged her to step into the Friends-of group and claim the space. From there, Journei started leading her home-schooling classes in the Foodway, joined the team, and helped shape its programming. She also built a foraged drinks business drawing on the park's edimentals, rooted in herbal knowledge and community support. 'We're not really shown what liberation can look like,' Nathan reflects. 'Journei showed what that looks like; finding this space gave her direction and enabled her to leverage opportunities for her family.' That arc – from showing up, to being seen, to leading – matters here more than any harvest tally. 'I track engagement, usership and outreach to tell the story of Foodway,' he adds. 'It's much better than pounds of produce.'

There are hard truths. Funding ebbs and flows. Volunteers, though essential, need training and guidance; good intentions can snap branches or pull out desirable edimentals. Urban soils demand testing and build-up before planting food. Land tenure is fragile; the climate now swings between drought and deluge. 'Parks are catch-alls for wicked problems,' Nathan says. 'Running a project like this will throw many challenges at you. My best advice is to be patient with the process, be detached from the issues and be compassionate with the people. Wake up the next day and do it again.'

If you wanted to start something like this where you live, you wouldn't need a barge or a whole public park. You'd need a sliver of land or a willing land partner (city, school, developer, faith group), and a clear agreement that harvesting will be welcomed and taught. Begin with one weekly stewardship window and a seasonal celebration. Plant for resilience and cultural meaning – your version of the Foodway's chestnut (*Castanea* spp.) plant combination. Create a foraging protocol. Pull weeds, add mulch and welcome anyone willing to get involved. Start small, make it public and let it grow.

The Bronx Foodway has changed the lives of many in the surrounding neighbourhood and leaves a legacy beyond its boundaries. It has sparked new food forests across the city, helped normalise edible plantings in public space and connected dozens of groups through shared work. But it also clarifies what a community garden isn't. 'It's not raised beds or a specific layout,' Nathan says. 'It's a place where people are seen, exchange skills and share resources. We make the unfamiliar familiar, and the familiar accessible – together – through planting, management and reciprocity.' The plants are the medium; the people are at the core of this garden.

The Foodway stands as proof that edible, beautiful, biodiverse planting belongs in the public realm, and that food is a generous gateway to nature connection at all scales. You don't need to own a garden or piece of land to feel it. Join a stewardship session at your nearest community plot. Volunteer. Co-lead. Or start a tiny Foodway on the edge of a park or an abandoned strip of land. If there's one takeaway from my visit to the Foodway, it was a sense of what becomes possible when food, people and place come together. If a former concrete plant flanked by highways can grow chestnuts and community, there's every possibility that an oasis of edible beauty can take root wherever you live.

School Gardens: Inspiring the Next Generation

Access to nature is a fundamental right every child should enjoy. And yet, access to green space remains unequally distributed. Many children grow up without the chance to build those deep connections to the living world. School gardens offer a way to democratise that access. With most children attending school, embedding food growing and nature connection into the school environment ensures more young people get the chance to plant a seed, nurture it and watch it grow.

Why Edimentals in School Gardens

Creating outdoor edible classrooms and growing edimentals helps foster future environmental stewards, children who understand their place within ecological systems and feel invested in protecting them. These spaces also enhance learning across the curriculum. Edible classrooms aren't just about gardening or science. They can bring lessons in maths, literacy, geography and art to life. Through the process of growing, observing and tasting, children come to understand the interdependence of knowledge, the importance of systems thinking and the richness of hands-on learning.

Creating an Edible Classroom

Employing the same layered, ecological approach to planting design, we can develop a palette of plants that is particularly child-friendly, one that features sweet and sour flavours, unusual textures and bright colours. The plants listed below are

An outdoor edible classroom at the Beacon Primary School, Liverpool, UK. One of the two school gardens created from the relocation of the 'School Food Matters' RHS Chelsea Flower show garden.

CONCLUSION

Honeyberry fruits ripening to a beautiful blueberry-like colour. They have a sweet, tangy flavour that makes them especially popular with children. They're easy to pick, delicious to eat straight from the bush and one of the first fruits of summer.

suggestions to engage children's senses and curiosity; they are not intended as a complete planting design. Instead, planting combinations can be drawn on to create full planting schemes for outdoor edible classrooms. Many will thrive in varying environments and require thoughtful placement depending on site and climate, but each offers something special to the edible learning experience.

TREE & SHRUB LAYER

Apple (*Malus domestica*): Familiar, seasonal fruit; perfect for storytelling and harvest-time activities.

Honeyberry (*Lonicera caerulea*): Early fruiting and tasty; ripens alongside strawberries.

Japanese pepper (*Zanthoxylum piperitum*): Sparkling, tongue-tingling flavour; a playful sensory experience.

STRUCTURAL & EMERGENT

Jerusalem artichoke (*Helianthus tuberosus*): Tall plant in the sunflower family with underground tubers; fun to dig and harvest.

Lovage (*Levisticum officinale*): Tall, architectural herb with a bold celery-like flavour and edible leaves, stems and seeds.

Sea kale (*Crambe maritima*): Striking glaucous leaves, early shoots and dramatic flower heads.

MID-LAYER & SEASONAL HITS

Anise hyssop (*Agastache foeniculum*): Liquorice flavour, attractive to pollinators and highly sensory.

Baldmoney (*Meum athamanticum*): Aromatic, feathery foliage with a sweet aniseed scent; also has edible roots similar to parsnip.

Lovage marches skywards, reaching awe-inspiring heights. Children love it for its towering scale and the strong, celery-like scent released when they brush against its leaves.

Anise hyssop engages children with its unique liquorice flavour.

Dainty flowers of wood sorrel create a magical carpet in woodland-style plantings.

Society garlic (*Tulbaghia violacea*): Mild garlic flavour with edible leaves and flowers; less pungent than traditional garlic or chives and attractive to pollinators.

LOW / GROUNDCOVER

Salad burnet (*Sanguisorba minor*): Rosette-forming perennial with small, cucumber-flavoured leaves; great in salads and holds well as an attractive, low edging plant.

Wild strawberry (*Fragaria vesca*): Small and sweet, spreading habit, perfect for covering soil.

Wood sorrel (*Oxalis acetosella*): Sour lemony leaves; children love the tangy taste.

CLIMBERS

Grape vine (*Vitis* spp.): Familiar fruit and interesting seasonal change; encourages vertical engagement.

Hardy kiwi (*Actinidia arguta*): Climbing vine producing smooth-skinned, sweet, mini kiwis; fun to grow and harvest.

Hops (*Humulus lupulus*): Fast-growing, textural climber with great architectural quality when grown up posts.

The rapid growth of hops makes them an enchanting climber for an edible classroom.

Case Study
Edible Classrooms
ALEC REED ACADEMY

In 2023, Alec Reed Academy, a bustling urban school in west London, was selected from a long list of applicants to become the new home of our RHS Chelsea Flower Show 'School Food Matters Garden'. What set them apart wasn't their plot, it was their commitment. Here was a school ready to welcome a new garden not simply as a beautifully planted space, but as a living, breathing classroom, with staff determined to embed it into the everyday life of the school.

'When we first heard about the project, we had no idea of the scale or opportunity,' recalls Katie, assistant headteacher of the primary school. 'But as soon as the children got involved – sketching their own designs, sharing their ideas – the excitement was electric.' After the buzz of Chelsea and the on-site build at the school, the garden became something much more than a beautiful space. It became an environment where learning, play, nature and creativity converge.

Today, the edible classroom hums with life. Science lessons unfold among the habitats hidden under logs; design and technology students harvest handfuls of herbs for soups they cook from scratch; even the rammed earth walls have taken on unexpected magic, helping children imagine the cool, textured surfaces of ancient Egyptian tombs. On sunny days, students scramble over the garden's boulders, delve their hands into the earth or rub the sensory, nonedible cola plant (*Artemisia maritima* 'Coca-Cola') leaves between their fingers, their faces lighting up at the fizzy, unexpected scent.

> What if every school had an outdoor edible classroom? The power of outdoor learning and nature connection through food is showcased here in Alec Reed Academy.

CONCLUSION

The weekly gardening club offers more than just horticultural skills. 'It's incredible to see which children are drawn to the space,' Katie says. 'We have one boy who struggles with classroom work, yet out here he absolutely comes alive. He's the "chief weeder", confidently guiding his classmates and proudly sharing what he knows. It's given him a place to shine and transformed his school life.'

Of course, creating and sustaining a garden in a busy, time-poor school isn't without its challenges. Early on, Katie found herself watering at lunchtimes, rallying staff and fundraising for gloves, tools and seeds. There were practical challenges to overcome, too: managing weeds, supervising children safely, deciding which plants could be harvested and eaten. But the garden's layered, edimental planting has proven to be a perfect fit for a resource-poor environment like a school. 'Once established, it really looks after itself,' says Jonathan, the school's newly appointed outdoor learning lead. Edimentals like globe artichokes (*Cynara cardunculus* Scolymus Group), society garlic (*Tulbaghia violacea*) and wild strawberries (*Fragaria vesca*) thrive with minimal input, while pollinator-friendly perennials create a sensory-rich ecosystem that holds its own through the seasons.

Perhaps most importantly, the garden democratises access to nature. 'Many of our children don't have gardens at home,' Katie reflects. 'School is the great leveller – here, every child has a chance to plant a seed, get their hands dirty and experience the magic of watching something grow.'

That magic has sparked something even bigger. Inspired by the success of the edible classroom, the school received funding for an ambitious new venture: transforming four acres of adjoining land into an urban community farm. Jonathan leads this new chapter, which includes an orchard, raised beds, wildflower meadows, special needs gardening spaces and plans for chickens, bees and even pigs. And the vision stretches beyond the school gates. 'We want this to be a place for the whole community,' says Jonathan, 'somewhere families can come, where local schools can visit, where we can grow food not just for learning, but for sharing.'

When asked what advice she would give other schools, Katie is clear: 'This kind of edimental, layered garden works really well; it's low maintenance, hardy and largely looks after itself. It adds an extra layer of richness to the school, a space that's so

A simple woodland walk that weaves among hazels and hawthorns creates a magical environment for imaginations to run wild.

much more engaging than grass alone. The children notice the bees, the colours and the wildlife. It creates a peaceful, sensory place where they can explore, imagine and feel calm. You don't need a huge space to make a difference – even small pockets can bring these benefits and help children feel more connected to the world around them.'

What began as a school garden has rippled outward, reshaping the school's culture, its sense of place, and its hopes for the future. It stands as a vivid example of what an edible classroom can offer - not just a space for growing food, but a space to foster nature connection, build resilience and inspire joy.

The 'School Food Matters Garden', freshly planted in its final home having been relocated after the 2023 RHS Chelsea Flower Show.

CONCLUSION

Gardens That Spark Change

If you've read this far, something in these pages has likely resonated with you. Perhaps it's the idea of growing food in ways that are as beautiful as they are productive. Maybe it's the thought of reconnecting with nature in a way that feels intuitive and joyful. Or it might be the realisation that our gardens can play a much bigger role – not just in our own lives, but in the health of our communities, ecosystems and the planet itself.

But this book isn't just about ideas – it's about action. And the best way to begin is simply to begin. You don't need acres of land or years of experience. You don't need perfect growing conditions or the latest tools. You just need curiosity and the willingness to give it a go. That might mean planting a single edible perennial in a pot. It might mean weaving herbs into a garden border, joining a local growing group or helping advocate for food growing in a local school or public space. Or it might mean shopping differently: supporting regenerative growers and celebrating local food.

Each small action contributes to a much greater shift.

A Call to Action: Maximising the Potential of Our Gardens

It's time to rethink what food growing looks like. Edimentals show us that edible plants can be beautiful, playful and productive all at once.

They bring joy, biodiversity and flavour – whether you're growing in a country estate or a city windowsill. They also invite us to test ideas on a small scale: to bring regenerative principles into our own gardens, our schools, our balconies and our public spaces.

We have the power to create change. So, plant something. Experiment. Get things wrong. Learn from it. Enjoy it. In doing so, you won't just be growing plants: you'll be growing a deeper connection to food, to nature and to the world around you.

This is your invitation to reimagine what's possible.

Acknowledgements

First and foremost, to my wife, Charlie – your support, patience and love are a constant. You make so much of our life possible while my work often devours time and energy. You're also my fiercest critic – always pushing for better and never letting me settle. And of course, thank you for coming up with the name of this book, *Eat Your Garden*, which perfectly captures the spirit of everything within its pages.

To the brilliant team at Harry Holding Studio: thank you for your support and commitment while I balanced writing alongside our busy design work. A special shout-out to Alex Horlick for your calm, capable presence throughout the process.

Huge thanks to Bronte Seller at Sylvie Design. Your magical digital illustrations brought The Edimental Garden to life, and your drawings and diagrams bring clarity to many of the ideas explored in this book. And to Marina Ralph: thank you for your dedication and expert eye in curating the images that thread through these pages.

To Caroline Michel and the team at PFD: this book would never have happened without your belief and guidance. And to the team at Chelsea Green: Muna, for your sharp editorial stewardship; Melissa, for your thoughtful design work; and everyone behind the scenes who brought it all together with such care.

To all the contributors who generously shared their time and knowledge: thank you. Particular thanks to Stephen Barstow, whose insight and generosity shaped so much of this book. And to Tim Smit, Josh Sparkes, Ben Falk, Mandy Barber, Vanessa Harmony, Sid Hill, Charles Dowding, Jerome Osentowski, Jason Williams, the team at Alec Reed Academy, and Nathan and the crew at Foodway: thank you for helping inspire the next generation of growers.

Thanks, also, to Matteo Ferrero for your expert botanical contribution to the plant list, and for your guidance across planting beyond this book.

To Clive Nichols and Alister Thorpe: your photography has captured the cssence of my gardens with beauty and generosity. Thank you.

To School Food Matters and Project Giving Back: thank you for making the 'School Food Matters Garden' a reality. It is featured throughout this book and was very much inspired it. Your ongoing work continues to make a real impact.

And finally, to my family. To my parents and sister, thank you for your unwavering encouragement and belief. And to my grandparents, thank you for planting the first seeds. You gave me the freedom, stories and space to fall in love with gardens. This book began with you.

Notes

Chapter 1: The Power of Edimentals

1. Vernon H. Heywood, 'Overview of Agricultural Biodiversity and Its Contribution to Nutrition and Health', in *Diversifying Food and Diets: Using Agricultural Biodiversity to Improve Nutrition and Health*, ed. Jessica Fanzo, Daniel Hunter, Teresa Borelli, and Federico Mattei (London: Routledge/Earthscan, 2013), 42–43.
2. Food and Agriculture Organization of the United Nations, 'Staple Foods: What Do People Eat?', in *Dimensions of Need: An Atlas of Food and Agriculture* (Rome: FAO, 1995), https://www.fao.org/4/u8480e/u8480e07.htm.
3. United Nations Department of Economic and Social Affairs, Population Division, *World Urbanization Prospects 2018: Highlights* (United Nations, 2018), 3, https://population.un.org/wup/assets/WUP2018-Highlights.pdf.
4. Eric Toensmeier, *The Benefits of Perennial Vegetables* (Chelsea Green Publishing, 2024), https://www.chelseagreen.com/2024/the-benefits-of-perennial-vegetables.
5. 'Perennial Crops', Project Regeneration, 1 April 2023, https://regeneration.org/nexus/perennial-crops.
6. Norman E. Borlaug, 'The Green Revolution Revisited and the Road Ahead', 8 September 2000, Special 30th Anniversary Lecture, The Norwegian Nobel Institute, Oslo, https://www.nobelprize.org/uploads/2018/06/borlaug-lecture.pdf.
7. Hannah Ritchie, Pablo Rosado, and Max Roser, "Environmental Impacts of Food Production," Our World in Data, December 2, 2022, https://ourworldindata.org/environmental-impacts-of-food; Tim G. Benton et al., *Food System Impacts on Biodiversity Loss: Three Levers for Food System Transformation in Support of Nature* (London: Chatham House, 2021), https://www.chathamhouse.org/2021/02/food-system-impacts-biodiversity-loss.
8. '10 Things You Should Know About Industrial Farming', United Nations Environment Programme, 20 July 2020, https://www.unep.org/news-and-stories/story/10-things-you-should-know-about-industrial-farming.
9. Office for National Statistics, 'UK Natural Capital: Urban Accounts', Census 2021, 8 August 2019, https://www.ons.gov.uk/economy/environmentalaccounts/bulletins/uknaturalcapital/urbanaccounts.
10. Paul A. Reinicke, 'Imagine a Lawn the Size of Georgia', Eco Idea Man, 30 June

2017, https://www.ecoideaman.com/imagine-lawn-size-georgia.

Chapter 2: Reimagining the Edible Garden

1. Marcia P. Jimenez et al., 'Associations Between Nature Exposure and Health: A Review of the Evidence', *International Journal of Environmental Research and Public Health* 18, no. 9 (2021): 4790, https://doi.org/10.3390/ijerph18094790.
2. Jimenez et al., 'Associations Between Nature Exposure and Health', 4790.
3. Stephen R. Keller et al., 'Adults Spend Little Time Outside Weekly', *The Nature of Americans National Report*, April 2017. https://natureofamericans.org/findings/viz/adults-spend-little-time-outside-weekly.
4. Marina Torjinski et al., 'Associations Between Nature Exposure, Screen Use, and Parent – Child Relations: A Scoping Review', *Systematic Reviews* 13 (2024): 305, https://doi.org/10.1186/s13643-024-02690-2.
5. Charles R. Clement et al., 'The Domestication of Amazonia Before European Conquest', *Proceedings of the Royal Society B* 282, no. 1812 (2015): 20150813, https://doi.org/10.1098/rspb.2015.0813; Chelsey Geralda Armstrong et al., "Historical Indigenous Land-Use Explains Plant Functional Trait Diversity," *Ecology and Society* 26, no. 2 (2021): art. 6, https://doi.org/10.5751/ES-12322-260206.
6. Stephanie Dalley, *The Mystery of the Hanging Garden of Babylon: An Elusive World Wonder Traced* (Oxford: Oxford University Press, 2013), 83–106; Annamaria Ciarallo, *Gardens of Pompeii* (Los Angeles: J. Paul Getty Museum, 2001), 52, 67–73.
7. Pedro Armillas, 'Gardens on Swamps', *Science* 174, no. 4010 (1971): 653–61, https://doi.org/10.1126/science.174.4010.653.
8. Liz Pickering, 'The History of English Gardens: Digging Through History', Discover Britain, June 17, 2025, https://www.discoverbritain.com/history/traditions/history-of-english-gardens.
9. Food and Agriculture Organization of the United Nations, 'Staple Foods: What Do People Eat?', in *Dimensions of Need: An Atlas of Food and Agriculture* (Rome: FAO, 1995), https://www.fao.org/4/u8480e/u8480e07.htm.
10. Margaret Spill et al., 'Repeated Exposure to Foods and Early Food Acceptance: A Systematic Review', *USDA Nutrition Evidence Systematic Review* (2019), https://www.ncbi.nlm.nih.gov/books/NBK582166.
11. Gary Paul Nabhan et al., 'Comparing Wild and Cultivated Food Plant Richness Between the Arid American and the Mesoamerican Centers of Diversity, as Means to Advance Indigenous Food Sovereignty in the Face of Climate Change', *Frontiers in Sustainable Food Systems* 6 (2022): 840619, https://doi.org/10.3389/fsufs.2022.840619.
12. J. Bélanger and D. Pilling, eds., *The State of the World's Biodiversity for Food and Agriculture* (FAO Commission on Genetic Resources for Food and Agriculture Assessments, 2019), http://www.fao.org/3/CA3129EN/ca3129en.pdf.
13. Justin Sonnenburg and Erica Sonnenburg, *The Good Gut: Taking Control of Your Weight, Your Mood, and Your Long-Term Health* (Penguin Press, 2015).
14. Martin Crawford, *How to Grow Perennial Vegetables* (Green Books, 2012).

15. Ron Sender et al., 'Revised Estimates for the Number of Human and Bacteria Cells in the Body', *PLoS Biology* 14, no. 8 (2016): e1002533, https://doi.org/10.1371/journal.pbio.1002533.
16. Daniel McDonald et al., 'American Gut: An Open Platform for Citizen Science Microbiome Research', mSystems 3, no. 3 (2018): e00031–18, https://doi.org/10.1128/mSystems.00031-18.
17. "Why Native Plants Matter," Audubon, 6 November 2024, https://www.audubon.org/content/why-native-plants-matter.
18. Jorge L. Leon-Cortes et al., 'The Distribution and Decline of a Widespread Butterfly *Lycaena phlaeas* in a Pastoral Landscape', *Ecological Entomology* 25, no. 3 (2000): 285–294, https://doi.org/10.1046/j.1365-2311.2000.00271.x.
19. Audubon, "Why Native Plants Matter."
20. Lionel Roques et al., 'A Population Facing Climate Change: Joint Influences of Allee Effects and Environmental Boundary Geometry', arXiv, 0907.0989v1, 6 July 2009, https://arxiv.org/abs/0907.0989; Jesse Chase-Lubitz, 'Invasive Species Could Replace Native Species in Extreme Weather', *Nature*, 10 November 2023, https://doi.org/10.1038/d41586-023-03708-w.
21. MSU Extension: Native Plants and Ecosystem Services, 'Ecosystem Services', Michigan State University, 17 February 2016, https://www.canr.msu.edu/nativeplants/ecosystem_services.
22. Richard Pyšek and David M. Richardson, 'Invasiveness and Its Relationship to Trends in Extinction', in *Fifty Years of Invasion Ecology: The Legacy of Charles Elton*, ed. David M. Richardson (Wiley-Blackwell, 2011), 317–340.
23. Peter Bellwood, *First Farmers: The Origins of Agricultural Societies* (Wiley-Blackwell, 2005).

Chapter 4:
Big Ideas from Regenerative Growers

1. Bill Mollison and David Holmgren, *Permaculture One: A Perennial Agriculture for Human Settlements* (Tagari Publications, 1978).
2. Arti Peyre et al., 'Dynamics of Homegarden Structure and Function in Kerala, India', *Agroforestry Systems* 66, no. 2 (2006): 101–115, https://doi.org/10.1007/s10457-005-2919-x.

Chapter 5:
Understanding Your Garden

1. Chris Arsenault, 'Only 60 Years of Farming Left If Soil Degradation Continues', *Scientific American*, 5 December 2014, https://www.scientificamerican.com/article/only-60-years-of-farming-left-if-soil-degradation-continues.
2. Fred Magdoff and Harold van Es, *Building Soils for Better Crops*, 4th ed. (Sustainable Agriculture Research and Education, 2014), 13–14, https://www.sare.org/wp-content/uploads/Building-Soils-for-Better-Crops.pdf.
3. Andy Simon and Robert White, *Beneath Our Feet: Exploring the Hidden World of Soil Microbes* (Soil Science Society of America, 2022), 45.
4. Lingwen Lu et al., 'Harnessing the Runoff Reduction Potential of Urban Bioswales as an Adaptation Response to Climate Change', *Scientific Reports* 14 (2024): 12207, https://doi.org/10.1038/s41598-024-61878-7.
5. WSU Extension: Rain Gardens 'What Is a Rain Garden?', Washington State

University, 15 February 2018, https://extension.wsu.edu/raingarden/featured-rain-gardens.
6. Food and Agriculture Organization, 'Chapter V: Special Forest Plantations – 2.1 Design of Windbreaks and Shelterbelts', in *Arid Zone Forestry: A Guide for Field Technicians* (FAO, 1989), 74–75. https://www.fao.org/4/t0122e/t0122e0a.htm.
7. Roger G. Barry and Richard J. Chorley, *Atmosphere, Weather and Climate*, 9th ed. (Routledge, 2009), 56.
8. Plants for a Future, '*Urtica dioica*, *Achillea millefolium*, *Rumex acetosella*', Database Plant Search, accessed 28 June 2025, https://pfaf.org.
9. US Department of Agriculture, Natural Resources Conservation Service, '*Andropogon gerardii*' and '*Bromus tectorum*', Plants Database, accessed 28 June 2025, https://plants.usda.gov.

Chapter 6: Designing with Edimentals

1. Jessica Gurevitch, Samuel M. Scheiner and Gordon A. Fox, *The Ecology of Plants*, 2nd ed. (Sinauer Associates, 2006).
2. Jeff Lowenfels and Wayne Lewis, *Teaming with Microbes: The Organic Gardener's Guide to the Soil Food Web*, rev. ed. (Timber Press, 2010).

Conclusion: Beyond the Garden

1. United Nations Department of Economic and Social Affairs, Population Division, *World Urbanization Prospects 2018: Highlights* (United Nations, 2018), 1, https://population.un.org/wup/assets/WUP2018-Highlights.pdf.

Image Credits

Unless otherwise noted, all photos and illustrations courtesy of the following contributors.

Pages iv–v, 62–3, 64–5, 112, 122–23, 139, 142, and 200–201 by Alister Thorpe.
Pages 2, 3, 49, 66, 86, 87, 97, 101 (*bottom*), 106–7, 118–19, and 222–23 by Harry Holding.
Page vi–1, Peter O'Connor, aka anemoneprojectors / Wikimedia Commons.
Pages 4, 5, 6–7, 8–9, 10–11, 44, 68, 71, 72, 141, 175, 238, and 263 by Clive Nichols.
Pages 12, 19, 22, 23, 24, 39, 51, 198–99, 217, and 218 by Stephen Barstow.
Page 13, Balise42 / Wikimedia Commons.
Pages 14, 17, 21, and 206 by Marina Ralph.
Pages 15, 45, 170, 179 (*right*), and 205, Agnieszka Kwiecień, Nova / Wikimedia Commons.
Pages 20 and 186, Jan Canty / Unsplash.
Pages 25, 26, 27, 30, 76, 85, 108, 109, 125, 126, 127, 128–29, 131, 134, 143, 151, 152, and 153 by Bronte Seller, Sylvie Design.
Page 25, James Baltz / Unsplash.
Page 28–9, Frank Vincentz / Wikimedia Commons.
Pages 31, 32, and 33 by Eden Project.

Page 34, Tina Xinia / Unsplash.
Page 36, USDA.gov / Wikimedia Commons.
Pages 37 (*top*) and 48, Markus Winkler / Pexels.
Page 37 (*bottom*), Barnabas Davotir / Pexels.
Page 38, Nick Fewings / Unsplash.
Page 40 (*top*), Albert Herring / Wikimedia Commons.
Page 40 (*bottom*), M. X. / Unsplash.
Page 41, Zeynel Cebeci / Wikimedia Commons.
Page 42 (*top*), Munkhbayar Dambajav / Pexels.
Page 42–3, Montse Olmos / Pexels.
Pages 46 and 193 (*right*) by Mandy Barber.
Page 47 by Emma Stoner.
Pages 53 and 54 by Josh Sparkes / Woolsery.
Page 56–7, Øyvind Holmstad / Wikimedia Commons.
Page 58, Daniel Seßler / Unsplash.
Pages 60 and 61 by Jason Cloud Gardener.
Page 67 by HHS.
Page 74–5 by Martin Crawford.
Page 78 by Whole Systems Design.

Pages 79, 80, and 81 by Ben Falk.
Pages 82, 88, 89, 90, and 91 by Vanessa Harmony.
Page 92 by Jacob Gibbins.
Pages 94, 95, and 96 by Sid Hill.
Page 98, Joe Hayes / Pexels.
Pages 99, 100, and 101 (*top*) by Charles Dowding.
Page 102–3, Gabriel Jimenez / Unsplash.
Page 105, Brandon Green / Unsplash.
Pages 111 and 201 (*right*), Eva Bronzini / Pexels.
Page 114–15, The Cosmonaut / Wikimedia Commons.
Page 116, Petruss / Wikimedia Commons.
Page 129, Annie Spratt / Unsplash.
Page 130 and 180, Stefan.lefnaer / Wikimedia Commons.
Page 132–33, Matt Baron-Thompson / Unsplash.
Pages 136 and 187 (*bottom*), Krzysztof Ziarnek / Wikimedia Commons.
Page 145, *top row left to right*, Plenuska / Wikimedia Commons; Plenuska / Wikimedia Commons;

245

Didier Descouens / Wikimedia Commons; Krzysztof Ziarnek, Kenraiz / Wikimedia Commons; by Clive Nichols. *Bottom row left to right*, Christian Fischer / Wikimedia Commons; Krzysztof Ziarnek, Kenraiz / Wikimedia Commons; Øyvind Holmstad / Wikimedia Commons; Wouter Hagens / Wikimedia Commons; by Marina Ralph.

Page 155 and 231 by Craig Atkinson.

Page 157, *top row left to right*, Gerd Eichmann / Wikimedia Commons; Jean-Pol GRANDMONT / Wikimedia Commons; Cephas / Wikimedia Commons; Tsungam / Wikimedia Commons; Krzysztof Ziarnek, Kenraiz / Wikimedia Commons. *Bottom row left to right*, Krzysztof Golik / Wikimedia Commons; Eric Hunt / Wikimedia Commons; Krzysztof Ziarnek / Wikimedia Commons; Agnieszka Kwiecień / Wikimedia Commons; Krzysztof Ziarnek / Wikimedia Commons.

Page 163, *left to right*, Pryma / Wikimedia Commons; by Krzysztof Ziarnek; Kenraiz / Wikimedia Commons; DoF CC-BY-X / Wikimedia Commons; Jac. Janssen / Wikimedia Commons.

Page 166–7, Maja Dumat / Wikimedia Commons.

Page 168, Georg Eiermann / Unsplash.

Page 169 (*top*), Colsu / Wikimedia Commons.

Page 169 (*bottom*), yulia-khlebnikova / Unsplash.

Pages 171, 176, 183 and 208, Krzysztof Ziarnek, Kenraiz / Wikimedia Commons.

Page 172, Meneerke bloem / Wikimedia Commons.

Page 173 (*left*), Wouter Hagens / Wikimedia Commons.

Page 173 (*right*), Eric Hunt / Wikimedia Commons.

Page 174, Annabell Hormann / Wikimedia Commons.

Page 177, Rob Hille / Wikimedia Commons.

Page 178, Qwert1234 / Wikimedia Commons.

Pages 179 (*left*) and 182, Krzysztof Golik / Wikimedia Commons.

Pages 181 and 194, Jean-Pol GRANDMONT / Wikimedia Commons.

Page 184 by Stand Shebs.

Page 185 (*left*), Olga Dudenko / Wikimedia Commons.

Page 185 (*right*), Tsungam / Wikimedia Commons.

Page 187 (*top*), Ryan Hodnett / Wikimedia Commons.

Page 188, DoF CC-BY-X / Wikimedia Commons.

Page 189, Cephas / Wikimedia Commons.

Page 190 (*left*), Andreas Eichler / Wikimedia Commons.

Page 190–91, John Rusk / Wikimedia Commons.

Page 192, Alpsdake / Wikimedia Commons.

Page 193 (*left*), Apios americana_Douglas Goldman / Wikimedia Commons.

Page 195, John Tann / Wikimedia Commons.

Page 196, ∑64 / Wikimedia Commons.

Page 197, USFWS Mountain-Prairie / Wikimedia Commons.

Page 203, B.navez / Wikimedia Commons.

Page 204, Marian Florinel Condruz / Pexels.

Page 207, Inge Poelman / Unsplash.

Page 209, Markus Leupold-Löwenthal / Wikimedia Commons.

Page 210, Walter Siegmund / Wikimedia Commons.

Page 213 (*top*), Devi Puspita Amartha Yahya / Unsplash.

Page 213 (*bottom*), Oziel Gómez / Pexels.

Page 214 by Jerry She / Unsplash.

Page 216, Lupus-huwiki / Wikimedia Commons.

Page 219 by Cihan Yüce / Pexels.

Page 220 by Denise Cusack / Pexels.

Page 225 by Jason Leung / Unsplash.

Pages 227, 228, and 229 by Andrew Oberstadt.

Page 232, Юлия / Wikimedia Commons.

Page 233 (*left*), Jamain / Wikimedia Commons.

Page 233 (*right*), Jasper Shide / Wikimedia Commons.

Page 234 (*top*), Von.grzanka / Wikimedia Commons.

Ppage 234 (*bottom*), Markus Spiske / Unsplash.

Pages 235, 236, and 237 by Britt Willoughby Dyer.

Index

Note: Page numbers in *italics* indicate photos and figures; page numbers followed by *t* indicate tables.

A

Achillea millefolium. See yarrow (*Achillea millefolium*)
Achnatherum hymenoides (Indian ricegrass), 35, *141*
acidity, of soil, 109, 110
Acorus calamus (sweet flag), 130, *130*
Actinidia arguta. See hardy kiwi (*Actinidia arguta*)
aesthetic considerations
  as constraint, 137
  design principles for, 141–44, *142*, *143*
Agastache foeniculum. See anise hyssop (*Agastache foeniculum*)
agroforestry
  at Central Rocky Mountain Permaculture Institute, *82*, 86–90, *86–89*, 91
  as design feature, 124, *125*
Ajuga reptans (bugle), 135, *136*
Akebia quinata (chocolate vine), 135
Alec Reed Academy, 73, 235–37, *235–37*
alexanders (*Smyrnium olusatrum*)
  in allotments, 98
  edibility of, 37, *198*
  as substitute crop, 218
allelopathy, 131
Allium × cornutum (St. John's onion), 218
Allium ampeloprasum var. *babingtonii*. See Babington's leek (*Allium ampeloprasum* var. *babingtonii*)
Allium angulosum (mouse garlic), 217
Allium moly (golden garlic), 218
Allium paradoxum (few-flowered garlic), 219
Allium schoenoprasum. See chives (*Allium schoenoprasum*)
Allium scorodoprasum (sand leek), *210*, 217
Allium stipitatum (Persian shallots), 189, *189*
Allium ursinum. See wild garlic (*Allium ursinum*)
allotments
  adding edimentals to, 97–98, *97*, *98*
  author's, 4, 13–14, 97, *97*
  edible meadows in, 49–50, *49*
Alnus cordata (Italian alder), 83, 158–59*t*
Aloysia citrodora (lemon verbena), 221
Amelanchier spp. (juneberry), 100, *142*, 227
Amelanchier alnifolia. See saskatoon (*Amelanchier alnifolia*)
Amorphophallus paeoniifolius (elephant foot yam), 84
ancient practices
  beauty and productivity combined in, 34–35, *34*
  foraging, 36, *36*, *37*
  permaculture inspired by, 76
angelica (*Angelica archangelica*), 205, *205*
Angelica lucida (seacoast angelica), 120
anise hyssop (*Agastache foeniculum*)
  edible parts of, 206
  harvesting, 214
  late-season flowering of, 41
  in school gardens, 232, *233*
annual vegetables
  at Birch Farm, 53, 54
  as design feature, *125*, 126–27
  edimental substitutes for, 216–18
  at the Falk homestead, 78, 79
  at Homeacres, 101
  in traditional food growing, 48–50, *48*, *49*, 126

247

Apios americana.
See groundnut
(*Apios americana*)
apple (*Malus domestica*)
    at the Falk homestead, 79
    grafted onto hawthorn, 63
    in school gardens, 232
apricot (*Prunus armeniaca*), 87, 89, 90
aquatic plants, profiles of, 195–97
Aquilegia vulgaris (columbine), 160–61*t*
Aralia cordata. See udo (*Aralia cordata*)
Arbutus unedo (strawberry tree), 119, 202
area for planting, calculating, 151–52, *152*
Aronia melanocarpa (chokeberry), 83, 228
arrowhead (*Sagittaria latifolia*)
    edible parts of, 209
    at the Falk homestead, 78, *81*
    profile of, 196–97, *197*
Artemisia dracunculus (French tarragon), 59
Artocarpus heterophyllus (jackfruit), 84
Asclepias incarnata (swamp milkweed), 228
Asimina triloba (pawpaw), 228
asparagus (*Asparagus officinalis*)
    in edible meadow plant mix, 146–47*t*
    edible parts of, 206, *207*
    harvesting, *15*, 214
    at Homeacres, 100
    in the School Food Matters Garden, 73
    for small spaces, 90
Asphodeline lutea. See king's spear (*Asphodeline lutea*)

Atriplex halimus (saltbush), 120
Atriplex hortensis (green orach), 89
autumn olive (*Elaeagnus umbellata*), 203
avocado (*Persea americana*), 87

B

Babington's leek (*Allium ampeloprasum* var. *babingtonii*)
    in allotments, *97*, 98
    edibility of, *198*, 210
    in edible meadow plant mix, 148–49*t*
    in food forests, 16, *17*, 83
balcony gardening
    Cloud Gardener UK, 60–61, *60*, *61*
    overview, 58, *58*
baldmoney (*Meum athamanticum*), 232
Balkan clary (*Salvia nemorosa* 'Caradonna'), 146–47*t*
bamboo (*Phyllostachys* spp.)
    edible parts of, 206
    harvesting, 214, *214*
    as substitute crop, 217
Barber, Mandy, 46–47, *47*
Barstow, Stephen, 19–24, *22*, 138, 139, 210, 216, 218
Barton Hills National Nature Reserve, 1, *1*, 132
basil (*Ocimum basilicum*), 58, 60, 127
Beacon Primary School garden, *231*
bee balm (*Monarda didyma*), 214, 221, 227
beech (*Fagus sylvatica*), 132, 133, *133*
beetroot (*Beta vulgaris*), 54, 73, 100
bergamot, wild.
    See wild bergamot (*Monarda fistulosa*)

Beta vulgaris. See beetroot (*Beta vulgaris*); chard (*Beta vulgaris* subsp. *vulgaris*, Cicla Group)
biennial evening primrose (*Oenothera biennis*), 59
Bimwala, Journei, 230
biodiversity
    among edimentals, 39–44, *39–44*
    at Barstow's edible garden, 20, 21
    baseline assessments of, 121
    at Birch Farm, 53, 54–55
    in challenging conditions, *107*
    design principles for, 138–140
    ecological niches role in, 129
    edimental contributions to, 16, 51
    industrial agriculture-related challenges, 25–26, *25*
    observing and nurturing, 120–21
biophilic design, *222–23*, 224
bioswales, 115–16
Birch Farm, 53–55, *53*, *54*
bistort (*Persicaria bistorta*)
    edible parts of, 140
    in food forests, 158–59*t*
    profile of, 179–180, *179*
black chokeberry (*Aronia melanocarpa*), 83
blackcurrant (*Ribes nigrum*), 79, 83
black salsify (*Scorzonera hispanica*)
    ecological niches for, 131
    profile of, 180–81, *180*
    as substitute crop, 218
blackthorn (*Prunus spinosa*), 124
bladder campion (*Silene vulgaris*)
    in edible meadow plant mix, 148–49*t*

profile of, 186–87, *187*
in the School Food Matters Garden, 73
as substitute crop, 218
Blitum bonus-henricus (Good King Henry), 52
bluebell (*Hyacinthoides* spp.), 133, *133*
blueberry (*Vaccinium* spp.), 79, 109
boundaries, as design feature, 124, *125*, 126
Brassica juncea (mustard), 97, 100
Brassica oleracea. See broccoli (*Brassica oleracea*); kale (*Brassica oleracea*)
Brassica oleracea Acephala Group (collard), 47
Brassica rapa Chinensis Group (pak choi), 61
Brassica rapa Pekinensis Group 'Yuki' (Chinese cabbage), 100
brassicas, perennial, 46–47, *51*, 52
Briza media (quaking grass), 148–49t
broad-leaved cuckoo flower (*Cardamine raphanifolia*), 217
broccoli (*Brassica oleracea*)
'Nine Star,' 46
romanesco, 97
sprouting, 100
Bronx River Foodway, 227–230, *227–29*
bugle (*Ajuga reptans*), 135, *136*
bulbs
edibility of, 209–10, *210*
harvesting, 215–16
Bunias orientalis. See Turkish rocket (*Bunias orientalis*)
Bunium bulbocastanum (greater pignut), 83, 176–77, *177*

C

The Cabin Charity, 67
calculations
percentage assignments in planting mixes, 149–152, 150t, *152*
quantities of plants, 151–53, *151–52, 153*
calendula (*Calendula officinalis*), 97, 100
Californian poppy (*Eschscholzia californica*), 71, 148–49t
Callirhoe involucrata (purple poppy-mallow), 183–84, *184*
call to action, 238
camassia (*Camassia quamash*)
for edible meadows, 96
edible parts of, 210, *210*
harvesting and processing, *216*
Campanula latifolia (giant bellflower), 219
Canadian goldenrod (*Solidago canadensis*), 130
canopy layers
in food forests, 82, 83, *85*, 157, 158–59t
indoors, 226
plant profiles, 168–170
in school gardens, 232
caper bush (*Capparis spinosa*), 120
Capsicum annuum. See chilli (*Capsicum annuum*)
Caragana arborescens (Siberian pea), 88–89
Cardamine pratensis (cuckoo flower), 189–190, *190*, 218
Cardamine raphanifolia (broad-leaved cuckoo flower), 217
carpet layer plants
design principles for, 135, *136*
in food forests, 157, 160–61t

Carya illinoinensis (pecan), 204
case studies
Alec Reed Academy, 235–37, *235–37*
Barstow garden, 19–24, *19–24*
Birch Farm, 53–55, *53*, *54*
Central Rocky Mountain Permaculture Institute, 86–90, *86–89*, 91
Cloud Gardener UK, 60–61, *60*, *61*
Colorado Edible Forest, 90–91, *90*, *91*
Eden Project, 31–33, *32*, *33*
Falk homestead, 78–81, *78–81*
Foodway at Concrete Plant Park, 227–230, *227–29*
Hill, Sid edible meadows, 94–96, *94–96*
Homeacres, 99–101, *99–101*
Incredible Vegetables, 46–47, *46*, *47*
School Food Matters Garden, 71–73, *71*, *72*
Castanea spp. *See* chestnut (*Castanea* spp.)
cattail (*Typha* spp.), 79
Caucasian spinach (*Hablitzia tamnoides*)
at Barstow's edible garden, 24
in medium-sized gardens, 63
profile of, 193–94, *193*
as substitute crop, 218
Celtis australis (European hackberry), 119
Centella asiatica (gotu kola), 226
Central Rocky Mountain Permaculture Institute, 82, 86–90, *86–89*, 91
Centranthus ruber (red valerian), 120, *139*, 206

Cestrum nocturnum (night-blooming jasmine), 87
Chaenomeles japonica (Japanese quince), 217
chamomile (*Chamaemelum nobile*), *116*, 213, 214
chard (*Beta vulgaris* subsp. *vulgaris*, Cicla Group), 54
'Chelsea Chop,' 211
Chelsea Flower Show. *See* Royal Horticulture Society Chelsea Flower Show
Chenopodium album (lamb's-quarters), 89
chestnut (*Castanea* spp.)
    at Bronx River Foodway, 227, 228
    at the Falk homestead, 79
    in food forests, 83
    nutrients in, 204, *204*
chicory (*Cichorium intybus*), 100, 219
children, 69–70
    See also school gardens
chilli (*Capsicum annuum*)
    in greenhouses, 127
    indoor growing of, 224, 226
    in small spaces, 58
Chinese artichoke (*Stachys affinis*)
    in food forests, 160, 160–61*t*
    profile of, 187–88, *187*
Chinese cabbage (*Brassica rapa* [Pekinensis Group] 'Yuki'), 100
Chinese yam (*Dioscorea polystachya*), 209
chives (*Allium schoenoprasum*)
    in edible meadow plant mix, 148–49*t*
    edible parts of, 206
    on green roofs, *68*, 69
    large container example planting design, 162–63*t*, 164
    multiple purposes of, 37, 44, *45*
    profile of, 183, *183*
    in the School Food Matters Garden, 73
    in small spaces, 60
    visual appeal of, 140
chocolate vine (*Akebia quinata*), 135
chokeberry (*Aronia melanocarpa*), 83, 228
Cichorium intybus (chicory), 100, 219
citron daylily (*Hemerocallis citrina*)
    in food forests, 158–59*t*, 160
    profile of, 178–79, *179*
citrus (*Citrus* spp.), indoors, 225, 226
Citrus × limon (lemon), 224, *225*
Citrus × paradisi (grapefruit), 87
clay soils, 108–9, *109*, 110
Claytonia sibirica (Siberian purslane), 83
Claytonia virginica (spring beauty), 219
climate batteries, 87, *89*
climate change mitigation and adaptation, 15–16, 25–26, *25*
climbing layers
    design principles for, 135
    in food forests, 82, 83, *85*, 157, 160–61*t*
    indoors, 226
    in medium-sized gardens, 62–63
    plant profiles, 192–94
    in school gardens, 234
Cloud Gardener UK, 60–61, *60*, *61*
clover (*Trifolium* spp.), 44, 131
coastal site conditions, 119–120
coffee (*Coffea arabica*), 226
collard (*Brassica oleracea* Acephala Group), 47
collating information on plants, 145–49, 146–49*t*
Colocasia esculenta (taro), 61
Colombia lily (*Lilium columbianum*), 190–91, *191*
Colorado Edible Forest, 90–91, *90*, *91*
columbine (*Aquilegia vulgaris*), 160–61*t*
comfrey (*Symphytum officinale*), 89, 90
common bistort (*Persicaria bistorta*), 96
communities of plants. *See* plant communities
community building, 227–230, *227–29*
community garden plots. *See* allotments
companion planting, 43
composting
    benefits of, 111, *111*, 124, *125*
    at Central Rocky Mountain Permaculture Institute, *86*
computer-aided design (CAD) software, for garden sketches, 105
connection to nature. *See* nature connection
constraints
    design principles for, 136–37
    food forest example planting design, 156–57
    large container example planting design, 163–64
containers
    as design feature, *125*, *126*, 127
    example planting design, 162–63*t*, 162–64, *163*
    for small spaces, 59
cooking with edimentals. *See* eating edimentals
coriander (*Coriandrum sativum*), 54

Cornelian cherry
  (*Cornus mas*)
    edible parts of, 202, 203, *203*
    in food forests, 158–59*t*
Corylus spp. *See* hazel
  (*Corylus* spp.)
cost considerations, 16
courtyard gardening, 59
crab apple (*Malus sylvestris*)
    at Central Rocky Mountain Permaculture Institute, 89
    in medium-sized gardens, 62, 63, *63*
    in the School Food Matters Garden, 73
    in small spaces, *142*
Crambe maritima. *See* sea kale (*Crambe maritima*)
Crataegus monogyna. *See* hawthorn (*Crataegus monogyna*)
Crawford, Martin, 82
creeping thyme (*Thymus serpyllum*)
    in containers, 59, 162–63*t*, 164
    profile of, 188, *188*
creeping vanilla orchid (*Vanilla planifolia*), 224
Cuban oregano (*Plectranthus amboinicus*), 226
cuckoo flower (*Cardamine pratensis*), 189–190, *190*, 218
cultural diversity
    ancient practices of, 35
    edimental contributions to, 16
    native plants, 41
Curcuma longa (turmeric), 84
currant (*Ribes* spp.), 90
Cydonia oblonga. *See* quince (*Cydonia oblonga*)
Cymbopogon citratus (lemongrass), 84, 226
Cynara cardunculus. *See* globe artichoke (*Cynara cardunculus*)

D

dame's rocket (*Hesperis matronalis*), 71, 73, 146–47*t*
Daubenton's kale (*Brassica oleracea* var. *ramosa*), 52
daylily (*Hemerocallis* spp.)
    in children's projects, 70
    edible parts of, 205
    at the Falk homestead, 79
    in food forests, 158–59*t*, 160
    at Homeacres, 100
    in medium-sized gardens, 62
    as substitute crop, 217, *217*
decks, as design feature, *125*, 126, *127*
deep shade light conditions, 113–14
density of planting, calculating, 151–53, *151*, *152*
Deschampsia cespitosa. *See* tufted hairgrass (*Deschampsia cespitosa*)
designing with edimentals, 123–165
    aesthetic considerations, 141–44, *142*, *143*
    constraints, 136–37, *136*
    design features, 124–28, *125–28*
    diversity considerations, 138–140
    ecological niches, 129–132, *129–131*
    edibility considerations, 140–41, *141*
    food forest example, 156–161, *157*, 158–160*t*
    large container example, 162–63*t*, 162–64, *163*
    layers, 132–36, *133*, *134*
    maintenance considerations, 164–65
    right plant, right place principle, 128–29
    step-by-step process of, 144–156, *145*, 146–49*t*, 150*t*, *151*–*52*, *153*, *155*

    successional planting, 137–38, *139*
dietary diversity, 36–38, *38*
Dioscorea polystachya (Chinese yam), 209
Diospyros spp. (persimmon), 228
Diplotaxis tenuifolia. *See* wild rocket (*Diplotaxis tenuifolia*)
Doellingeria scabra. *See* Korean aster (*Doellingeria scabra*)
dots and fillers
    design principles for, 135
    in food forests, 157, 160–61*t*
    plant profiles, 189–191
Dowding, Charles, 99–101, *99*, 111, 153
drumstick primula (*Primula denticulata*), 218
Duchesnea indica (false strawberry), 83
Dunnett, Nigel, 94, 136, 155
Dystaenia takesimana (Korean celery), 47, 217

E

eating edimentals
    edibility considerations, 200–202
    fruits, nuts, seeds, and flowers, 202–6, *203*–*6*
    harvesting, 200, 210–16, *213*, *214*, *216*
    overview, 199–200
    practical tips for, 216–221, *217*–*222*
    roots, tubers, and bulbs, 208–10, *208*, *210*
    shoots, stems, and leaves, 206–8, *207*, *208*
ecological niches
    in food forests, 82
    in planting design, 129–132, *129*–*131*
Eden Project, 31–33, *32*, *33*, 94

edible meadows
   in the author's allotment, 49–50, *49*
   beauty and productivity combined in, *10*, 11
   as design feature, *125*, 126
   on green roofs, *68*, 69
   Hill, Sid work, 92
   at The Lodge, *4*, 68–69, *68*
   overview, 93
   sample plant mix for, 146–49t
edible plant parts
   bulbs, 209–10, *210*
   diversity of, 11
   flowers, 205–6, *206*
   fruits, 202–3, *203*
   leaves, 207–8, *208*
   nuts, 203–4, *204*
   overview, 200–202
   roots and tubers, 208–9, *208*
   seeds, 204–5, *205*
   shoots and stems, 206–7, *207*
edimentals
   author's childhood involvement with, 1–4, *2*, *3*
   challenges of, 18
   defined, 4
   key features and benefits of, 12–18
   origin of term, 19
   overview, 11–12
Elaeagnus multiflora (goumi), 83
Elaeagnus umbellata (autumn olive), 203
elder (*Sambucus nigra*)
   in agroforestry, 124
   at Bronx River Foodway, 228
   at Central Rocky Mountain Permaculture Institute, 89
   edible parts of, 202
   in medium-sized gardens, 63
Eleocharis dulcis (water chestnut), 64, 195, *195*

elephant foot yam (*Amorphophallus paeoniifolius*), 84
emergent layers. *See* structural/emergent layers
environmental conditions. *See* site conditions
Eschscholzia californica (Californian poppy), 71, 148–49t
Eugenia uniflora (Suriname cherry), 87
European hackberry (*Celtis australis*), 119
exposed, windy sites, 116–17
external inputs. *See* inputs

F

Fagus sylvatica. *See* beech (*Fagus sylvatica*)
Falk, Ben, 78–81, *78*
false strawberry (*Duchesnea indica*), 83
Farmers Arms pub, 53, 55
fennel (*Foeniculum vulgare*)
   in the author's allotment, 97
   in edible meadow plant mix, 146–47t
   edible parts of, 205
   at Homeacres, 100
   profile of, 172–73, *173*
   in the School Food Matters Garden, 73
   suppression of competing plants, 131
fermenting edimentals, 219, *219*, 221
few-flowered garlic (*Allium paradoxum*), 219
fig (*Ficus carica*)
   at Bronx River Foodway, 228
   at Central Rocky Mountain Permaculture Institute, 87
   placement of, 42, *42–43*
fillers and dots. *See* dots and fillers

Florence fennel (*Foeniculum vulgare* var. *azoricum*), 173
flowers
   colours and shapes of, 144
   edibility of, 205–6, *206*
   harvesting, 213–14, *213*
Foeniculum vulgare. *See* fennel (*Foeniculum vulgare*)
food forests
   biodiversity in, 139
   Bronx River Foodway, 227–230, *227–29*
   Central Rocky Mountain Permaculture Institute, *82*, 86–90, *86–89*, 91
   as design feature, 124, *125*
   example planting design, 156–161, *157*, 158–161t
   role in permaculture, 82–85, *85*
   in small spaces, *142*
food production, global
   industrial agriculture-related challenges, 25–26, *25*, *26*
   regenerative food systems vision, *26*, *27*
food security
   edimental contributions to, 16, 18
   fertile food systems vision, *26*, *27*
   industrial agriculture-related challenges, 25–26, *25*
Foodway at Concrete Plant Park, 227–230, *227–29*
foraging, 36, *36*, *37*
forest gardens. *See* food forests
'Fortunei Hyacinthina' hosta, 185–86, *186*
foxtail barley (*Hordeum jubatum*), 141
Fragaria spp. *See* strawberry (*Fragaria* spp.); wild strawberry (*Fragaria vesca*)

French tarragon
  (*Artemisia dracunculus*), 59
fruits
  edibility of, 202–3, *203*
  harvesting, 212–13
  See also specific types
fuchsia (*Fuchsia* spp.), 217
full sun light conditions,
  113–14
function stacking
  permaculture principle, 80
fungi layers, in food forests,
  83, *85*, 133

G

Galium odoratum (sweet
  woodruff), 160–61*t*, 185, *185*
garlic, wild. *See* wild garlic
  (*Allium ursinum*)
Geranium × *johnsonii*
  'Johnson's Blue,' 148–49*t*
giant bellflower
  (*Campanula latifolia*), 219
giant Korean celery (*Dystaenia
  takeshimana*), 47, 217
ginkgo (*Ginkgo biloba*), 119, 204
global food production
  industrial agriculture-
    related challenges, 25–26,
    25, *26*
  regenerative food systems
    vision, *26*, 27
globe artichoke
  (*Cynara cardunculus*)
  at Alec Reed Academy, 236
  in edible meadows, 49,
    146–47*t*
  at Homeacres, 100
  in the School Food Matters
    Garden, *71*, 73
  visual appeal of, *14*, 140
golden garlic (*Allium moly*), 218
goldenrod (*Solidago* spp.)
  at Bronx River Foodway, 228
  ecological niches for, 130
  familiarity with, 12
  herbal teas of, *13*, 221

gomchwi (*Ligularia fischeri*),
  221
Good King Henry
  (*Blitum bonus-henricus*), 52
gooseberry (*Ribes uva-crispa*),
  90, 217
gotu kola (*Centella asiatica*),
  226
goumi (*Elaeagnus multiflora*),
  83
grape (*Vitis vinifera*)
  at Central Rocky Mountain
    Permaculture Institute,
    87, 89
  in medium-sized
    gardens, 63
  in school gardens, 234
grapefruit
  (*Citrus* × *paradisi*), 87
grasses
  in edible meadows, 96, 132
  in groundcover layers,
    140–41
greater musk mallow (*Malva
  alcea*), *95*, 217
greater pignut (*Bunium
  bulbocastanum*), 83,
  176–77, *177*
greenhouses
  at Central Rocky Mountain
    Permaculture Institute, 87
  as design feature, *125*,
    127, *127*
green infrastructure, 67–69,
  67, *68*
green orach (*Atriplex
  hortensis*), 89
green roofs, 68–69, *68*
Green Walls in Schools
  initiative, 67–68, *67*
groundcover layers
  design principles for,
    134, 135
  in food forests, 82, 83, *85*,
    157, 160–61*t*
  grasses in, 140–41
  indoors, 226

large container example
  planting design,
    162–63*t*, 164
  plant profiles, 183–88
  in school gardens, 234
groundnut (*Apios americana*)
  in food forests, 83, 160–61*t*
  profile of, 192–93, *193*

H

Hablitzia tamnoides. *See*
  Caucasian spinach
  (*Hablitzia tamnoides*)
Hamamelis spp.
  (witch hazel), 228
Hansen, Richard, 136
hardy kiwi (*Actinidia arguta*)
  in food forests, 83
  profile of, 192, *192*
  in school gardens, 234
Harmony, Vanessa, 90–91,
  90, *91*
Hart, Robert, 82
harvesting edimentals
  basic information about,
    200, 210–12
  fruits, nuts, seeds, and
    flowers, 212–14, *213*
  roots, tubers, and bulbs,
    215–16, *216*
  shoots, stems, and leaves,
    214–15, *214*
hawthorn (*Crataegus
  monogyna*)
  at Alec Reed Academy, *237*
  apple or pear grafted
    onto, 63
  at author's grandparents'
    house, *2*
  ecological niches for, 132
  as native plant, 41, *41*
  in the School Food Matters
    Garden, 73
hazel (*Corylus* spp.)
  in agroforestry, 124
  at Alec Reed Academy, *237*
  edible parts of, 203, *204*

INDEX   253

hazel (*continued*)
   at the Falk homestead, 79
   in medium-sized gardens, 63
   multiple purposes of, 44
   in the School Food Matters Garden, 73
   in small spaces, *142*
health benefits of edimentals, 36–38, *38*
heartnut (*Juglans ailantifolia* var. *cordiformis*), 204
hedges, 63, 124
Helianthus annuus (sunflower), 70
Helianthus tuberosus. *See* Jerusalem artichoke (*Helianthus tuberosus*)
Hemerocallis spp. *See* daylily (*Hemerocallis* spp.)
herbaceous perennial layers, in food forests, 82, 83, *85*
herbal edimental teas, *213*, 214, *220*, 221
Hesperis matronalis (dame's rocket), *71*, 73, 146–47t
Hill, Sid, 92, 93, 94–96, *94*
Himalayan water creeper (*Houttuynia cordata*), 196, *196*
Hippophae rhamnoides. *See* sea buckthorn (*Hippophae rhamnoides*)
Hitchmough, James, 94
Homeacres, 99–101, *99–101*
home gardens (Kerala, India), 83–84
honeyberry (*Lonicera caerulea*), 91, 232, *232*
hops (*Humulus lupulus*)
   at Central Rocky Mountain Permaculture Institute, 89
   climbing nature of, 62
   edible parts of, 207
   in food forests, 160–61t
   harvesting, 214
   profile of, 194, *194*
   in school gardens, 234, *234*

Hordeum jubatum (foxtail barley), 141
hosta (*Hosta* spp.)
   at Barstow's edible garden, *20*, 24
   edibility of, *198*
   fermenting, 221
   in food forests, 160–61t
   profile of, 185–86, *186*
   as substitute crop, 216
houseplants, in biophilic design, 222–23, 223–26, *225*
Houttuynia cordata (Himalayan water creeper), 196, *196*
Hull, Chris, 92
Humulus lupulus. *See* hops (*Humulus lupulus*)
Hunter, Nathan, 227, 228, 229
Hyacinthoides spp. (bluebell), 133, *133*
hydrangea (*Hydrangea macrophylla*), 110, 120
Hylotelephium spp. *See* sedum (*Hylotelephium* spp.)

I

identification of plants, importance of, 199–200
Incredible Vegetables, 46–47, *46*, *47*
Indian ricegrass (*Achnatherum hymenoides*), 35, 141
indoor use of edimentals, 222–23, 223–26, *225*
industrial agriculture
   challenges from, 25–26, *25*, *26*
   limited number of crops in, 38
inputs
   low needs of edimentals, 15
   traditional food growing, 50
invasive plant concerns, 42, 167
Italian alder (*Alnus cordata*), 83, 158–59t

J

jackfruit (*Artocarpus heterophyllus*), 84
Japanese pepper (*Zanthoxylum piperitum*), 232
Japanese quince (*Chaenomeles japonica*), 217
Japanese wineberry (*Rubus phoenicolasius*), 42
Jerusalem artichoke (*Helianthus tuberosus*)
   at the Falk homestead, 79
   harvesting, 215, *216*
   late-season colour of, *28*, 29, 41
   prairie origins of, 93
   in school gardens, 232
   as substitute crop, 218
Johnson's Blue cranesbill (*Geranium* × *johnsonii* 'Johnson's Blue'), 148–49t
Juglans spp. *See* walnut (*Juglans* spp.)
Juglans ailantifolia var. *cordiformis* (heartnut), 204
juneberry (*Amelanchier* spp.), 100, *142*, 227

K

kale (*Brassica oleracea*), 47, 52, 54, 215
Kerala home gardens, 83–84
king's spear (*Asphodeline lutea*)
   in edible meadow plant mix, 146–47t
   edible parts of, 140
   profile of, 175–76, *176*
   in the School Food Matters Garden, 73
kitchen gardens, adding edimentals to, 97–98
Korean aster (*Doellingeria scabra*)
   beauty and productivity of, *12*

at Birch Farm, 54
profile of, 177–78, *178*
Korean celery (*Dystaenia takesimana*), 47, 217
Korn, Peter, 113

L

lablab bean (*Lablab purpureus*), 87
Lactuca sativa 'Batavian Red' (lettuce), 100
lamb's ear (*Stachys byzantina*), 181–82, *181*, 228
lamb's-quarters (*Chenopodium album*), 89
large gardens, 65–66, *66*, 138
lavender (*Lavandula* spp.), 43, *97*
layers of plants
    in allotments, 98
    in balcony gardens, 61
    at Central Rocky Mountain Permaculture Institute, 88–89
    design principles for, 132–36, *133*, *134*
    at the Falk homestead, 79
    in food forests, 82–83, *82*, *85*, 157
    indoors, 224, 226
    in Kerala home gardens, 84
    large container example planting design, 162–63*t*, 164
    in large spaces, 66
    in medium-sized gardens, *64*
    overview, 43
    percentage assignments in planting mixes, 149–152, 150*t*, *152*
    in the School Food Matters Garden, 73
    setting out plants by, 154
    in small spaces, 59, *142*
    See also specific types of layers

leaves
    edibility of, 207–8, *208*
    harvesting, 215
lemon (*Citrus* × *limon*), 224, *225*
lemon balm (*Melissa officinalis*), 83, 221
lemongrass (*Cymbopogon citratus*), 84, 226
lemon verbena (*Aloysia citrodora*), 221
lettuce (*Lactuca sativa* 'Batavian Red'), 100
leucaena (*Leucaena leucocephala*), 87
light conditions, 113–14
Ligularia fischeri (gomchwi), 221
Ligustrum scoticum (Scots lovage), 120
lilac (*Syringa vulgaris*), 89
Lilium columbianum (Colombia lily), 190–91, *190–91*
lime tree (*Tilia* spp.), 221
Little, John, 113
living walls, 67–68, *67*
loam, 109, *109*, 110
The Lodge, 68–69, *68*
Long Barn Farm, 65, *66*
long lists of plants, 144–45
Lonicera caerulea (honeyberry), 91, 232, *232*
Lost Gardens of Heligan, 31
lovage (*Levisticum officinale*)
    in allotments, 98
    edible parts of, *198*, 205, 207
    in school gardens, 232, *233*
low/groundcover layers. *See* groundcover layers

M

maintenance of edible gardens, 96, 164–65
Malus domestica. *See* apple (*Malus domestica*)

Malus sylvestris. *See* crab apple (*Malus sylvestris*)
Malva alcea. *See* greater musk mallow (*Malva alcea*)
mango (*Mangifera indica*), 84
mapping
    light conditions, 114
    water movements, 115
marigold (*Tagetes patula*), 100
Matteuccia struthiopteris. *See* ostrich fern (*Matteuccia struthiopteris*)
meadow-style plantings. *See* edible meadows
medium-sized gardens, 62–64, *63*, *64*
medlar (*Mespilus germanica*), 202
Melica uniflora f. *albida* (wood melick), 160–61*t*
Melissa officinalis (lemon balm), 83, 221
Mentha aquatica (water mint), 113
Mespilus germanica (medlar), 202
Meum athamanticum (baldmoney), 232
Microbiome Garden, *92*, 93
microclimates, 117–18, *118–19*
mid-layers
    design principles for, 134, *134*
    in food forests, 157, 158–59*t*
    indoors, 226
    large container example planting design, 162–63*t*, 164
    plant profiles, 175–182
    in school gardens, 232
mint (*Mentha* spp.), 60, 113, *142*
Monarda didyma (bee balm), 214, 221, 227
Morus spp. (mulberry), 87
mouse garlic (*Allium angulosum*), 217

mulberry (*Morus* spp.), 87
multipurpose plants, 44, *44*
musk mallow
  (*Malva alcea*), 95
mustard (*Brassica juncea*),
  97, 100
Myristica fragrans
  (nutmeg), 84
Myrrhis odorata. See sweet
  cicely (*Myrrhis odorata*)

N

nasturtium
  (*Tropaeolum majus*)
    in children's projects, 70
    in kitchen gardens, 97
    in small spaces, 58
Nasturtium officinale
  (watercress), 61, 64, 79
native vs. non-native
  edimentals, 39–43
*Naturalistic Planting Design:
  The Essential Guide*
  (Dunnett), 136, 155
nature connection
  ancient practices of,
    34–35, *34*
  biophilic design,
    222–23, 224
  Eden Project, 31–33, *32*, *33*
  foraging, 36, *36*, *37*
  importance of, 29–30,
    30, 34
nettle (*Urtica dioica*), 120, 130
niches, ecological. *See*
  ecological niches
night-blooming jasmine
  (*Cestrum nocturnum*), 87
'Nine Star' broccoli (*Brassica
  oleracea* [Botrytis Group]
  'Nine Star Perennial'), 46
no-dig growing methods,
  99–101, *99–101*
non-native vs. native
  edimentals, 39–43
nutmeg (*Myristica fragrans*),
  84

nuts
  edibility of, 203–4, *204*
  harvesting, 212–13
Nymphaea spp. (water lily), 79

O

oak (*Quercus* spp.), *34*, 35
observation
  of biodiversity, 120–21
  for garden management, 165
  in large spaces, 65–66
  of site conditions,
    104–5, *105*
oca (*Oxalis tuberosa*)
  edible parts of, 209, *209*
  harvesting and
    processing, *216*
  as substitute crop, 218
Ocimum basilicum (basil), 58,
  60, 127
Ocimum tenuiflorum
  (tulsi), 84
Oenothera biennis (biennial
  evening primrose), 59
oregano (*Origanum vulgare*)
  on green roofs, 69
  large container example
    planting design,
    162–63*t*, 164
  in pots, 59
  in small spaces, 58
organic matter, for improving
  soil, 111, *111*
Origanum vulgare. See
  oregano (*Origanum vulgare*)
Osentowski, Jerome, 82, 84,
  86–90, *86*, 91
ostrich fern (*Matteuccia
  struthiopteris*)
  in food forests, 158–59*t*
  hostas combined with, 186
  moisture needs, *115*
Oxalis acetosella (wood
  sorrel), 135, 234, *234*
Oxalis tuberosa. See oca
  (*Oxalis tuberosa*)
oxlip (*Primula elatior*), 219

P

pak choi (*Brassica rapa*
  Chinensis Group), 61
partial shade light conditions,
  113–14
parts of plants, edible.
  See edible plant parts
passionflower
  (*Passiflora caerulea*), 58
passionfruit
  (*Passiflora edulis*), 226
patio gardening, 59
pawpaw (*Asimina triloba*),
  228
pear (*Pyrus communis*)
  in the author's allotment,
    97
  in food forests, 83
  grafted onto hawthorn, 63
pecan (*Carya illinoinensis*),
  204
peppercorn (*Piper nigrum*),
  84, 226
percentage assignments in
  planting mixes
    calculating, 149–152,
      150*t*, *152*
    food forest example
      planting design, 157
perennials
  annuals substituted by,
    216–18
  benefits of using as
    edimentals, 14
  brassicas, 46–47, *51*, 52
  chef use of, 55
  ecosystem services
    performed by, 79
  edimentals vs., 51–52, *51*
  slow nature of, 18
*Perennials and Their
  Garden Habitats* (Hansen
  and Stahl), 136
perennial wall rocket.
  See wild rocket
    (*Diplotaxis tenuifolia*)
Perilla frutescens (shiso), 187

permaculture
  author's journey to, 75–77
  Central Rocky Mountain Permaculture Institute, *82*, 86–90, *86–89*, 91
  core concepts of, 76, *76*
  at the Falk homestead, 78–81, *78–81*
Persea americana (avocado), 87
Persian shallots (*Allium stipitatum*), 189, *189*
Persicaria bistorta (common bistort), 96
Persicaria odorata (Vietnamese coriander), 226
persimmon (*Diospyros* spp.), 228
pH, of soil, 109, 110
Phyllostachys spp. (bamboo). *See* bamboo (*Phyllostachys* spp.)
Pictorial Meadows, 69
Piper nigrum (peppercorn), 84, 226
plant communities
  at Barstow's edible garden, 22
  defined, 129
  ecological niches for, 129–132, *131*
  See also polycultures
plant identification, importance of, 199–200
planting design. *See* designing with edimentals
Planting in a Post-Wild World (Rainer and West), 136
planting mixes
  balancing ornamental and edible qualities, 140
  biodiversity in, 139–140
  food forest example, 158–161*t*
planting plants, 154–55, *155*
plant parts, edible. *See* edible plant parts

plant profiles
  aquatic plants, 195–97
  climbing layers, 192–94
  low/groundcover layers, 183–88
  mid-layers and seasonal interest, 175–182
  overview, 167
  structural/emergent layers, 171–74
  trees and shrubs, 168–170
Plants for a Future, 18, 62, 202
Plectranthus amboinicus (Cuban oregano), 226
plum (*Prunus domestica*), 79, 90
polycultures, 53, 54–55, *54*
  See also plant communities
Polygonatum biflorum. *See* Solomon's seal (*Polygonatum biflorum*)
pomegranate (*Punica granatum*)
  at Central Rocky Mountain Permaculture Institute, 87
  in edible meadow plant mix, 146–47*t*
  indoor growing of, 226
  in pots, 59
  in the School Food Matters Garden, *71*, 73
ponds
  in balcony gardens, 61
  as design feature, *125*, 128, *128*
  at the Falk homestead, 78, 79, *81*
  in medium-sized gardens, 64
  for water management, 116
primrose (*Primula vulgaris*), 219
Primula denticulata (drumstick primula), 218
Primula elatior (oxlip), 219

Primula vulgaris (primrose), 219
profiles of plants. *See* plant profiles
Project Giving Back, 5, 72
prostrate rosemary (*Salvia rosmarinus* 'Prostratus'), 59
Prunus armeniaca (apricot), 87, 89, 90
Prunus domestica (plum), 79, 90
Prunus spinosa (blackthorn), 124
public realm edimentals, 227–230, *227–29*
Punica granatum. *See* pomegranate (*Punica granatum*)
purple poppy-mallow (*Callirhoe involucrata*), 183–84, *184*
Pyrus communis. *See* pear (*Pyrus communis*)

Q

quaking grass (*Briza media*), 148–49*t*
quantities of plants, calculating, 151–53, *151–52*, *153*
Quercus spp. (oak), *34*, 35
quince (*Cydonia oblonga*)
  large container example planting design, 162–63*t*, 164
  in medium-sized gardens, 63
  need for cooking of, 202

R

Rainer, Thomas, 136
rain gardens, 116, *125*, 128, *128*
ramsons. *See* wild garlic (*Allium ursinum*)
raspberry (*Rubus idaeus*), 79, 90

red valerian (*Centranthus ruber*), 120, *139*, 206
red-veined sorrel (*Rumex sanguineus*), 98, 160–61*t*
regenerative food systems
    Birch Farm, 53–55, *54*
    Homeacres, 99–101, *99–101*
    vision for, *26*, *27*, 76–77
    See also agroforestry; edible meadows; food forests; permaculture
relocalised food systems
    at Birch Farm, 53–55, *54*
    vision for, 16, *26*, 27
    See also allotments
researching plants, 144–45
resilience of edimentals
    overview, 14, 15–16
    in the School Food Matters Garden, 73
    traditional food growing combined with, 51
The Resilient Farm and Homestead (Falk), 78
Rheum × hybridum. *See* rhubarb (*Rheum × hybridum*)
rhizosphere layers, 82, *85*
rhubarb (*Rheum × hybridum*)
    edible parts of, *201*, 202
    at the Falk homestead, 79
    familiarity with, 37
    at Homeacres, 100
Ribes spp. (currant), 90
Ribes nigrum (blackcurrant), 79, 83
Ribes uva-crispa (gooseberry), 90, 217
ricegrass (*Achnatherum hymenoides*), 35, 141
right plant, right place principle, 128–29
Ringve Botanical Garden, 21
romanesco broccoli, 97
rooftop gardening
    green roofs, 68–69, *68*
    for small spaces, 58, *58*
root crop layers, 82, *85*

roots and tubers
    edibility of, 208–9, *209*
    harvesting, 215–16, *216*
rosemary (*Salvia rosmarinus*)
    drought tolerance of, 113
    in edible meadow plant mix, 146–47*t*
    harvesting of, *200–201*
    at Homeacres, 100
    placement of, 43
    in the School Food Matters Garden, 73
    in small spaces, 58, 59, *142*
Royal Horticulture Society Chelsea Flower Show
    awards given by, 5
    'Chelsea Chop,' 211
    Microbiome Garden display, *92*, 93
    overview, 71
    See also School Food Matters Garden
Rubus idaeus (raspberry), 79, 90
Rubus phoenicolasius, 42
Rudbeckia laciniata (sochan), 174, *174*, 217
Rumex acetosa. *See* sorrel (*Rumex acetosa*)
Rumex acetosella (sheep's sorrel), 120
Rumex sanguineus (red-veined sorrel), 98, 160–61*t*

S

safety considerations, plant identification, 199–200, 202
Sagittaria latifolia. *See* arrowhead (*Sagittaria latifolia*)
salad burnet (*Sanguisorba minor*)
    at Homeacres, 100
    for living walls, 68
    in school gardens, 234
salads
    Barstow super salads, *19*, 21, 218, *218*

    edimental crops for, 218–19
    at Homeacres, *101*
salsify (*Tragopogon porrifolius*), 37
saltbush (*Atriplex halimus*)
    for coastal conditions, 120
    edible parts of, 208
    profile of, 169, *169*
salvia (*Salvia* spp.), 60
Salvia nemorosa 'Caradonna' (Balkan clary), 146–47*t*
Salvia rosmarinus. *See* rosemary (*Salvia rosmarinus*)
Sambucus nigra. *See* elder (*Sambucus nigra*)
sand leek (*Allium scorodoprasum*), *210*, 217
sandy soils, 108–9, *109*, 110
Sanguisorba minor. *See* salad burnet (*Sanguisorba minor*)
saskatoon (*Amelanchier alnifolia*)
    edible parts of, 203
    in food forests, 83, 158–59*t*
    profile of, 168–69, *168*
School Food Matters charity, 5, 72
School Food Matters Garden
    at Alec Reed Academy, 235–37, *235–37*
    awards for, 5
    at Beacon Primary School, *231*
    case study, 71–73, *71*, *72*
    naturalistic design for, 6–9, 99
    percentage of edible plants in, 9, 140, *141*
    research for, 19
school gardens
    edible classrooms, 235–37, *235–37*
    edimentals for, 69–70, 231–34, *231–34*

Green Walls in Schools
initiative, 67–68, *67*
See also School Food
Matters Garden
Scorzonera hispanica.
See black salsify
(*Scorzonera hispanica*)
Scots lovage (*Ligustrum scoticum*), 120
sculptural habitats, as design feature, *125*, 126
sea buckthorn (*Hippophae rhamnoides*)
at the Falk homestead, 79
nitrogen fixing by, 131
profile of, 169–170, *169*
vitamin C in, 42, *42*
seacoast angelica (*Angelica lucida*), 120
sea kale (*Crambe maritima*)
alkaline soil needs, 109
in the author's Bristol garden, *139*
at Barstow's edible garden, 20, *21*, 24
at Birch Farm, 54
early-season growth of, 41
in edible meadow plant mix, 146–47t
edible parts of, 205
harvesting, 215
profile of, 171–72, *172*
in school gardens, 73, 232
seasonal interest layers
design principles for, 134, *134*
in food forests, 157, 158–59t
large container example planting design, 162–63t, 164
plant profiles, 175–182
in school gardens, 232
successional planting for, 137–38
sedum (*Hylotelephium* spp.)
in edible meadow plant mix, 146–47t

edible parts of, 208
in food forests, 161
at Homeacres, 100
in medium-sized gardens, 62
sedum (*Sedum* spp.), green roofs of, 69
seeds
edibility of, 204–5, *205*
growing plants from, 153–54
harvesting, 212–13, *213*
self-seeding plants, 211
The Self-Sufficient Gardener (Seymour), 20
serviceberry/juneberry (*Amelanchier* spp.), 100, *142*, 227
setting out plants, 154–55, *155*
Seymour, John, 20
shade and sun conditions, 113–14
sheep's sorrel (*Rumex acetosella*), 120
shelterbelts, 117
Shepard, Mark, 90
shiso (*Perilla frutescens*), 187
shoots and stems
edibility of, 206–7, *207*
harvesting, 214–15, *214*
short lists of plants, 145, *145*
shrub layers
in food forests, 82, 83, *85*, 157, 158–59t
indoors, 226
plant profiles, 168–170
in school gardens, 232
Siberian pea (*Caragana arborescens*), 88–89
Siberian purslane (*Claytonia sibirica*), 83
Sichuan pepper (*Zanthoxylum simulans*), 170, *170*
Silene vulgaris. *See* bladder campion (*Silene vulgaris*)
silty soils, 109, *109*, 110

site conditions, 103–21
biodiversity, 120–21
as constraint, 137
food forest example planting design, 156
large container example planting design, 162
light, 113–14
location, 105–6
microclimates, 117–18, *118–19*
observation of, 104–5, *105*
overview, 103–4
soil, *102*, 103, 106–13, *107–9*, *111*, *112*
specialist conditions, 118–120
water, 114–16, *115*, *116*
wind, 116–17
Sium sisarum (skirret), 37, 98
size of plant, in planting design, 143, 153
sketching the garden
for observation, 105
for planting design, *143*, 144, 145
for refining layers and species percentages, 150–51
skirret (*Sium sisarum*), 37, 98
sloe (*Prunus spinosa*), 124
smallholdings, 65–66, *66*
small space growing
edible meadows, 96
food forest principles applied to, *142*
recommendations for, *57*, 58–59, *58*
successional planting for, 138
Smit, Tim, 31–33, *31*
Smyrnium olusatrum.
See alexanders (*Smyrnium olusatrum*)
sochan (*Rudbeckia laciniata*), 174, *174*, 217

INDEX

259

society garlic
  (*Tulbaghia violacea*)
    profile of, 182, *182*
    in school gardens,
      234, 236
soil health, 106–13
  assessment of, *102*, 103,
    109–10
  biodiversity, *107*
  at Central Rocky Mountain
    Permaculture Institute, 90
  at the Falk homestead,
    79–80
  importance of, 77, 107
  improvement of, 111
  overview, 106–7
  resilience of, 111, *112*, 113
  soil layers and types, 107–9,
    108, *109*
soil moisture, 110
soil pH, 109, 110
soil types, 108–9, *109*
Solidago spp. *See* goldenrod
  (*Solidago* spp.)
Solidago canadensis
  (Canadian goldenrod), 130
Solomon's seal
  (*Polygonatum biflorum*)
    edible parts of, 207
    in food forests, 158–59*t*
    harvesting, 214
    profile of, 173–74, *173*
sorrel (*Rumex acetosa*)
  in balcony gardens, 61
  ecological benefits of,
    40, *40*
  edible parts of, 208
  at the Falk homestead, 79
  familiarity with, 37
  harvesting, 215
  in salads, 219
sourcing plants, 153–54
space-maximising benefits of
  edimentals, 14, 57
Sparkes, Josh, 53–55, *53*
specialist site conditions,
  118–120

spreadsheets
  for calculating plant
    quantities, 152
  for collating information,
    145–49, 146–49*t*
spring beauty
  (*Claytonia virginica*), 219
sprouting broccoli (*Brassica
  oleracea* [Italica Group]
  'Claret'), 100
spurge (*Euphorbia* spp.),
  toxicity of, 113, 139
Stachys affinis. *See* Chinese
  artichoke (*Stachys affinis*)
Stachys byzantina (lamb's
  ear), 181–82, *181*, 228
Stachys floridana
  (wild artichoke), 187
stack functions permaculture
  principle, 80, *81*
Stahl, Friedrich, 136
stems and shoots. *See* shoots
  and stems
step-by-step planting design
  process, 144–156
    collating information,
      145–49, 146–49*t*
    order vs. disorder,
      155–56
    percentage calculations,
      149–151, 150*t*
    plant quantity calculations,
      151–53, *151–52*, *153*
    researching plants,
      144–45, *145*
    setting out and planting,
      154–55, *155*
    sourcing, 153–54
St. John's onion
  (*Allium × cornutum*), 218
strawberry (*Fragaria* spp.)
  early season harvesting
    of, 202
  for groundcover, 91
  for living walls, 68
strawberry, wild. *See* wild
  strawberry (*Fragaria vesca*)

strawberry tree (*Arbutus
  unedo*), 119, 202
structural/emergent layers
  in containers, 162–63*t*, 164
  design principles for,
    134, *134*
  in food forests, 157, 158–59*t*
  plant profiles, 171–74
  in school gardens, 232
subsoil, 107, *108*
substitute crops, 216–18
successional planting
  design principles for,
    137–38, *139*
  at the Falk homestead, 79
  in the School Food Matters
    Garden, 73
sun and shade conditions,
  113–14
sunflower
  (*Helianthus annuus*), 70
Suriname cherry
  (*Eugenia uniflora*), 87
swamp milkweed
  (*Asclepias incarnata*), 228
sweet chestnut
  (*Castanea sativa*), 204, *204*
sweet cicely (*Myrrhis odorata*)
  for edible meadows, 96
  edible parts of, *198*, 205
  in food forests, 158–59*t*
  in salads, 219
sweet flag (*Acorus calamus*),
  130, *130*
sweet woodruff (*Galium
  odoratum*), 160–61*t*, 185, *185*
Swiss chard (*Beta vulgaris*
  subsp. *cicla*), 97
Symphytum officinale
  (comfrey), 89, 90
Syringa vulgaris (lilac), 89

T

Tagetes patula (marigold), 100
taro (*Colocasia esculenta*), 61
Taunton Deane kale (*Brassica
  oleracea* var. *acephala*), 52

'Terracotta' yarrow (*Achillea millefolium*), 175, *175*
thyme (*Thymus vulgaris*), 58, 69
Thymus polytrichus (wild thyme), 113
Thymus serpyllum. *See* creeping thyme (*Thymus serpyllum*)
Tilia spp. (lime tree), 221
Toensmeier, Eric, 90
topsoil, 107, *108*
traditional food growing
    benefits and challenges of, 50–51
    edimentals vs., 48–50, *48*, *49*
Tragopogon porrifolius (salsify), 37
trailing plants
    for living walls, 68
    for small spaces, 59
trees
    harvesting from, 212
    indoors, 226
    in medium-sized gardens, 62, *63*
    in school gardens, 232
    See also canopy layers
Trifolium spp. (clover), 44, 131
Tropaeolum majus. *See* nasturtium (*Tropaeolum majus*)
tubers and roots
    edibility of, 208–9, *209*
    harvesting, 215–16, *216*
tufted hairgrass (*Deschampsia cespitosa*)
    in edible meadow plant mix, 146–47*t*
    in food forests, 158–59*t*, 160
Tulbaghia violacea. *See* society garlic (*Tulbaghia violacea*)
tulsi (*Ocimum tenuiflorum*), 84
Turkish rocket (*Bunias orientalis*)
    at Birch Farm, 54
    edible parts of, 208, *208*
    in food forests, 83
    as substitute crop, *217*
turmeric (*Curcuma longa*), 84
Typha spp. (cattail), 79

U

udo (*Aralia cordata*)
    at Barstow's edible garden, *22*
    edible parts of, 206
    profile of, 171, *171*
understorey layers, 82, *85*, 157
    See also mid-layers; shrub layers
Urtica dioica (nettle), 120, 130

V

Vaccinium spp. (blueberry), 79, 109
Væres Venner garden, 21
valerian (*Valeriana officinalis*), 158–59*t*
Vanilla planifolia (creeping vanilla orchid), 224
Vietnamese coriander (*Persicaria odorata*), 226
viola (*Viola tricolor*), 100
violet (*Viola* spp.), 228
visual aids for planting design, 145, *145*, 150–51
Vitis vinifera. *See* grape (*Vitis vinifera*)
'Vranja' quince (*Cydonia oblonga* 'Vranja'), 162–63*t*, 164

W

walnut (*Juglans* spp.), 88, 203, *204*
water chestnut (*Eleocharis dulcis*), 64, 195, *195*
watercress (*Nasturtium officinale*), 61, 64, 79
water lily (*Nymphaea* spp.), 79
water management
    at Central Rocky Mountain Permaculture Institute, 87
    at the Falk homestead, 78, *79*, 80, *81*
    for new edible gardens, 165
    understanding site conditions, 114–16, *115*, 116
water mint (*Mentha aquatica*), 113
water storage, 115
weed management, 164–65
West, Claudia, 136
wild artichoke (*Stachys floridana*), 187
wild bergamot (*Monarda fistulosa*)
    at the Falk homestead, 79
    in food forests, 158–59*t*, 160
    prairie origins of, 93
    uses of, *74*, 75
wild cabbage (*Brassica oleracea*), 221
wild garlic (*Allium ursinum*)
    ecological niches for, 131
    fermenting, 221
    in medium-sized gardens, 64
    for pesto, *40*, 41
    as substitute crop, 217, *217*
wildlife
    garden health indicated by, 120
    protecting harvest from, 212
wild rocket (*Diplotaxis tenuifolia*)
    edible parts of, 208
    at Homeacres, 100
    for living walls, 68
wild strawberry (*Fragaria vesca*)
    ecological niches for, 131
    in food forests, 160–61*t*
    in medium-sized gardens, 64, *64*
    profile of, 184–85, *185*
    in school gardens, 73, 234, 236
    in small spaces, *142*

wild thyme (*Thymus polytrichus*), 113
Williams, Jason, 60–61, *60*
Wilson, Andrew, 136–37
wind, 116–17
windbreaks, 117
windowsill growing, *56*, 57, 58
witch hazel (*Hamamelis* spp.), 228
Witloof chicory (*Cichorium intybus* 'Witloof'), 219
wood melick (*Melica uniflora* f. *albida*), 160–61*t*
wood sorrel (*Oxalis acetosella*), 135, 234, *234*
World Garden, 21

worm farms, *86*, 88

X

Xanthoceras sorbifolium (yellowhorn), 204

Y

yarrow (*Achillea millefolium*)
  in the author's Bristol garden, *139*
  in edible meadow plant mix, 146–47*t*, 148–49*t*
  at the Falk homestead, 79
  in herbal teas, 221
  as indicator plant, 120
  multiple purposes of, 44, *44*
  profile of, 175, *175*
  in the School Food Matters Garden, 73
yellowhorn (*Xanthoceras sorbifolium*), 204
yield
  obtain a yield permaculture principle, 80
  traditional food growing vs. edimentals, 50

Z

Zanthoxylum piperitum (Japanese pepper), 232
Zanthoxylum simulans (Sichuan pepper), 170, *170*

About the Author

HARRY HOLDING is a leading voice in contemporary garden design and a pioneer of the edimental movement – the fusion of edible and ornamental planting. Since founding Harry Holding Studio in 2016, he has been named among *House & Garden*'s Top 50 Garden & Landscape Designers and received multiple accolades from the RHS, the Society of Garden & Landscape Designers and other industry bodies. His School Food Matters Garden at the RHS Chelsea Flower Show 2023 won the People's Choice Award, earning praise from *BBC Gardeners' World*, *The Times*, *The Telegraph*, and *Financial Times*. In 2024, the RHS invited him to return and design their Feature Garden, further cementing his reputation as a leading figure in sustainable, plant-led design. Harry and his studio are designing a garden for RHS Chelsea 2026 in collaboration with the Eden Project.

Harry's work spans private gardens, public landscapes and international commissions, including a dedicated area of the new Shuttleworth Botanical Garden on the Isle of Man and an area of the new Eden Project in Morecambe. In 2025, the British Library selected him as one of ten international designers to contribute to *Gardens of the Future*, for which he envisioned a Future Food & Medicine Garden exploring sustainable community food systems. A regular tutor at the London College of Garden Design, Royal Botanic Gardens, Kew, Harry is also a sought-after guest speaker on ecological design. *Eat Your Garden* is his debut book.

First published in 2026 by Chelsea Green Publishing | PO Box 4529 | White River Junction, VT 05001 | West Wing, Somerset House, Strand | London, WC2R 1LA, UK | www.chelseagreen.com
A Division of Rizzoli International Publications, Inc. | 49 West 27th Street | New York, NY 10001 | www.rizzoliusa.com

Copyright © 2026 by Harry Holding Studio LTD.
All rights reserved.

No part of this book may be transmitted or reproduced in any form by any means without permission in writing from the publisher.

Publisher: Charles Miers
Deputy Publisher: Matthew Derr
Commissioning Editor: Muna Reyal
Project Manager: Natalie Wallace
Developmental Editor: Sara Bader
Copy Editor: Susan Pegg
Proofreader: Jacqui Lewis
Indexer: Shana Milkie
Designer: Melissa Jacobson

ISBN 978-1-64502-334-0 (hardcover) | ISBN 978-1-64502-335-7 (ebook)
Library of Congress Control Number: 2026001607 (print) | 2026001608 (ebook)

Our Commitment to Green Publishing
Chelsea Green sees publishing as a tool for cultural change and ecological stewardship. We strive to align our book manufacturing practices with our editorial mission and to reduce the impact of our business enterprise in the environment. We print our books using vegetable-based inks whenever possible. This book may cost slightly more because it was printed on paper from well-managed, FSC® forests and other controlled sources, and we hope you'll agree that it's worth it. *Eat Your Garden* was printed on paper supplied by Bell & Bain Ltd, Glasgow that is certified by the Forest Stewardship Council®.

Authorized EU representative for product safety and compliance
Mondadori Libri S.p.A. | www.mondadori.it
via Gian Battista Vico 42 | Milan, Italy 20123

Printed and bound in Great Britain by Bell & Bain Ltd, Glasgow.
10 9 8 7 6 5 4 3 2 1   26 27 28 29 30